FREYA STARK

THE COAST
OF INCENSE

Autobiography 1933–1939

LONDON
JOHN MURRAY
ALBEMARLE ST

FIRST EDITION . . . 1953

PRINTED IN GREAT BRITAIN BY
WYMAN AND SONS, LTD., LONDON, FAKENHAM AND READING
AND PUBLISHED BY JOHN MURRAY (PUBLISHERS) LTD.

To

STEWART

"Era gia l'ora che volge il disio
A 'naviganti, e 'ntenerisce il core
Lo dì c'han detto ai dolci amici addio . . ."

Contents

Illustrations

xi

facing page

★

SKETCH MAP BY H. W. HAWES

★

WOOD ENGRAVINGS BY REYNOLDS STONE

Foreword

IN this third and, for the present, last volume of autobiography, I have followed the previous system of alternating letters from the past with my present-day impressions, so that the result may be, as I hope, the composite one of memory and reflection, present and past, plaited in together, as they are in actual life: for it is usually a chord and not a note that we remember.

I have brought it up to 1939, when the "iron curtain" of the last world war closed down. This full stop comes from no belief that the world at that moment came to an end, even for my generation. It is perhaps for the opposite reason: for no iron curtain yet discovered will stand against the pressure and persistence of life, and I still hope to live long enough to write about an opening door. Meanwhile this book travels mostly in South Arabia, whose distant, severe and unimaginable beauty lives in my heart, so that I have been glad to write about it once more, and to paint, while doing so, as honest a portrait of myself as I can.

ASOLO.   1953.

The Coast of Incense

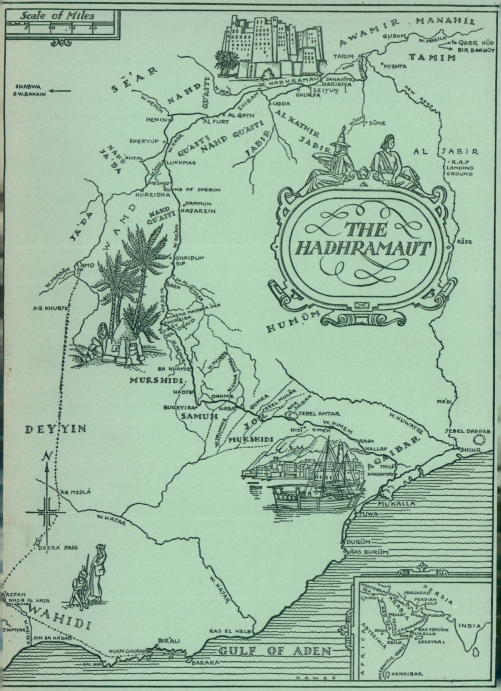

SKETCH MAP BY H. W. HAWES TO ILLUSTRATE THE CHAPTERS ON SOUTH ARABIA

1

First Journey to the South, 1933–35

THE most beautiful river poem to my mind is the description, in Sohrab and Rustum, of the Oxus:

"Rejoicing through the hushed Chorasmian waste,
Under the solitary moon."

It is, to the geographer, the picture of his life. Geologists may see their years in terms of time; musicians in some echo that dies in air; the poet strains language beyond the bounds of telling; the physicist sees diagrams of force rather than forms; the historian watches himself as one wave among waves of sea: but to us, who delight in maps, the idea of life inclines to be spatial—we see it moving from point to point, like a road if we are disposed to attribute its shaping to men, like a river, if we have more feeling for the unexpectedness of nature. Because I have lived free of institutions or a 'planned economy', I incline to the river. Its downhill course does not trouble me; the act of birth is implicit with death and I look with hope on the ultimate smooth sea. That is ever in sight, though the bends and turns that reach it may be hidden. I watch them in the past—swift corners where the current gathers in wrinkles like a worm and sweeps by bridges and landmarks: or curves that lead gradually to new reaches: or the few stretches that make straight for the polar star. Unwanted waters are left behind, in pools and eddies or swampy marshes. Tributaries tumble in from their private sources, and are involved in the majestic solitude in which each human soul sweeps to its estuary. And if the current is true

B

enough and strong, the last clogging sand bars will not hinder its peaceful entry into the waters from which it came. In this volume my river, in its middle course, distant from its 'mountain cradle', already well past many 'banks of sand and matted rushy isles', sweeps—with whatever splitting of current and stemmed stream—towards the Arabian south.

I have often been asked what first turned me towards Arabia, and the explanation usually seems inadequate though I cannot find a better. At the back of the adventure lay a curiosity for things in general which I had even as a child, and a desire, justified I think by the unusually harassing surroundings of my youth, to escape into an emptier, less fretful life. I had leaned towards music and then drawing, and had shown no talent for either: had written something and—encouraged by my godfather, W. P. Ker—sent it to *The Cornhill* to be rejected: the little spark, with no one about to blow it to a flame, went out for the time being. But there was a creative impulse, which is strong as love and deep as life, and if it finds no road available in art will turn to life itself for its shaping. Not wholly consciously, but not quite unconsciously, as far as I can remember, I determined to fashion my future as a sculptor his marble, and there was in it the same mixture of foresight and the unknown. The thing in the mind of the artist takes its way and imposes its form as it wakens under his hand.

And so with life. With my requirements, the answer I found was sure to be remote. It was also bound to include danger, for I remember wishing often to find what might silence fear, and to reach the end of my days free from that mortal weakness. This is no addition of later years, for I have found references to it in notes and diaries, and can remember at the age of fourteen the tranquillity which a first reading of the Phaedon, the death of Socrates, gave me—a widening of the bounds of life which even then I felt to be essential. To turn this widening from a mere concept into a reality remained sometimes consciously, and always, I think, subconsciously, one of my chief desires: and how deep and permanent it was I realized through my joy and relief during the second war, when a rather hopeless operation found me, by some happy coincidences, free from anxiety and ready. My parents were both perfectly gallant in their separate ways, and so was my sister; in all my youth fear seemed to be unrecognized and non-existent except obscurely and ashamed in my own heart: and perhaps, strangely enough but not as unusually as one might imagine, it was this unavowed timidity which made me seek out dangerous things and made me find—even in mountaineering—that the chief delight was *not to be afraid*. Only a person both adventurous and timid can feel this.

With such ingredients, and a love of research for its own sake, a liking for people and language, a habit of travel, and a deep diffidence in social relations which yet I was drawn to—it is not surprising that the adventures came: that they came in Arabia was accident. I wanted space, distance, history and danger, and I was interested in the living world: I think it was some stray conversation with a young man I liked—Gabriel de Bottini—just home from north Africa; the coincidence of a teacher in San Remo; the realization of the wide reach of the Arab lands and the drama of their future, involved in oil: all these things were sufficient to localize those deeper desires which would otherwise have found their outlet equally spontaneously in China or Peru, or anywhere where space, distance, history and danger existed.

In Asolo, on the edge of the Venetian plain, the gift of the house I still live in brought with it a mellowness, a feeling of home. The happiness of a livable world in which one is at ease had existed at L'Arma, but there it had been my own making: my mother, torn from Dronero and unhappy, always felt it as exile. In Asolo she came to a place where many people had loved her in her youth. A life she liked, and was meant for, gradually wound itself about her; she turned from all that she had cared about and made herself anew. Sir William Goodenough, a friend in these years, once said of someone: "He has courage, and that is all that matters." It might have been said of my mother, for this gift of hers brought everything in its train. She never tired of life nor feared it, but met all with acceptance, crisp gaiety, zest, and humour. The deep sorrow, and even remorse, over my sister's death; the distress for the children kept out of our way; the blatant evidences of her son-in-law's duplicity—all dug themselves within her, with suffering and an ever-widening charity, an absence of blame for others and that humility which wastes little time on its own concerns. The most casual visitor could feel her nobility; and she had that supreme goodness which carries unimpaired into old age the capacity to love.

Her conversion to the Roman church, a discipline and, I believe, a hard effort in the years of her sadness, now became her comfort and support. She would descend with a happy serenity after mass on Sundays into the peace of our garden in the sun. Perhaps the pleasantness of gossip in the church porch, the friendly interests of local affairs, contributed to the benefits of prayer: my mother loved to expend herself in uncomplicated feelings of charity. Our Monsignor, an old man with an amethyst ring, the brogue of a peasant and the mind of a diplomat, and behind his simplicity a feeling that all the panoply of Rome was there, would sit with her for hours, discussing some quite practical problem—communists, illegitimate babies, or drains. Like Wordsworth in the Ode to Duty, my mother laid aside her will—as much as so vital a person could do so—and for the first time in her life took advice: and Monsignor's advice was strictly sensible. On one occasion she asked him whether it was justifiable for her to acquiesce in the fascist habit of making out two bills, a genuine and a tax-payer's bill, for the clients of her little factory, where the Asolo silks were woven: without a moment's hesitation he absolved her from any remnant of Anglo-Saxon scruple. In those days honesty was easy in Britain: many of our friends have now come round—in practice if not in theory—to the old Monsignor's view.

Herbert Young and I remained Protestant, and this impeded the intimacy of our household during the first Asolo years.

But tolerance prevailed. My mother's generosity, her sense of humour and the long independence behind her, held their way; both Herbert and I had a love for the old religion, livable as a rambling house that every age has touched and altered, so that the roots of history, of human nature itself, seem built into its stones. Among its porches and outer shrines and gardens we could happily wander, and watch my mother disappear into the privacy of inner places that gave her peace.

The fascist politics of these years were not nearly so easy. In 1924 the socialist deputy Matteotti was murdered, and the mock-trial of his assassins followed: I turned from Mussolini and his methods, nor did the punctuality of trains seem to me to make up for the abolition of the constitution and of every democratic guarantee. My journey to Syria in 1927 opened my eyes to Italian ideas in the Mediterranean. In 1933 I told someone in London that there was a plan for Abyssinia and that it would inevitably entail conflict with us—and was told that I might be sure our Foreign Office had the question well in hand. Through the years that followed there was a growing anguish; a certainty that war lay at the end of this long totalitarian run; and despair when I went to England to see the apparent favour with which Mussolini was considered as a prop of the Conservative party.

These rigid feelings made my life difficult in Asolo, where my mother cared nothing for politics and everything for the people with whom she lived. I listened, exasperated almost beyond endurance, to descriptions of the fascist regime made to our travelling English with a disregard, innocent but total, of any fact at all. Monsignor was all for bowing to every Rimmon in sight; and when an order came on the national day that only Italian flags were to be shown, my mother obediently took down the Union Jack from our balcony; I put it up again, as soon as I noticed, and she submitted, not from conviction but love.

Because of her little factory, she was involved with and attended to by every sort of fascist official interested in the great game of advertisement which lay at the root of Mussolini's success. The Italians had not been used to slogans: unobtrusive pictures, bad and small, recommended *Olio Sasso, Fernet Branca, San Gemini* or *Cinzano*—but there was nothing to correspond to English hoardings; the pæans and invocations that now began to stalk in large black letters across every blank wall acted as a new bacillus in virgin soil.[1] Before 1939 the effect had worn itself away and a cynicism born of three thousand years of civilization was brought to bear on the simple and mostly ridiculous words; but in the first instance I am convinced that a large part of Mussolini's power was due to his introduction of the methods of advertisement to an inexperienced people.

I once saw Mussolini during these years. He came to open an industrial fair at Treviso, where my mother was given a stall—a little room like a box in a theatre. Here she set up a loom and spread some of her silks, and I dressed as a peasant girl and sat with the weavers. I spent a long time the night before wondering whether I should take our little revolver and shoot the Duce as he came by. I am glad I did not try, partly because I should certainly have missed; and partly because a deep un-reasoned feeling for the immensity of life, too sacred to be touched by human judgment deterred me, and even more, a feeling for the unreliability of history which might exalt a man equally by his living or his dying: it would be disappointing to ennoble that ignoble man by killing him—and the thought of my mother and myself no doubt added their weight in his favour. So he walked past benignly, surrounded by black escorting shirts,

---

[1] A few of these slogans may be worth noting before they are forgotten:
"*Molti nemici, molto onore.*"
"*Credere, obbedire, combattire.*"
"*Ogni casa un corpo di guardia.*"
"*Quando si ode il tuono del cannone, è proprio la voce della patria.*"
"*Libro e moschetto, fascista perfetto.*"
"*Mussolini ha sempre ragione.*"
"*Se avanzo, seguitemi; se indietreggio, fermatemi; se muoio, vendicatemi.*"
"*Meglio un giorno da leone che cento anni da pecora.*"
"*La pace riposa su otto milioni di baionette.*"
"*Il Duce comanda; Vittorio Emanuele eseguisce; e Dio approva.*"

tassels and sabres, and I watched him and thought how he would look without a uniform to distinguish him, in a crowd. Like a good, bullet-headed, Roman centurion, I thought, who had seen some service, but not so very much. The people danced folk-dances before him, and he relaxed into a benevolent, elderly man, with sagging lines: until he remembered the photographers and the Public, and straightened, and pushed out his chin.

Among the better things stimulated by the fascist publicity was an interest in Italian handicrafts; they were encouraged and exhibited as well as being almost suffocated by regulations, and both these processes brought small swarms of visiting officials to the silk weaving in Asolo, which my mother had made the best of its kind in Italy. Uneasy little people came, unaccustomed to command: my mother saw in them only the struggling, decent humanity, while to me they were an advance-guard in the downfall of Europe. Our divergence was more apparent than real—as if one of us were looking at a waterfall and the other at its drops. In the end I think my mother was right: the world belongs to those who see its individual beauty; personal goodness is safe, and the abstract is full of danger; and when the test came in 1939 my mother's uncritical generosity had its reward in the love of all. Long before that, she and I found each other in a region of pure affection beyond the range of ideologies; we realized that the foundations were the same, and that differences in the superstructures, accidents of temperament or the mere friction of living, could be eased by management and absence so as to disappear.

Absence is one of the most useful ingredients of family life, and to dose it rightly is an art like any other. In the years between 1933 and 1939 I was most often away from home, and yet the happiness received and given, the planning and remembering, were greater than anything that might have come through an unbroken stay: the domestic masochist who refuses to take a holiday may consider whether a fear of not being found indispensable does not lie at the bottom of his or her constancy.

[7]

The relation between parents and grown-up children is anyway artificial, a novelty in the animal world which requires most delicate handling. My mother now concentrated on me all the affection which her nature was bound to bestow, selfless and overwhelming: other objectives had disappeared, and I sometimes felt—with regret for my ingratitude—that the amount of this affection was more than I could manage. If I happened to dine out, she would lie awake till I came in, to say good-night; and however late I might sit after dinner, would never go to bed before me. These silly things oppressed me. I felt like a small raft—inadequate to be alone to support a human soul on the deep sea where it swims. It also made me egotistical, for I knew that the greatest pleasure I could procure my mother was to let her *give*—her time, her thoughts, her love: my letters in these years are full of vanities and make me, in fact, less modest that I am and far more snobbish, for I told her everything about myself that I thought might please her. And when now some unexpected flattery comes upon me, a sense of loss comes with it, for there is no one left to whom it can give that innocent satisfaction.

At L'Arma, on the Riviera, where most of the summer of 1933 was spent, a change had also crept in; the sun, the sea, the leisure, the hot scents under the pines were good as ever, but they had lost their feeling of permanence: it was a holiday place and no longer a home, and as we were still far too poor to keep a house merely for pleasure, there was a weight attached to it. The necessity to sell or let it was in our minds and it gave a sensation frequent in the possession of two houses—the sort of strain visible on the face of the lady in the circus who is riding two horses at once. New friends from the East came—Gerald de Gaury, standing with his paintbox in his hand and his hat over his eyes, decorating our palm tree with a frieze: and Christopher Sykes, a young man about to try his luck in Luristan, whom I had met and liked in Teheran as an honorary attaché with a reputation for never working, because of his preference for a world not enclosed in files.

[8]

In 1933, when the bathing and the drives were over, days with the Biancheris across the border at Eden Rock or Monte Carlo, or visiting Mrs. Robertson at Vence, or picnicking in and out of Alpine ridges that looked south to the Mediterranean and north to Europe; when the olives were blackening on trees that in shadow take the colour of the patina on bronze, and the vines were turning again to sticks after their summer's wealth—I went to Asolo by Dronero, with a long two-day walk with my sister's children in the hills on my way.

October was spent quietly, and then came Geneva and London, and I was not back till May of 1934, for another Italian summer broken only by a fortnight in Bavaria and first climbs in the Bavarian Alps. We drove to Innsbruck across the Brenner and reached Partenkirchen, where the outsides of houses are frescoed with saints and madonnas under wide eaves, and every walk in the pastoral mountains is cheered by an 'Alp' that sells beer or coffee by the way. I hope and think that this may still be so, for it made the country pleasant, like a garden on somebody's show day, and the Bavarians enjoyed and walked about their mountains as if they found them new and enchanting and did not think of them as being there all the time. The Bavarian husbands enjoyed them, walking with pointed sticks and *lederhosen* and open vests and glistening hot necks, like statues of the Roman decadence by barbarian craftsmen who have no longer the skill to make the head the right shape or put expression in the features: but they were happy and ready to 'grüss Gott' instead of 'Hitler' when they saw we liked it better: and their wives, out of reach of conversation ten steps or so behind, in the pretty *dirndl* that suits all figures, were happy too. They were friendly and strangely unlike what one thought of as a modern world; and in spite of the good food and clean service and up-to-date appointments of Dr. Wigger's Kurheim where we stayed, we felt like travellers of the Middle Ages, who found a way of life and a tradition entirely different from their own only a few days' journey away, across half a dozen ranges. During these weeks, in a bleak supernational atmosphere, beyond the comprehension of these rather insensitive valleys, the Austrian Anschluss was being organized.

I was joined by Lucy Selwyn, a mountaineer and friend, and we spent ten hours over the Alpspitze and Hochblassen during our last days and then, having crossed back to Italy, walked from Siusi by the Schlern to Vajolet and climbed the Stabler and the Winkler Turm on two successive mornings. The Winkler is a hard tower, and the few little creases that are by way of being footholds on the worst stretch were very far apart for my small size: I was the last on the rope, which is left long in the Dolomites to allow for escalading and fastening on to rock: it led, solitary and uncompromising, up a smooth face to the region into which our guide and my companion had vanished out of sight—and somehow I had to join them. I tried and slipped, and the rope, holding me like a pendulum under the armpits, swung slowly out over the valley far below; it swung with a circular movement round a sort of bastion and back again, and I had plenty of time to look about me—with slight nausea—and to plan to grip the mountain face before we swung again. I did so, and with inelegance managed to scrabble somehow up the side, so pale that Lucy noticed it when I reached her: I said nothing to lower morale at the time, but sucked some lumps of sugar—and I have often found that the best way of dealing with emotion is to eat. In a letter to Jock Murray a week or two later I describe the Dolomites as 'finicky', which seems a peculiar adjective for that strenuous morning: but there is a lot of detail about them which makes them look, beside the Alps, as a Japanese garden might look beside the old trees of an English park. To me, the great and simple lines of the granite are ever the most satisfying: yet the Dolomites have a domestic loveliness; old age can walk about their meadows, where no distance is too unmanageable; and when I revisited them lately, and looked across to the Schlern and Rosengarten from the top of Latemar, and saw the varied pastoral forest-scattered region that slopes from Trent to the Brenner, it seemed to me that few countries in the world look more happy or more beautiful. The Winkler

Turm has been my last adventure on rock, and it ended happily with an *abseilung*, which I had never tried before: the rope runs through the hand smoothly and lets one down and makes the mountain seem intimate and easy—and it was borne in upon me that a rope, like one's digestion, imagination, and many other things besides, is not really one sort of object but two, according to whether it is under control or no.

I saw new bits of Europe and especially Germany during the next two years, for I chose a different route to and from England whenever I went there. Munich and the Amalienburg—gone like last year's snow—a train journey through the vine-lands of Würtemburg, Cologne and its cathedral, a drive up the western border by Freiburg and Trier in 1935. What I best remember is the peacefulness of the frontier hills, with autumn orchards laden, and dusty lanes cut by the frontier pole; and the same sort of men on either side in their different uniforms, turning out to let our car through with the same friendly boredom; and wayside inns where one drinks kirsch of the Vosges, or villages whose vintage creaks over cobbled streets under timbered houses where the baby Rhine still goes gay, an uncontroversial stream. We stayed a few days in Belgium, rebuilt and prosperous, and saw the tapestry-like Brussels square, the castle of Ghent and the pictures in Bruges, with a recurring wonder that so much has come through—the stones of the walls scarce chipped, the painters' colours merely softened by time. Sometimes, when looking into shops that deal in antiquities, I have been overcome by the number of *objects* the world, with all its vicissitudes, has managed to collect and preserve, and have felt it almost a blessing that things are destroyed: but now, while our ruins stand raw and naked, with the humanity that belongs to them bleeding like a wound, it is a comfort to remember that debateable land lying between its two wars in the sun, preserving itself, reshaping the rhythm of its towns and rivers, tillages and harvests, till the torn edges are healed into new tissue, and none but the historian will guess the covered gap, where the plough cuts its usual furrow, whatever the hand behind it.

[11]

After my return from the East, in June 1933, I reached London to be presented with the Back Grant by the Royal Geographical Society, and stepped into a world of encouragement and publicity for which nothing had prepared me. I was old enough to take it quietly and cared more for the new friendships, the feeling of being less on the circumference of life, the discovery above all that people I met were ready to give the best of themselves, than for the platform ingredients of success. "The great point about being a traveller", I wrote to my mother, "is that everyone tells you the amusing things *they* have done . . . they know that one can understand and sympathize, and I find it much nicer than being expected to talk myself."

I stayed with the Rhuvon Guests whom I loved, and saw Vyvyan Holt who was over with King Faisal from Iraq, in cheerfulness until the Assyrian massacres threw a shadow. At the Royal Geographical Society or through the Goodenoughs I met explorers—Bertram Thomas, Philby for whom I have a liking, Douglas Carruthers who became a friend; and Sir Percy Cox—thin, with long face and long nose a little crooked, like an old portrait badly painted where the character is so strong that it shows through. An Arab told me that he was called 'The One of Forty Ears and One Mouth' because he spoke so little and knew so much—but he would ask for me in the R.G.S. when he heard I was in the building, and I would go in to the little Presidential study, and find that he liked to talk at his own pace and about his own ground; there was a great atmosphere of fine spacious days about him, of the gulfs and coasts of Arabia.

I stayed with the Julian Huxleys in Highgate, in a gay little house where the people one could wish to meet were sure sooner or later to appear. Juliette has the art and Julian the zest for living, and both are unselfish enough to prefer companionship to an audience. I met Lady Ottoline Morrell there with a Gainsborough sweep from a past that has vanished; and Ruth Draper with fine sad eyes, too sensitive to escape without grief in this world; and James Stephens, fragile and elusive as if he stood on the universe on tiptoe—but unfortunately always interrupted by his wife.

At Sir John and Jock Murray's, in Albemarle Street, where friendship was growing as *The Valleys of the Assassins* was being printed, in a good atmosphere of Lord Byron and Victorian solidity combined, I met Peter Quennell and Peter Fleming, Hector Bolitho, Osbert Lancaster and a number of other friends of to-day; and Dr. Munthe, who gave his publisher more trouble than I did, for he had to be *packed* for. I found him so padded in charm that one could never reach him.

I lunched with the Allenbys, made shy by the hot eyes and great domed forehead and the sensation of a will more powerful than any other part of the soldier; even a quiet observer felt it in full force, and the sense of *safety* was lacking, which the greater but more evenly proportioned character of Lord Wavell was to give, when years later I came to know him. Sir Ronald Storrs, also a stranger to me then, sat on my other side at this luncheon party, and made me feel sandwiched between *suaviter in modo* and *fortiter in re*.

To old friends in Scotland, Cambridge and Devon, I now added visits to the Iveaghs, who had become pillars of the little world in Asolo and very dear to my mother, and who asked me for many good week-ends during the next few years. I saw orientalists, and studied the elements of Sabæan script, and in London made friends with Husain 'Ala, Persian Minister at that time. I was asked by him to a dinner commemorating the poet Firdausi, and watched him as he listened inscrutably to Sir John Simon, the guest of honour, making one of the most tactless speeches I have ever heard, praising the Persian nation for all that it had ever copied from the West.

When the Back Grant was given me, Viva Jeyes, who had been so good to me in my youth, began to reproach me for conceit. It was not want of affection—but perhaps the sight of my life opening out made her feel old, and she spent most of the time we were together reminding me of anything that might depress me. Like a pony that means to get its canter anyway, I put my head down and pretended not to mind, but it distressed me, and I hated to see cheerfulness wasted which I would so gladly have shared. The reproaches did not hit their mark, for they were unjust. Perhaps a detached perspective comes to me by nature; I felt surprise and pleasure over what was happening to me, but not conceit; I think that I felt it fair to cash in on the good things, having had to put up with so many of the bad: and I am delighted anyway to welcome pleasantness without the arrogance of wanting to feel that I deserve it.

Publicity in itself had no head-turning qualities as far as I was concerned. At college, the mere answering to my name for the morning roll call had given me a suffocating uneasiness: to walk up to a platform and take my parchment from the kind hands of Sir William Goodenough was like a dive into deep water—in spite of reason, I could not believe that it would turn out well. On the day after this ceremony a voice over the telephone asked if I would speak for the BBC. "Have you ever heard of this institution before?" it asked. I was taken into a little padded room, to 'talk naturally', and for the first time in my life was paid a guinea a minute for my time. My inhibition about speaking in public must be entirely visual, perhaps an early vanity, conscious of plainness and badly made clothes; for in moments of excitement I forget it, and over the air, where the speaker is unseen, I feel no timidity at all.

I pulled myself together and lectured at the Royal Central Asian Society, in November, to one of the gentlest audiences, full of my friends. Charles Ker came to fetch me in a luxurious car, dined me on champagne, and handed me to my chairman Sir Denison Ross, who led me up some steps to contemplate a packed room, completely silent, below. How different are the feelings with which one reaches some nick in the hills and sees the empty ranges of travel before one: and how incongruous that one of these moments should lead to the other. Next year, in 1934, I spoke again at the BBC, in a Persian miscellany arranged by Lionel Fielden, which I enjoyed entirely, for it was done in company—with Sir Denison, and old General Dunsterville who had built the road of the Paitak Pass to Kermanshah, and A. T. Wilson who had become a member of Parliament and managed in a downright, argumentative, yet not disagreeable way to insult every member of the team separately before the rehearsals were over. The pleasure of this comradeship took away all the uncomfortable (and I think pernicious) Simon Stylites element of solitary publicity.

In the same month of October, the Royal Asiatic Society gave me the Burton Medal. This was an immense pleasure, a sort of consecration into the fellowship of Arabia, and again astonished me with the strangeness of being rewarded for what one likes to do—though it is, perhaps the best thing to be rewarded for. Lord Lloyd gave me the medal—"very alert and decided, neat little man," I wrote at the time, "he spoke charmingly about me, in fact everyone was too good and I felt that it couldn't be me. Captain Burton rescued me and gave me a cocktail afterwards, and I ended the evening at the Goblet with the Geoffrey Youngs."

Three publishers, besides John Murray, now asked to see my work, which had been appearing in *The Cornhill, Spectator, Contemporary,* and *Illustrated London News.* Between 1929 and 1934 I made £272 by writing (and spent £155 on dress): it does not seem very much, but I thought it affluence. Even then, poor as I was, and ever since, I have looked on the gain of my writing as something to be spent exclusively on superfluous things. I would rather live poor with good surprises than melt my comforts down into an average and take variety away, and in the winter of 1933 I put this theory to the proof.

I had been half scalped in a machine as a child, and a nerve in the head now gave trouble. An operation was recommended, though not urgently essential: but the surgeon said that by removing some of the scar, my appearance would be greatly improved, and this magic promise took away all hesitation. The want of a regular education has never caused me any regret, but the absence of beauty has always been disappointing; I have managed without it, but even now I cannot help thinking

[15]

how much more fun to myself and others I might have procured, but for the absence of a few pigments, a millimetre here or there, a tiny tilt of chin or eyebrow, which those who possess them often scarcely know how to manipulate, and which I felt I might have animated to very great advantage. I was still much in love at this time, neither dropped nor requited, and therefore unhappy; and I nursed the sad little useless feminine illusion that improved looks might make a difference. The difference is scarcely ever in the object; it is in the eye that sees and clothes what it loves in its own enchantment, so that Aphrodite herself may leave a man cold and some little tip-tilted nonentity find a way to his heart. This is a happy arrangement, and a comforting one too, for it means that love seeks, however clumsily, for something more essential than the trappings of time. Yet beauty is certainly useful, if only to create illusion; and with this lure, and with the wish to be as sound as possible before my next expedition, I went into hospital on the 18th of December.

I wished to tell no one except Minnie Granville, Venetia, and my mother, for I meant to be operated on from a public ward and to save my income for my Arabian journey, and had no wish to be forced by my friends to take a private room. With the determination of not wasting more money than necessary on the merely useful, I said nothing, left the gaiety of London, packed a little underwear and some books, reached Dollis Hill Hospital in a taxi, and was taken with my suitcase in my hand to a bed in the long white row of a ward.

I spent eleven weeks there, a longer time than I or anyone else had expected. Twelve beds stood in two rows in a high, light, airy room. The only strain was a want of privacy: in the early morning, with the winter darkness lying like a wild creature outside the curtainless windows, we washed with our basins perched on the beds between our knees. I came to know how the early waking, deplored by convalescent sleepers, is longed for by those in pain; and I still think with gratitude of the first mug of tea. The patients were kind people, good to each other, helpful as soon as they could move about, touchingly self-con-

[16]

trolled so as not to increase the general discomfort, decent in every way. The feeling for differences of class was much stronger then than now, and they constantly did small things for me saying: "We know that you're a lady", with the gentleness that belongs to all the world and lives in the heart. And when a shocking woman was thrown in upon us by a street accident and spent four days without a word to anyone right or left, except to say: "See where they have brought me" to the young man who came to carry her away—her departure was greeted with a kindly sort of contempt; and "she thinks herself too good for us" was the worst that was said.

I learned a great many things, many that pleased and some that shocked me. Among the latter was the fact that no one, myself excepted, ever mended their underwear; they bought it cheap and threw it away, which entails a slatternly period of holes. I was also pained but amused at the pink, paper-bound novels that went about: I asked my neighbour to read me a paragraph, and this was it: "'Good God,' said Susanna: 'what will my mother say when she hears that I have dropped my new eyelashes into the champagne?'" To me everyone was kind, perhaps because I was alone except for a visit from Minnie and from Viva. The operation took three hours, late in the evening, and the whole ward, which had kept awake after its bedtime to watch for my return, told me next day that I was the only patient they had seen to be wheeled back smiling in her sleep. They kept quiet for a day or two after, so as to let me rest as I lay with my eyes bandaged and in pain. They did this for anyone who was really suffering: but the people in the beds near me also kept quiet during the days before the operation, when I lay busily reading about South Arabia, and this delicacy I have always remembered with gratitude.

My deprivation of sight lasted less than a week, but it had an instantaneous effect of removing me into a far world, where not only visible boundaries, but the landmarks of hearing, of taste and smell too seemed to be removed: all food was alike, and the ear, unaided and unaccustomed, could not tell from where a footstep came; touch alone remained reliable. I fell back on the poems I had once learned, and pulled them out bit by bit from their forgotten crannies, until—by the end of the week— about five thousand lines had returned to me.

A second operation had to be performed, and the weeks went on. I became the Oldest Inhabitant and arbiter of the ward, a sort of final court of appeal. I was in distress, apart from this delay, for the man I cared for nearly died at this time and I waited for news every day. I would have gone to him, and planned to do so if I recovered soon enough; and dreams of his illness joined themselves to mine and galloped like horses all night through my heart. In that stress, which I could only keep to myself, my useless love burnt itself out: only love that is answered can last for ever. There was still one meeting in the summer full of pain; and then suddenly, the thing that had been a part of me and had hurt so much was outside me, like a dead puppy which the mother can turn over and sniff at and know that it is dead. With ecstasy and surprise I felt that I was free.

By the end of February, my cropped head wrapped in a velvet hood, I was riding to hounds with Venetia in Wales. I was in London a month later, and spent a happy spring, the work of my book behind me, no immediate task on my hands, surrounded by friends. On my last evening, Jock Murray gave a party which somehow ended in Lord Byron's mews, in a room where the door by which Augusta used to enter can still be seen; and on November the 8th I left, seen off at Victoria, and sailed from Venice on the 24th. In my luggage I had a mass of notes on South Arabia and letters of introduction to the sultans in the Hadhramaut. They had been obtained in a roundabout way through the kindness of Lord Halifax, who wrote to Sir Akbar Hydari, who procured them from the Sultan of Mukalla, then in the bodyguard of the Nizam of Hyderabad. I knew that without some definitely open door I could never get a British administration to let me wander as I pleased, and but for these letters I would have had great difficulty in jumping that barrier

[18]

which makes our civilization a sanctuary or a prison according to the side from which one sees it. I should have had difficulty, but I think I should have succeeded, for I was now recognized as a traveller and met everywhere with kindness.

The journey, largely told in *The Southern Gates of Arabia*, is described in the letters that follow. I reached Aden in November, and spent a few weeks studying the Arabic of the south; on the 13th of January with 13 packages, after dinner at the Residency, I changed my silver slippers for canvas shoes and started in a small coasting vessel belonging to M. Anton Besse for Mukalla. The country was still wild; a temporary truce had soothed it to allow of the Sultan's visit to his almost unknown towns of the interior—but the weeks of the truce were running out and the little towns were preparing again for their perpetual wars. The state of the country was rather like that of England under King Stephen: beyond the quiet but desert emptiness of the *jōl*, north of Du'an, every fortified spur, house, or city boasted an independence of its own, until one reached the wider but equally unsafe reaches of the great wadi Hadhramaut. From Mukalla I made my way with a small caravan of donkeys, inland to the wadi Du'an.

Clear of cross currents, I was now out again and happy in the freedom of the world. But in Du'an I sickened, and in the great wadi Hadhramaut I very nearly died. I lay there for a fortnight facing, like someone condemned, a death that seemed both impossible and inevitable. In the intervals of weakness I read Virgil:

> Vivite felices, quibus est fortuna peracta
> Iam sua: nos alia ex aliis in fata vocamur.
> Vobis parta quies: nullum maris aequor arandum.
>
> > (*Aen. III*, 493)

> Deserta per ardua dulcis
> Raptat amor.
>
> > (*Georg. III*, 290)

[19]

Largior hic campos aether et lumine vestit
Purpureo, solemque suum, sua sidera norunt.

(*Aen. VI*, 640)

These quotations, written in my notebook at the time, still bring back the sharpness of those days, the hard, remote and noble valley so tremendously separated from the world, the heroic quality of its life, so like the Aeneid—"the little towns; the surrounding enmity; the holding to custom and one's own people; and the unreasonable women kept separate, while men watch the games."

*   *   *

HOSPITAL, LONDON, 6 January, 1934.

Dearest Venetia [Buddicom],
I am able to do a little work but not much and devote much time to thinking. It is more and more borne in upon me how wrong people are to judge events from the time of their accomplishment and not from the moment of their *thought*: the real action is when one *thinks* a thing—the rest just an unrolling of consequences. It is sometimes frightening to see the consequences come rolling in so inevitably after the thought which had started them is already so far past. I am sure that the misconception leads to half the troubles in the world—in human and all relationships: people try to deal with actions, which are merely consequences and cannot therefore be any longer vitally affected: and leave the actual causes of events lying unnoticed and untended around them all the time.

9 January, 1934.

Dearest B [My Mother],
I am glad I am not in a private ward. They all have biblical names and the one now vacant is called "The Agony in the Garden"!

12 January, 1934.

I got your letter but was *thoroughly shocked* by your plea that for the sake of obtaining even most valuable prayers one can give away

[20]

other people's secrets! I am sure too that the Father Eternal takes my more conventional view of the matter and no sooner got those illicit supplications than he sent me my relapse. As for John, I don't know whether he prays or not, but I know he knows about my operation.

31 January, 1934.

Dearest Venetia,

I am getting better. It is mysterious, where one gathers strength after such absolute prostration, but somehow or other the little cells go on with their business, and to-day I can sit up and look round

"Rescued awhile from Death though pale and faint"

—every sudden movement still makes my heart feel like a bird trying to escape, but the head is mending all over and the eyebrow I hope will be elegant!

c/o VENETIA, FLINTSHIRE, 28 February, 1934.

Dearest B,

The great moment of the Wig's arrival came this morning—a lovely auburn creation all shining in waves like a peaceful sea, with a few ripples of curl at its edge. When I put it on I looked so exactly like a tart that I felt desperate. By careful tying in with a ribbon however, and pinning down the curls tight to my face, it now looks more like me, and no doubt in time you will all refuse to let me go back to my own modes and efforts. If we get a sunny day I shall get Venetia to take a snapshot and you shall see the loveliness for yourself! When I get to London again I will go and talk it over with Mr. Vasco and see if he can't make it smaller to the head—though with the ribbon it looks quite nice and Grecian.

ASOLO, 5 *May,* 1934.

Dearest Venetia,

I don't know what has happened to all these days. They have melted away in my hands! I am only just straight and unpacked this morning—really because instead of coming as I hoped to rustic peace, there was a festival in honour of Duse's anniversary in full swing and an Aunt and Uncle arriving on Vicenza platform simultaneously with me—and they have only just gone. We had defiles of young and budding fascists, ministers to make speeches, and tea in the

Municipio, which developed into a sort of football scrum, everyone fighting their way in after the ministers. I don't think they will ever turn Italy into a Military Nation: you never saw anything so bored and slipshod as these soldiers of the future: they had not even taken the trouble to shine their boots, and they are so obviously satiated with speeches and trumpet-blowing that it leaves them completely inert. In the evening Emma Grammatica, who was a friend of Duse's, gave a play—a cheerful little thing supposed to represent life in Canada, where the stepfather falls in love with his stepdaughter and shoots himself. And we had more speeches, and felt how comparatively restful London is.

20 May, 1934.

I am sorry about your old head. I know well what you felt like: it happens so often, especially at our time of life when everyone is so busy leading their own little show and there is neither the leisure of youth nor age. I don't think one should worry too much, or think of the drifting apart as more than temporary: one is so apt to think of people's affection as a fixed quantity, instead of a sort of moving sea with tide always going out or coming in but still fundamentally *there*: and I believe that this difficulty in making allowance for the tide, is the reason for half the broken friendships.

I had a telegram on the 17th, the day the book came out, from Mr. Murray saying, "Best wishes for birth of a swan." So I wired back: "Mother doing well. Congratulates other parent." I hope he did not think it too indelicate! They have sold 737 copies already, so I *hope* it may go on.

I am going to Venice to have a heart to heart talk with the Leica agent to see what is the minimum I can do with in the way of lenses etc. And also to see the result of the use of the electric light-meter: a man here has the very best one, and lent it me for a day, and I went about taking as many different sorts of pictures as I could. I have also tried taking an artificial light picture but fear my lens has not got a large enough opening. I think I shall get quite clever with the camera by the end of the summer.

I am also trying to do some botany—and it is very fascinating but rather improper—to pry so minutely into all the plants' private life!

[22]

27 *May*, 1934.

Did I tell you that I have discovered a third route—into Arabia by the Indian Ocean. The people of that district furnish the body-guard to the Nizam of Hyderabad, and I have got a letter to him from Lord Halifax asking for introductions: so there is hope there if the other fails.

PARTENKIRCHEN, 26 *June*, 1934.

Dearest B,

We [Lucy Selwyn and I] are starting rather incorrectly by train, as it has poured with rain all day and is only clearing now: the excuse was welcome, as we can both hardly move after 10 hours climbing yesterday. We started up the Alpspitze, and got up in 2½ hours, finding it so easy that it was really disappointing: so then the sight of Hochblassen, a real good pyramid of rock and only 2 hours more up was too tempting. Then the guide said that sometimes it can be done by a little ice couloir that looked very steep and engaging on the North face—what a pity we had no ice-axe to attempt it! By the time we got near the decisive col, the absence of the axe became of less and less importance in all our eyes, and the end was that we went up without, a really exciting hour of snow work and definite proof that my head is all right after all! The whole of the mountain was as good as could be—another hour of rock ridge with mist-filled abysses on either side: a bit of ice to come down over (where I had to lead the way too being first on the rope), and then a wonderful rock descent on to the Hollenthal Hütte, which would have been really difficult but for the rope banisters they stick in all over this landscape. I found I got back into my stride very quickly and it was a great delight to be searching for handholds in the rock and twisting round corners again.

2 *July*, 1934.

My dear Lionel [Smith],

My friend Lucy Selwyn and I have been walking about in the mountains, meeting in Bavaria and coming down the valleys by train and the mountains on foot, until I twisted my ankle yesterday and have to do the rest in a charabanc. But we got two days on the Rosengarten, doing two 'towers' to satisfy ourselves that our heads are still steady: it was rather terrifying. The only thing that made me feel a little sick was Lucy's hat, suddenly floating past—looking so very disembodied and alone with all the landscape behind and below it. One crawls up chimneys looking down on valleys far below, and really rather relieved when one follows the rope round its last corner to the top (especially when one's hands and wrists are as weak as mine), and then comes down in a sort of rope cradle, steering with one's feet against the mountain. It was 9 years since I had done anything in this way, and I was so glad to feel I could still face a height. The weather rather varied and not too good, but flowers lovely: little white soldanellas in the turf, and everything so much brighter than lower down.

Their 'quaint enamelled eyes'—is that Lycidas, or am I making it up?

ASOLO, 6 July, 1934.

My dearest E,

Your letter came just after we got home, and makes me very sad. It will not matter in time, but it does hurt dreadfully I know: and perhaps even more so, when it is just a dream that we relinquish. It happened to me, a few years ago now, and I remember one evening on the Punta at Mortola, coming on a little poem of Heine's which said to his own heart: "grieve no more, for whatever you lose, no one can take from you the freedom to love *anything, everything* in the world:" and it gave me great comfort: for after all it is *our* capacity for love which matters, and that is independent of anyone else. I feel also about marriage that we will soon have passed the age when the need of it is felt most hardly, and soon we will get into an age when all the things that are best followed in freedom will matter more and more: so that unless there is a very real companionship, we are probably better without it. I do not know—but if we are strong, and have faith in life and its richness of surprises, and hold its rudder steadily in our hands, I am sure we will sail into quiet and pleasant waters for our old age. Dearest, I *am* so sorry.

I have been awarded a medal: The Burton Memorial Medal— great honour—but all so expensive! I feel too that I have done nothing to deserve it.

21 July, 1934.

Dearest Venetia,

It is fun that you are beginning to collect a travel fund! It will be very necessary, as I foresee complete penury ahead: I think I must get an annuity for Mama (as Mario will *never* pay up) and that will leave me with no income at all. However, apart from this gloomy subject, what good news it is that you are able to think about it in a tangible form. I hope that by next year the journey to Asolo will be possible at any rate.

It is dreadfully hot and stuffy here now and I am rather worn and tired as I have so much work to do—all this added lecture business is just what breaks the donkey's back as I had as much as I could manage before. But the Arabian project gets more and more exciting: the old map is coming to life as it were: I can find enough existing land-marks to see its outlines very clearly, and there is an enormous field of discovery practically untouched. I hope I may reach it, though it is a grim little corner of aridity and wars. All the ancient fertility where the Great Route went is being submerged by the sands drifting south and is desert now.

I saw the *Merchant of Venice* the other day, given in the open air in a Venetian Piazza: I have never seen anything more beautiful—a little bridge across the Canal, where the gondolas slipped to and fro, and a palace and Jessica's balcony behind. Romance: the beautiful dresses strolling up and down, and masques and dancers. And the Italian, taking away from the play the magic of its verse, still left Shakespeare incomparably greater than anyone else: it was interesting to see him standing so, as it were, on the intrinsic merit of his *matter*, apart from the magic of words.

29 July, 1934.

What a bloody world we are living in! To read the papers makes one quite sick and here one cannot help feeling that the horror over poor little Dollfuss is largely mixed with eagerness over the excellent excuse for waving flags on the Brenner. I hope the British idea of civilization will win through in the end, for the more I see of other nations the more I feel that we are the only one ever actuated by any remotely decent motive at all.

I have done nothing this week but pore over Arab maps and I am quite worn out by it in this hot steamy summer weather. Also a feeling of loneliness. Also the worry of contemplating Mama's finance which, however, I hope to get settled on a very small but more or less trustworthy basis before I leave. Also the lecture which hangs like a millstone.   How *lovely* it would be if one could gather medals without lectures, roses without thorns.

The map of Arabia is very exciting.   There is no doubt that the S.W. corner is practically *full* of things to discover.   It is rather trying that three English people have just gone and vanished into space there.

A horrid reviewer says I have the "nose of an explorer" : he means to be kind, but *how* misguided, and so regrettably true.

28 *September*, 1934.

My dear Lionel,

I am hoping to go to Yemen in the winter.   Everybody tells me I *must* travel, now that I feel quite inclined to sit still!   But I have been rather feeble and depressed all summer, and it will probably do a lot of good to walk about the hills of Arabia.   I have been reading books about it and it sounds a good country though uncomfortable.

We did a proper Dolomite tower, with average footholds of about three inches, and felt quite happy but frightened and I had the unpleasant moment of dangling in space on a rope: I think I must have a scientific mind, because the only thought I can remember in the crisis was: "It can't be so unpleasant to be hung after all!"

28 *September*, 1934.

Dearest Venetia,

I am rather depressed, as after weeks of pain I went yesterday to be X-rayed—thought it might be an ulcer, but it is colitis—not so acute but quite tiresome enough, and not really desirable to take to Arabia. However I hope that care and self control in the matter of food may make it better before I start.

18 *November*, 1934.

The day after you left was very hectic as you can imagine: at lunch at the Ladies' Club, I sat between Lady Ampthill (whom I liked very much) and Elizabeth Robins who told me how she went to nurse her sick brother in the Klondyke years ago.   She was a frail pathetic little old lady with blue eyes and white hair that made one think of a lake in a snowy landscape.   I rushed away from lunch to go with John Murray to see the cinema camera, of which he is presenting half, and the rest to come out of the Assassins' Valley: the precious thing is to go straight to Aden where I shall have time enough to practise. I was so excited over this affair, that I completely forgot my tickets and passport and went and had tea with the Persian Legation family instead; then sherry with friends who had an R.A.F. man who wants to motor through Hadhramaut (but not for a year yet) and then home, and had to get the ticket on the way to the station next morning: Viva so tamed by then that all she could do about it were little protesting noises but nothing articulate.

We got across Europe quite comfortably: it is really an easier way because not crowded, and very lovely climbing up from Lake of Lucerne, with a powdering of new snow on the pines and the cherry trees red—and so here all well and not too many tea parties.

I don't think I shall ever get my things into anything *like* two saddle bags and I am now busy trying to compress.

My next letter will be from ship.

Nr. BRINDISI, 25 *November*, 1934.

I thought I should never get through in time and have had to bring various jobs with me, but the map got done, and the packing, and the beautiful white ship sailed out from the middle of Venice in the sunset, and I almost *ached* with the wish that you were with me. I felt as if you were too, in a way. It was very wonderful sailing by Venice just as her lights were lit: as if a Canaletto had suddenly come to life. It is a wonderful approach: the *Salute* cupolas against the western sky, and one looks right into the Piazza and at the Ducal Palace as one drifts by.

It was a wrench to leave Herbert: but he is very well, and so is Mama, so I hope all may be well till I return. Thank you again my dear for all—I can't tell you what a help you have been both moral and material. The sea is very blue, with a small wrinkle on it, but more than I like.

c/o W. J. BRAMLY, BURG AL ARAB, EGYPT, 29 *November*, 1934.
Darling B,

I am rather delirious this morning, having arrived here yesterday in the dark and slept in a well-curtained room, and only when I got up and drew the curtains, saw the sudden vision of the lion-coloured desert and a band of sea, almost black, beyond. The wind whistling in the sunlight over emptiness—quite different from the European wind that rustles in trees: it is all a hard gaiety not made for weaklings. It was agreeable enough to get here yesterday, to get away from the feeling of general degradation of Alexandria and push on and through all her rubbish heaps and suburbs, banana fields and cabbages, to the empty country in the sunset. The luminous sky that I now recognize, with a light, a quality of light shining *in* it as it were, and the dun coloured sands getting darker: we stop at little stations of ten or twelve houses with not a light showing, though it's only 6 o'clock: a bigger station where we meet the down-coming train (mostly empty water tanks as water has to be carried here): we go slowly from a long way out, so as not to run over all the village youth which is playing about on the line: the down-coming train puffs by with a dog trotting contentedly beside it: the ticket collector, one traveller, and the porter, help me out, and the station master (who has so much gold braid and is so smart that he quite overshadows his station) receives me, and soon Whiffy[1] and a nephew come up in a bumpy Ford; they have bread to give to the station dogs, and after this operation we set off over desert track, and through the mediæval arches of Whiffy's town, to the top of his hill, where his *qasr* stands like a palace in the Arabian nights. It is really fine, with great arched rooms, all white, and parquet, or black and white tiles, and in it all sorts of lovely furniture and rugs, with plenty of spaces between—and outside the desert.

1 *December*, 1934.

Dearest Venetia,

I am sitting on the seashore—the sea the colour of a green turquoise if you can imagine that as being luminous: everything is luminous, the white sand, made of microscopical fragments of shell all polished and rounded, the sky with soft cloudy layers, and the square walls of an old Egyptian temple to Osiris in the background—now called Abusir—on a ridge behind us. The sea is only three miles from the house: I see it from my window, an almost black horizon appearing here and there behind the desert ridge—and an old ruined lighthouse against it built in the time of the Ptolemies and on the same principle as the one of Alexandria. It is a view which makes one

[1] W. Jennings Bramly.

[28]

feel happy in spite of oneself and come down to breakfast in an optimistic mood—so wide and clear and empty—just the yellow desert with a thin scattering of scrub like heather, and the gentle ridges, and the old tower and sky. I wish you could see it. After breakfast I sit out in a summer house built of stone: all the house is built square of stone (a quarry of the Ptolemies is close by), and the walls around; heavy front door made of sheets of iron, so that one has half the feeling of being in a fort. The trees are all still small —no taller than I am, one has no feeling yet of anything to interfere with the desert freedom. And the house is full of empty spaces too, with lovely bits of furniture and rugs here and there. A young nephew, Akers Douglas, takes me down to the sea where there is even more solitude—miles of empty sands with crabs rushing about in and out of the water: Alexandria is on the right, 40 miles away, and on the left there is nothing worth speaking of before Tripoli.

The day after I got here, Mr. Bramly took me to call on Sayyid Idris the head of the Senussi, who has fled from the Italians and lives in exile in another square house alone on a hillside. My Arabic having vanished for the time being, I could only understand about half what he said, but it was very pleasant to be listening again and he was a charming figure, very slender and brown and gentle, with a red skull cap and slippers, and a white sort of toga they wear here in lieu of abba, thrown over his head and shoulder—a kind man, with the Arab sense of humour, and long well-bred hands and easy manner and no *louange* at all for the Italians. He left, and his lieutenant Omar Mukhtar went on fighting them until they got him and hanged him, and got everyone in from the countryside to see them do it—about 20,000 people, so that he is even more of a national hero after death than before. The Arabs said of him that "he could drive one to one's death more surely in a day than Time can in a hundred years"

3 *December,* 1934.

Dearest B,

The days here have gone very quickly and I am leaving to-morrow. I had meant to do so before, but Sayyid Idris, the Senussi, was going to visit us and I waited for that as I should have liked to have seen him again: but he is ill: the chief inspector, an urbane nervous little brown Egyptian who gave us coffee at the centre of the

[29]

district this morning, said that it was nothing of any importance, but his intestines, heart, liver, lungs, and kidneys were affected: but, said he, "I am twice as ill as he is and still cheerful."

The Italians are not popular here, and the advice I gave you about investments is very earnestly repeated. The Sayyid of the Senussi is of course very anti-Italian. His lieutenant went on fighting them after he left the country and became a national hero. He was a fine fighter and was once seen going into battle with no weapon at all: "I will find plenty to pick up from those who run away," he said.

Whiffy is full of all sorts of amusing stories. He has been in dozens of tight corners, and has met all the interesting people about here for the last generation at least. It is a charming combination to be so away from everything and everyone, and yet so interested in it all.

I am struggling with my notes: have got forty-five pages copied but so much still to do.

CAIRO, 4 *December*, 1934.

I add this from Cairo—I was to have arrived at 12 and got up to catch the little desert train at 7, Whiffy rattling me down in the old Ford through a beautiful sunrise-pink desert. The train however had to wait for the other train and we missed the *coincidenza*: the station master was on board, and he and the guard did their best for me (not that I cared): "Every minute shall be half a minute" said the guard, and waved and shouted to our engine: passengers were hustled down and off in the twinkling of an eye: signal boxes, as we rushed past, were screamed at in Arabic and told to stop the express: we saw the express steam in to the station from ever so far off: "It is waiting, you see," said my guard: "it must wait. Perhaps Bramly Bey will get me a transfer to Alexandria?" But sad to say, the Cairo express got tired of waiting and steamed out just as we arrived. I had to console the station master, he was so sad about it—the guard said: "This is a *bad* station." Anyway we had a good run for our money, and nearly derailed ourselves in the effort, and I had quite a nice morning walking about down to the sea.

Here I have just been out to see Cook's who are very superior and say there are no cargo boats and anyway there is a rule against taking ladies alone. I shall see about this however.

I lost my way and was taken back to the hotel by a stray young man who told me he had never heard such good Arabic from an Englishwoman. But he was a very dull young man.

7 December, 1934.

Dearest Venetia,

I have been thinking of you such a lot and wishing you were here again, yesterday going in to Sultan Hasan—the beautiful mosque with the straight square lines—do you remember? And the morning before when I really did get into the Tutankamen things. I am glad to have seen them and some are most beautiful—but on the whole it is more the cumulative effect which tells—the *mass* of objects rather than the loveliness of the period: and some are impressive just by the sheer value of the gold, like the enormous tomb-chambers of beaten metal, and the mask, and enamelled coffin of the king. But there are one or two really perfect things—a black dog-God Anubis, with tall ears, gilt inside and standing up, and gold rimmed eyes looking away through everything into space, lying with its paws out before it: such a triumph of simplicity, everything essential left there and nothing *but* the essential; even the four little delicate ripples of his ribs under the smooth black. There was another charming little gilt statue of the king throwing a harpoon, striding out, one leg forward, one arm raised, one sandalled foot bent on the ground: they seem to have the secret of giving movement without the restlessness of motion. And there were lovely models of boats, and chairs and chariots: the jewels looked like their own imitations in the Tottenham Court Road.

Mr. Guest gave me the names of various old Sheikhs to visit, but their addresses are all such as "in the school so and so, near the citadel". It takes a lot of wandering in slums to find them. A nice old bookseller I have got at and sat this morning in his shop, looking at books on Hadhramaut: he had very little, but an old man with a grey beard dressed in complete rags who was sitting in a corner turning over books suddenly recommended Maqrizi, a classic—as it might be if someone dressed far worse than a crossing sweeper were suddenly to say that one would find a quotation in Chaucer.

I can't get a boat till Wednesday, and shall reach Aden on the 19th d.v. I have got a passage for £11 instead of £21 (the P. & O. tourist fare) and am going to wipe the floor with Mr. Cook's young man before I leave.

[31]

I am being socially entertained: lunching and dining out and everyone very pleasant: no detectives visible this time! Do you remember how we teased the poor man? I have been given three doses of serum against scorpions, twenty-three against snakes, and the Bank Manager has cashed my cheque (though he did say that he would advise me to make more arrangements beforehand next time). In fact everyone is being as nice as can be—and a young man has just been to tea who is living here among the Egyptians and doing research work, and will take me into mosques I hope. Ramadhan begins tomorrow, and I wish I had time to see more of it. He knows a lot about the country—and was telling me how interesting it would be to go and live for a time at Tanta where is the shrine of the patron saint of prostitutes and all sorts of peculiar customs. He also tells me how they bring hashish from Syria: the horses are made to swallow it and it is then evacuated this end.

He tells me that the Italians are thoroughly disliked and the French too: and quite a strong pro-British party growing up. He seemed to think that unless this present Egypt government succeeds, the only other way out will be for us to return—invited by the Egyptians. Anyway, I can't understand people who think that the interesting time is over in the East: it seems to me that we are just on the threshold of all the excitement.

It is still like the Arabian Nights too. I went to the scent shop in memory of our visit and then fell for a small piece of amber (probably faked) in the bazaars, and was given coffee and invited to the cinema by the owner of the shop on the strength of my Baghdad accent: he showed me his portrait in Arab dress (he had been evicted for political reasons from Iraq)—and we parted like friends, though I believe he got rid of his worst piece of amber.

12 December, 1934.

Darling B,

George Cattaui and his brother took me through the Arab quarter full of lovely bits of noise and colour, bazaars with over-hanging wooden eaves—a narrow strip of light above; by old carved stone-work of mosques, into the most lovely mosque and tomb of Sultan Kala'un. The Arab makes everything one harmony, treating wood, stone, metal, and colour all the same in intricate pattern: the earlier however keeps a simplicity, and the good mosques here are places of peace, where the eye can rest on quiet proportions of smooth grey wall between the richness, and see up above the dim glitter of the gilt and painted ceilings. I went by myself afterwards and looked at other mosques in the Arab bazaar—a lovely one with school attached called Sultan Ghur:—and a friendly old Sheikh showed me round: as one goes in, one can look through a barred window down into a little roofed bazaar. The people are very good about showing their mosques and quite friendly. Though I was turned away from the Imam Shafa'i: he is the Imam for the Yemenis (one of the four great teachers whose ritual is accepted by the Sunni Moslems) and he is buried right away at the edge of Cairo through miles of slums. I was very late in getting to him because the tram ran over a donkey cart: a woman was rolled off backwards and bounced about but with no injury, even to her voice—but the poor donkey was dragged along in an unpleasant way for some yards and when finally extracted stood there, with a patient expression as if it were all in the day's work and a huge gash down its leg: I looked at both the woman and it, and as there seemed nothing useful to do, got back into the tram while the crowd gradually worked itself up—from quite quiet beginnings into a state of frenzy, luckily tempered by the expectance of the police. The tram conductors gathered together as one tram after another came up: the donkey owner went for the tram man and pulled his hair: luckily it was short and thick and did not give a very good hold, and the tram man was bullnecked and well able to bear it. But meanwhile I sat in the tram, and thought I was going to be late for lunch: a man with the groceries in his hand was thinking the same: we fraternized—when finally we went on he took me up to the mosque, where a horrid fat sheikh refused admittance without a pass. I told this tale to Mrs. Devonshire, a friend of the Guests with whom I lunched next day. She studies Islamic art and has the entrée, and happened to be taking a young Frenchman next day—so I got in after all and was rewarded by its being I am sure the most lovely tomb in Cairo, built by the daughter-in-law of Saladin who is buried there too with her son. It is all lined, dome and all, with richly painted woodwork. Everything except the modern screen round the tomb is old and lovely and in harmony. The sheikhs all knew Mrs. Devonshire and gathered in a friendly way, and we then went and looked at a very early tomb just behind and rattled away in the young man's car to the tomb of a female saint called Nafisa—there are five or six

D   [33]

female saints buried in Cairo. The car was a two-seater and I sat in the dicky, and we rushed at a mad and wicked speed but luckily missed the Arab ladies by inches: they all flutter about in veils in the middle of the road and look (and are) stupid.

The Murrays, who came to the Bramlys at Burg, have been taking me round to Pyramids—first to the near ones, which are much tidier than the others with sharper edges, and then to Sakkara further off; I enjoyed both. The Gizeh ones had a bank holiday air, as it was Sunday afternoon, and to see one's semblables moving about near them gives one a small idea of the human race. Mr. Murray quoted, I forget from whom, that the trouble with the human species is that it has so many duplicates. But when we had done our duty by the Sphinx we went up to tea with the archaeologists who live in little hutments at the back, in desert: and there one does not see the tourists and one does see the sunlit slope of the pyramids against the peacock-coloured Egyptian fields, and looks out on the other side over the sand which stretches to the Atlantic, and this was worth the afternoon call which happened simultaneously with that of twelve American Jews all in a bunch. Sakkara was far lovelier, and we descended into a tomb and saw its walls covered with delicate and most beautiful reliefs, some painted but the most pleasing, to my mind, not. All the dinners the man was to eat through Eternity were being brought to him, chiefly bread and goose: it was an awful thought that so long a series of menus was in the hands of your heirs and survivors; one would think carefully about what sort of a housekeeper one married. The birds and oxen were most beautifully done, with a perfection of simplified line which makes the later Greek seem vulgar.

The Archaeologist is a dear old patriarch—Mr. Quibell, who gave us tea. He is crushed under the weight of several tons of alabaster (Allah blaster he calls it) which used to be vases but appears to have been shattered by an earthquake under the pyramid, and out of the chaos complete vases have to be reconstructed. There were five heaps in separate parts of the courtyard. The world will be flooded with alabaster vases, and they are very precious, over 3000 B.C. I said I would bring him a piece of alabaster from Yemen, but he pretended not to hear! He has asked me to Cambridge where he lives. Everyone has asked me to come again and one can live cheaply at the Suore S. Carlo Borromeo (tell Lavinia): as it is I have been spending £2 a day what with one thing and another: some of it in medicines—30/- on a preventive of dysentery called Yatren: it seems to be very good and I am taking it now for my colitis: whether it is that or the really *excellent* food I don't know, but I begin to feel well again.

I have been giving every spare moment to my notes, and shall have them all done by the time I reach Aden (sitting up several evenings till midnight: they were like a nightmare).

Posted at PORT SUDAN, 14 December, 1934.

Dearest Venetia,

Do you remember looking from the Palestine-Egypt train at many parallel ranges running along our southern horizon? The mountains of Sinai? I am looking at them from the Red Sea, dark sapphire blue between us. The Mountains are even grander than they looked in the distance—reddish, with jagged crests running in saw edges, and no visible signs of human life—though no doubt if one were wrecked there, there would soon be a lot of those little black Howeitat Beduin or their cousins ready to do something unpleasant. We are getting into warmer weather and the misguided stewards put fans on to us at luncheon; the sea is getting calmer and calmer and a blacker blue: they have put awnings over the deck; we are in a state of coma, all sleeping figures in deck chairs, and not one of them looking ornamental. I am travelling tourist and they are all going back to offices in Mombasa or beyond and very dull.

The boat was twelve hours behind time coming through the canal, and I had over twenty-four hours in Suez. I got there late on Wednesday night and went to the hotel, and found myself an object of some interest next morning, as the servants—on the strength of my Arabic such as it is—had said I came from Jedda! The hotel would make a Somerset Maugham story. It was all a little dingy, but with obviously British efforts at comfort, and the black servant told me it was run by Mister Carew. He turned out to be an old stout naval cripple with a white pointed beard, who greeted me next morning. He had a leg shot off and many injuries guarding the canal here during the war. His wife had a blonde wig on and nondescript clothing, but a rather nice face and gentle manners: she wore black glasses and was quite blind. The poor old couple sat all in and out of their guests in a sort of central hall with a litter of magazines, sewing

machines, and an old old family friend who did the laundry: they take
quite a non-commercial interest in their guests and spend the days
telephoning to ask how far the various boats have got in the canal.
The last of the daughters was just away to be married; and a stage
Irishman, very bluff and squat, was looking after them out of friendship in a quite amateurish way. He was elderly, and had spent
twenty years as pilot on the canal, and had a little greyish wave very
much plastered into position on the top of his head, and china blue
eyes with an innocent expression. He thought me a spy at first and
came and sat with me in a little garden full of sparrows and oleanders
where the family cat, Peter, was trying to sit on my notepaper while
I wrote some Christmas letters. It was very funny to be suspected
once again: it seemed quite familiar. I had rather asked for trouble
by saying I wanted to see a man there who is a notorious smuggler of
pearls; I suggested asking him to lunch—Captain Macleavy came up
with an air of mystery and said that as a Man of the World he would
advise me not to do this; he said this with the solemn air of a wise
elderly baby and made a great effort not to say any more. But
having so started on my moral welfare, he was soon calling me 'my
dear child', and telling me all about life in Suez, and the poor old
couple who keep this hotel on though they have quite a good pension
—only it would bore them so to give up. And how he loves the
Bohemian life (east of Suez) and can't bear to live with his wife in
Worthing, which is nothing but whist drives "and Oim Oirish me
dear, but it leads to an extrangement"; and by the time he had telephoned ten times and found the boat still sticking in the canal, and had
seen that I got through the customs, and visas and quarantine, and had
worried himself over the fact that I thought of going all alone to
places like Hodeida, his affectionate heart completely adopted me as
well as the one-legged Captain and his blind wife. He took me up
for a drive to Suez itself, from which Port Tewfik, the harbour, is
built out on a long headland; and after we had gone to enquire about
the undesirable pearl smuggler and not found him, he took me
round the badly lit streets and bazaars, which his untidy Irish heart
likes so much better than Worthing, gave me a vermouth, got a little
boy to polish my shoes, pressed a box of chocolates upon me, drove me
back by a détour to see in the moonlight the white cenotaph to our
Indian troops on the Canal with two tigers snarling at Asia, and
finally lent me a pair of pyjamas to sleep in till the boat should get

clear! All this out of sheer effusiveness and the need for expression, for the kindly feeling poured itself with equal warmth over the old blind lady; and he was mismanaging the hotel with the same irresponsible devotion.

By the time we got back, the dubious M. Claoué had arrived: he is a friend of Henri de Monfreid who is looked upon as one of the most dubious characters in the Red Sea. He was a curious man, with lids coming very low down over his eyes, a rather nice, very decided mouth, and little round tilt to his nose, and the back of his head completely straight down into his neck. He looked as if he might stick at nothing if it were in his way so to say. He liked, he told me, the excitements of a life of adventure: he must have a lot just now as the Egyptian government found him with a sack of £4,000 worth of pearls and no explanation of how they came, and is trying to get £1,000 duty on them out of him. We did not refer to these topics, but kept to H. de M. who is giving 'des Conférences' in Belgium, but would in any case not be very accessible just now as he is embêté with the English (and French and Italians and all) because they want to deport him. We discussed the difficulties of a life of crime in an abstract way, and I must say I rather liked the man. He told me that he had tried ever so often and never yet succeeded in going to Mecca —but is going to do it next year with Ibn Saud's son—and when I spoke about Kessler's book on slavery, he looked a little sceptical and smiled when I said it did not ring quite true. There was certainly something to be said for him. De M. apparently has been trying to dethrone the Negus in Abyssinia and failed. "That will be very inconvenient," said I, "because the Negus might poison him now." "It is indeed inconvenient," said M. Claoué and explained that this is why the moment is not good for me to be shown the slave trade. It was altogether an amusing talk for the civilized (?) twentieth century.

My Irish friend sat up till midnight and took me to the launch— after providing me with hot tea which the Captain got very specially from another retired Captain in China. We walked down to the wharf: I shall not forget the sight of the boat coming with lights, moving as if she were motionless through the motionless water, her big light shining like a halo and the little lights on her masts all up among stars—

[37]

"Without a breath, without a sound
She steadies on upright keel."

Captain Macleavy pressed an orange into my hand; we parted as bosom friends; the Greek Company agent took me over and shattered all the harmony by telling me his philosophy as we went along. "All pleasures are as nothing to me if there is not a girl." "I see the English misses go two or three together with nothing to amuse them but books, and I do not understand." He then told me that the English are as slaves ground down by three or four hundred families who only shoot, and do not allow one to buy a house for more than ninety-nine years. I tried to explain freehold and leasehold. "Then I have been misinformed?" he said, as if such a thing were quite unthinkable. I assured him he had, and was glad to reach the boat, where I was put into a 4-berth cabin with two quite nice but dull women going to Mombasa. And that is all the adventures so far.

Nearing ADEN, 18 *December, 1934.*

Darling B,

It seems like an enchantment to say to myself that I am now in the Indian Ocean. When I came up after breakfast, we were running along on a sea full of small foam flecks, dark blue, and otherwise harmless, and we had the mountains of Yemen on one side and Africa on the other—misty horizons, with faint wild peaks. We skirted round the island of Perim and through the straits: a little God-forsaken island, with a few square hutlike houses and a few round grey tanks for oil: a few British live there, and get long holidays, I hope, as it is a dreary habitation; and since then we have been skirting Yemen, and the mountains are jagged behind a sweep of sand, and I have worked at those notes and maps so long that I feel as if I knew it all already. This morning, by a last effort, I finished my notes: over 140 double sheets, all with cross references in red ink: I hope it may profit me. I have been an object of wonder and it saved me from playing any games or being at all sociable, so that perhaps it was a blessing in disguise. The temperature is *lovely*: cool enough to-day to sit on deck with my little grey jacket; people are in shorts and pyjamas. Although I have had it explained I suppose, I don't think I ever really took in the roundness of the world and the rotation of the equator till now: the Great Bear is nearly off the sky, and we are

[38]

rushing round almost as near the sun as we can get, and you wouldn't think that a thousand miles or so would make such a difference considering the universal spaces. I am reading the Periplus of the Erythrean Sea (how much prettier a name than Red Sea): it was an old commercial chart by an unknown Greek of Alexandria in the first century—the first account of these shores, which the Arabian traders tried to keep wrapped in mystery so that Roman commerce should not enter. It is very pleasant to sit and read it on deck while the gulfs and bays unroll before one.

People on this boat have heard of my book; I am dreadfully notorious and treated like an Author—it is rather awful. Will keep this for Aden.

ADEN, 20 December, 1934.

Dearest Herbert [Young],

I am most beautifully settled here for three weeks. M. Besse,[1] to whom Mary gave me a letter, is more than charming: he is a Merchant, in the style of the Arabian Nights or the Renaissance; all day long telegrams come to him from India, America, China, Yemen, Africa, Europe. His own ships go steaming about these coasts (and one will take me to Mukalla)—and his agents are everywhere: he tells me I shall be looked after when I get into the inner Hadhramaut and he has friends among the rivals of the Mukalla Sultans (who live and shoot just over the border) so that the second step of my journey is clearing up beautifully. He lives here in the Arab quarter of the town with a beautiful young daughter, in a house built with a deep verandah al round it to keep the heat out, and filled with books, gramophone records, and comfortable chairs: in one corner of the room is a lamp shining through a red alabaster chalice to illuminate a photograph of the Venus of Cyrene: I am sure the native servants must think she is the family Goddess. He is a real Epicurean, in the good sense of the word; and has made himself here a world of his own—not belonging even to the British club, but knowing everyone who is worth knowing, and having immense power all over the country. He gave me the most delightful welcome, and immediately found me a house nearby and a boy to look after me, and sends me my food unless I come to

[1] Sir Anton Besse, who later became the founder of the College of St. Anthony in Oxford.

eat here—which I have done these two evenings. We are in what is called the Crater; in photographs taken from the air, one can see how it is so really, a wild circle of cliffs and rock with only one opening out to sea where the lava must have poured away. No green is visible, but the full moon over these wild black crags is very fine, and the soft deep sky. On a spur above the town is the Zoroastrians' tower of silence where they expose their dead. There are not many here but M. Besse tells me he has seen the funerals in India, where every tower has its own particular band of vultures: when the friends and relations of the dead have left him, the guardian of the tower tears the shroud and the vultures come lower and wait for a few seconds: then their chief old vulture advances, and after that they all swoop down and in a few hours nothing but bones is left.

23 December, 1934.

This interruption was due to a slight indisposition. It kept me lying down flat and not in a convenient position for writing, but all is well again now.

I have seen a few of the people here when I went to a cocktail party at Mrs. Portal's—the Resident Sir Bernard Reilly was there, and told me he had been hoping I would stay at the Residency: he was very pleasant, with a sense of humour. Everyone here has been into the Hadhramaut, and say the people are very friendly. They have not been to my city of the temples however; but seem to think it quite feasible if one has plenty of time and tact. Colonel Lake and Captain Hamilton, politicals, were there too and very pleasant. M. Besse tells me they are all rather relieved to find me an ordinary human being, as they had so many letters announcing my arrival, they feared I might come with trains of camels and be a dreadful nuisance.

I have a nice little flat and it is quiet. A young Yemeni teacher comes three hours a week and Arabic is pouring back into my brain. I had quite a long talk with a man from Nejd, called Khalid Abd-el-Latif—a charming Arab with long refined face and good manners, all dressed in flowing spotless white and delightful to talk to. He is if not a Wahabi then very much that way, and talked to me about the folly of worshipping tombs of Saints, because, said he, "we cannot tell what they were really like. Their words seem good to us, but

[40]

Allah alone knows the heart. Why should one worship anyone but Allah?"

Meryem Besse took me to see the building of a dhow: the ribs are made of natural bits of tree-trunk or branch from Malabar, chosen for its curve. There is a little harbour with the old craft, I should like to explore more fully. I have not been about much yet, except to write my name at the Residency and buy a night-gown and some canvas shoes.

23 December, 1934.

Dearest Venetia,

I can't begin to tell you everything—the chief news is that my journey promises quite well—that I am just in time, as everyone is now going to the Hadhramaut, but no one has been to Shabwa, and everyone here is ready to help. I have been adopted so to speak by M. Besse—a wonderful person who lets life play upon him as if he were an instrument responsive to all its variations. His daughter took me into their storehouse of frankincense and myrrh. Doesn't that mere statement thrill you? An old Jew with a curly short beard and little curly ringlets on his cheeks, all dusty from the powdered spices, showed us round. The myrrh is dark and sweet and parti-coloured browns like very old amber; the best frankincense is very pale yellow, almost white—called *samr*: the storehouse was piled with great stacks of it in sacks. The whole trade depends now, as it has for so many ages that no one can count them, on the wind. When the monsoon blows the little dhows cannot land, and so they wait till this season, and now begin to arrive in little fleets from all the incense bays along the coast.

You can have no idea of what a sunset is in Aden. Imagine one half of the sky a luminous green—I can't tell you how luminous, like green water when you are in it and looking through it to the sun: and this green shoots up fanlike in rays towards the other half of sky where night is lying already, deep blue. Above the sea along the horizon are pink ripples of cloud; the sea heaves with the sweep of the coast past the mouth of Aden bay, with flat lights on it as it catches the west. And half bathed in the light, half black in their own volcanic shadows, the rocks of Aden stand up like dolomites, so jagged and old. M. Besse took me for a long walk over these jagged ridges; they are all lava, spongy and unsafe; we came down to the sea where

[41]

the beach is undercut and a coating of barnacle shells makes the edge quite delicate pink: here the launch met us and we came back towards the sunset, and the full moon came up behind the great natural rampart of Aden. There is a feeling of gigantic and naked force about it all, and one thinks what it was when these hills were boiling out their stream of fire, hissing them into the sea, and wonders at anything so fragile as man living on these ancient desolations.

Christmas Eve.

Darling B,

In the afternoon I went with the Besses for a 'little walk' over the edge of the Crater down to the beach where millions of shells are heaped up by the monsoon: one can see here how limestone is formed of once living creatures. Such beautiful shells too. Meryem found one like pale grey agate, a sort of conch. Her father was as pleased over it as a child or more so. He has a passion for everything beautiful. He is indeed a charming person, so impulsive and kind, but not just with words, for he always follows out his proposals. He is very much what Mario [my brother-in-law] might have been if he carried out what he said, and if he cared only for the immaterial side of things: these two enormous ifs M. Besse does carry out, but keeps the extraordinary practical impetus, the exacting *everything* from those he cares for, the absolute domination: it makes him no doubt difficult to live with, and I am sure there is trouble coming with Meryem who has her father's character and will not long be bound to anyone's chariot wheels. At present she is his slightly rebellious but really devoted slave and he adores her. He sits at work from early in the morning—six o'clock or before—seeing people of every sort and dealing with problems from every country. He speaks with a charming French accent, very quietly but with no mistake at all about whether or no his mind is made up. It is most fascinating to watch. When he was seventeen his father died leaving debts, and from being wealthy they were desperately poor: he served four years in the army and then got a job here, and decided that whatever happened he would never face that agony of poverty again: and he has made several fortunes—and does not care for money a bit. He has grey hair, very curly round a small bald patch: his eyebrows go up and he looks out from under them: he walks very lightly on the

[42]

tips of his toes; and his mouth has a little tight-lipped cynical curve to it that might well make fools afraid of him. He has a Scottish wife who is not here. His staff are all obviously nervous and his servants devoted. What the English here think of him I don't know: they probably dislike him with a few exceptions among the best of them.

26 December, 1934.

Christmas day is over. I spent it with nothing particular about it till the evening, except that Nagi brought me in a pair of delightful slippers from Meryem with my tea. I have given your scarf, which was much appreciated. Poor Meryem had all the staff to dinner—twenty-two people, including me. She rather likes a little indiscriminate gaiety, poor child, and hardly ever indulges in it.

"Elle est superficielle d'une façon étonnante," says M. Besse, while she struggles over his cablegrams, and says no to all the parties: he adores her with complete possessiveness which is bound to lead to trouble. They were working all day yesterday and this dinner party loomed larger and larger as the afternoon drew on.

"Je ne le supporterai pas," said M. Besse: "you and I will leave them; we will go in the launch on the sea." I made a feeble effort to stand by Meryem, who had sixteen men and only four women: she however said that it was well worth while to get rid of her father, who would cast gloom over all the young clerks' efforts at cheerfulness. After tea he took me out for a drive to the mainland—Sheikh Othman —where the sea character of Aden changes to desert filled with little bushes and coloured pebbles. It was a lovely sunset, in a sky so golden that the disk of the sun itself could not be seen—it was all one molten colour. He comes riding here with his wife when she is here: she must be a rather charming woman by what he says of her. We came back in a more peaceful frame of mind, but at a pace which penetrated even to my ignorance: I looked at the speedometer and saw it just touching fifty miles an hour. M. Besse relapsed into gloom as the hour drew near: I found him all ready dressed like a sacrificial victim and a lovely table laid on the roof: all the young clerks, very shy and naturally not a bit at their best. I had a rather nice young man next me: Meryem was enjoying it, her father looking at her with a mixture of pain and adoration quite disarming to behold, Meryem saying things that made even the Scotch sea-captain beside her blush.

We played consequences and read them out—pulled crackers—and then when they started to dance M. Besse murmured to me: "Je ne le supporte plus: est-ce que vous venez?" He vanished and got into white clothes: seized an armful of coats for me, opened a trap door down the back stairs, and crept out to the car, leaving the party to its fate. Herbert will sympathize. We motored down to the port: found the launch and Somali chauffeur waiting with the rising moon, and were off with a most delightful feeling of escapade. It was such fun. We passed by all the lights of Aden—people dancing in bungalows, sailors feasting on the ships: we made for the entrance point; the sea and wind freshened, we were round the corner under the black hill and rocks—Orion above, and Taurus and the Pleiades. Then no lights at all, except three yellow and a green from some travelling ship at sea: the spray in a light rain on our faces: M. Besse and I lying in great comfort on cushions, while he kept the tiller with one hand— the Somali with his big turban sticking up in a little 'ciuffo' looking out to sea ahead of us. "On se lave l'âme," said M. Besse, and made a little gesture of horror every time I mentioned the party. We went on and on. "I know a cave, we could sleep on the sand," said M. Besse, "but Meryem would be anxious." I thought this quite as well, as I may just as well keep some shred of reputation while I am about it. But we still went on—the sea getting more of a swell while M. Besse told me how he and his wife had just saved their lives round this corner. We saw a sort of halo round a bend, and suddenly opened a long spit of land and a little solitary lighthouse as black as the rocks it stood on: it was a peculiar lighthouse, worked by a black shutter which went down over its light and up again instead of a circular movement: the effect was indescribably malignant, as if a hooded figure were masking and unmasking itself, a kind of Moloch idol waiting for victims: the spit of rock came down like a snout with a hole like an eye through which the sky shone: the moon hid behind clouds; the water boiled round the headland, several currents meeting: and the clockwork regularity of that malevolent black figure of the lighthouse gave an eeriness quite inexpressible.

"This corner is what we always call the *chaudron*, because the water bubbles up," said M. Besse. "It is very difficult to steer. I used to like to hold my life by a thread, but now I do not think it right to do so any longer"—and we were tossed about by a broadside wave like a coracle.

[44]

"I do not like the way our motor works" he chose this moment to say.

It was really great fun: we were tossed from side to side, the waves heaved their backs all round us, I had not the faintest idea where we were, what time or what world we were in. We made for a cleft between the mainland and an island; shot through with great skill; saw a little sleeping beach and tall houses. I couldn't think where we were. M. Besse refused to say: he suggested it might be the moon: he went through some tortuous little lanes by a small white mosque, by a few sleeping goats who looked familiar, and landed at his own door: we had come right round the Aden volcano, which is attached to the land by only a very narrow neck. I don't believe I have ever enjoyed a Christmas evening quite so much.

27 December, 1934.

Yesterday we went after tea to see the route of our nocturnal expedition, and it looked so ordinary and different in the light of day. The lighthouse, a neat smooth structure of black stone, a signal station above, and steps down as it might be Brighton. The sea was smooth, there was nothing of the mystery to show. M. Besse told me that I and his wife and daughter were the only women whose courage he would trust to take that round with the sea as it was—but I must say I was blissfully unconscious of any heroism!

Yesterday morning his old Arab friend Makkawi came to call— a most beautiful face, long, with great almond-shaped eyes, a manner of rather abstracted, indescribable dignity. He is coming one evening with his hubble-bubble for a talk, and he is going to arrange for a visit for me to the Sultan of Lahej in the hills. He told me about the Aden water supply, how the plants get it for nothing but the people have to pay. At one time he said the water was used for watering the streets, and the people had to pay so much that they mostly used sea-water for washing: but this was stopped by representation to the authorities and now it is the sea water which waters the streets. M. Besse told me that the old man is known and respected by everyone in Aden; that he never budges an inch, if the whole world is against him: "he is like you in that," said M. Besse—though what has brought him to this opinion of my rock-like character I have no idea.

[45]

I have been to the Doctor here who has discovered chronic dysentery: I must have had it inside me for a long time, but he says it can be dealt with and I am taking a cure and hope to be far better than ever before now that the bug is known. The Doctor and his wife are dining to-night (I always dine at the Besses and lunch by myself). To-morrow Colonel Lake is dining. He is nice, *very* silent, and devoted entirely to Beduin. Poor man, he has just heard of the death of his mother—a telegram of condolence came before the news. It is so dignified—he goes on just as usual, and says nothing about it.

Last night M. Besse read Anatole France—the charming tale of Celestin and Amicus, the hermit and the faun.

27 December, 1934.

Dearest Venetia,

How I wish you were here. I am enjoying myself so much. My little flat all to myself with a verandah of trellis work through which the sea breeze blows. In the morning, so silently that I never hear him, Nagi brings my tea; I then wander down the street to the Besses' house and sit there and write, while he sits at his desk across the room and settles huge enterprises in a quiet way—where his ships are to go, whether or not to buy up all the incense of his coast, to send tar and petrol to Abyssinia. The office is on the ground floor, an arcaded room with lots of compartments with desks, each with some huge business of its own, a Parsi, an Arab, French, German, Englishman, Russian running them. The incense trade is immense; it deals with the gum from Africa and Arabia and soon the dhows will be bringing it in now that the monsoon and Ramadhan will be over. Then he supplies all these coasts with petrol, etc. Then in the other parts of this house are millions of skins, which make the finest gloves in the world (Mocha). He has a soap factory: is agent for all sorts of things —and has three steamships going to and fro. It is fascinating to see so huge and varied an affair and one brain the centre of it all—and to watch how quietly definitely and rapidly he deals with the people as they come. It was fun to watch him with the Italian agent for the Somali incense—an oily creature who thought his statements were meant as a basis for bargaining and tried diplomacy—one going straight as an arrow, the other all in curves. He hates the Italians: and his manager, who was in Italian Somaliland, tells me they have made a rule there that every native must salute a European (which is very fatiguing as the European has to answer all the salutes) and must get off the sidewalk for him! It looks very much as if England and France had been *squared* and Italy given a free hand in Abyssinia, and it makes one quite sick.

30 *December*, 1934.

Dearest B,

A charming noble old Arab came to call last night after his dinner (it is now Ramadhan, so that dinner is an important event). He has the most beautiful old face, with a great brow and long quiet eyes— all very fine lines, long and thin, as if Life has worn them down until nothing but the beautiful essence is left. He had a big white and red turban pushed off his forehead and sat in his long white gown smoking an enormous hubble-bubble, four feet high, all carved black and silver from Malabar—and told us that when he went to see the Wembley exhibition and then travelled to Edinburgh to visit a son who is employed there, the people in the hotel looked from his turban to his hubble-bubble and from his hubble-bubble to his turban and laughed. So that he went to the manager and complained of this want of manners. The manager said he had better take no notice, but this old man, who is grand in his own country, asked in his gentle voice, almost inaudible when he speaks English, for the address of the head office. Whereupon the manager said he would talk to the scoffers, descended into the hotel lounge, and brought back apologies and the assurance (I am ashamed to say) that the delinquents were not Scottish but English. This sort of thing, the old man said, never happened with the well-born, though sometimes, when walking over a Scottish moor and meeting someone, he would see that they turned round after he had passed and, if he turned too, there would be a smile interchanged. My host here tells me that he is a man who has never once compromised his opinion for anyone; he has stood out for British against Muslim or vice versa quite regardless of consequences. Once a year he gives a banquet to all his English and Arab friends on the roof of his house in the desert behind Aden. He complained to me of the state of things in the Yemen; the rulers are trying to stop the constant raiding "and the tribes are so poor that if they cannot raid they have nothing to live on". I couldn't help feeling that this is a fallacy, like that of taking in each other's washing—but my Arabic

[47]

isn't good enough yet—after two years' rusting—to go into these abstruse things.

30 December, 1934.

I had a lovely day in Little Aden on Friday. It is just across at the opposite mouth of the bay, but the size of the bay will be clear to you when I tell you that the little motor boat takes an hour to get there. The Besses did not come, but three girls and three men of the staff came, and I went with a young Frenchman who, in his little sailing boat, has H. de Monfreid as his life's ideal. It is what they call a *zarug,* with a point at each end, and a triangular sail tied by old ropes to any old bit of woodwork, as it seemed to me. We had "the Pilot and the Pilot's boy" Muhammad (who managed the party, being about ten years old), and a brigandish-looking assistant, all dressed in a futah (which is a loin cloth), a turban, and their lovely mahogany skin. The Frenchman in a blue shirt, shorts, and a red and green turban looked quite thrilling against the dark sea, but of course there was no wind and our triangle of sail billowed about and pitched lazily till we finally reached the rocks in over two hours, and were met by fishermen and boys with even less on (only 3 turbans between about 20 of them) and they took us off in what they call *huris,* which are canoes also pointed both ends and very wobbly; they have oars made by nailing a round disk of plank on a pole, and a little sail they can rig up, and skim through these waters like fish. One of the small boys told me that the way to keep off sharks was to have a bold heart: if you cringe, said he, the shark gets you, but if you are bold (and he pushed his thin little chest out as far as it would go) they never touch you.

Muhammad ordered our small crowd of admirers about, and they gambolled round us while we left the shore (all strewn with mother of pearl among the rocks) and walked across a sandy neck to the village of Little Aden. It is a lonely attractive promontory—spiky like Dolomites only darker in colour, with long low bits of sand slung like hammocks between the pinnacles, and the blue sea along the curving shore. The little village is all of palm-matting huts, with two little wooden shops and one solid one-roomed building, which is the prison. Two policemen live there and boss the place. Muhammad took us into his mother's house, which was beautifully clean, furnished with two sorts of bedsteads of coco-fibre, and a shelf with a

[48]

row of plates below, a row of cups above, and a row of old electric-light bulbs as ornaments in between. The women came crowding —some very pretty; one has to be very pretty to stand having blue lips and yellow daubs under the eyes. Some had all their faces dusted over with yellow, which made them look as if they had been brushing through pollen. They have a very graceful walk, swinging from side to side (the Arabs have a special word for it) and they wear bright colours—reds and yellow, thrown over one on top of the other, so that the sandy little village of huts is transformed as soon as they all come to their doors. There must be a lot of negro among them. We walked along the sands and examined a boat for sale: it was about 9 metres long, and all made by an old man in two months, quite nicely carved, though in poor wood, and it costs 1,000 rupees (£75) sails and all. Then we went along the shore, while our escort, now quite large, picked up shells for us: they are lovely shells of many sizes and colours, but all inhabited by crabs and running about in an unpleasant manner. I took some home the other day, not noticing the crab, and couldn't think why they kept on falling off my dressing table—till I saw the horrid little thing running about my carpet.

We had a gorgeous lunch under the shadow of a rock and then slept, and woke up to find the silent and blond English boy, Mr. Coleman, playing rounders with the village boys: they were very good at it, and we soon all joined in the game except one girl who was obviously shocked at this familiarity with natives and simply disgusted at our return to the village encircled in a swarm of small and friendly boys. I must say I felt a little sad to see my coat clasped to a very shiny small damp bosom in the enthusiasm of holding it safe.

I haven't yet been to the British Club, but am going to-day to be taken by Colonel Lake. He came to dine the other night and was pleasant—shy and slow and opening out as slowly and tentatively as a shell fish, ready to retreat at the slightest shock. He looks rather engaging, with hair plastered in the middle, very smooth on either side of a parting, and a very soft hat and nice bony hands—and a very deep voice which comes out after long consideration.

E

[49]

1 January, 1935.

The Besses' old skipper from Dis in Dhufar came this morning: dark mahogany, with a red turban tinsel-edged and a blue check cotton thrown over one shoulder. Such a charming face. He has been in the house for years and when Meryem came he embraced her on one cheek and then on her shoulders: it was so charming. M. Besse told me that the man once refused to take his dhows to Africa because he said the season was dangerous. M. Besse was annoyed and said he would get another skipper if this one refused: the poor man was miserable, but still he refused and said: "I can't, I *can't* go." M. Besse got another one, and the ships got caught in a gale and were battered and very nearly wrecked—and the old Nakhuda never even said "I told you so".

1 January, 1935.

Dearest Venetia,

Every morning as I come down to the Besses, I pass two long strings of camels, the first bearing rushes, or rather canes, in two trailing rustling faggots slanting down from either side and hiding almost all except the animal's neck; the second with two sacks of charcoal on either side, that looks exactly like coal and comes from the Audhali country N.E. of here. Little dark men, walking very straight and elf-like, with curly black hair tied with a fillet and nothing much on except a loin cloth and some indigo, come walking by the camels' side: and a kid or goat is often sitting on top of the load, only its horns and soft ears appearing, and an interested little face looking out on the world as it undulates along.

My dysentery is being very drastically treated and I feel quite ill but hope to get rid of it this fortnight.

3 January, 1935.

Dearest B,

We had the end of Ramadhan and the feast day yesterday. You never saw anything like the dresses down our street—the colours and variety. The children were too adorable—the little girls with mittens painted up their arms in patterns in dark brown colour which lasts a few days and they call it *hudhar*. They are friendly now and come running out to take my hand for a hundred yards or so as I walk down. The preparation for the feast is very accidental; one

[50]

will have her arms painted, another one her hair buttered, another has new glass bracelets, or a pair of *mules* with pompoms, two sizes too big so that she can grow. The little *Bohra* boys wear caps like inverted flower pots all covered with tinsel embroidery. The Somalis all walk with a ridiculous little walking stick: they are very lank and angular, like modern art, and I don't like their figures so much as the beautifully made Arab who is all spring and movement. They are small here, but Colonel Lake says that up in the Aulaki hills you could easily enlist a regiment of 5 ft 10 or 6 ft. men. The tribesmen came swaggering down yesterday looking as if simply everything belonged to them, their curls shining with butter and tied in a classical manner with a fillet, their new cotton kilts bright yellow with huge curved daggers tucked in the front, and a cotton or woollen scarf folded lengthwise and carried carelessly and superbly over one shoulder.

When I got here to the Maison Besse I saw the ceremony of good wishes—all the employees coming up in rows—and such a variety, though of course this day is not for the Indian or European staff. There were three men from Mukalla, a nice but wild looking little lot, very dark, with long faces. One of them saw me in the street and asked if M. Besse was upstairs, and I brought him up confidingly and did M. Besse out of four rupees, as all he wanted was a free passage. They are tiny little people, small-boned and very like grasshoppers.

We dined with the Ingrams in the evening and saw what they brought from Hadhramaut: the contents of a grave (though the people kept back the best pieces), and some bits of flint and obsidian which look very much as if worked by the hand of man. They are very pleasant and live in a house full of books and objects on the top of the ridge where they get the breeze from both sides.

I had an amusing time in the market with Meryem the other morning, looking into all the little shops, buying bracelets from Bombay (glass), watching the Sudanese beating out shoes and belts with an old nail, seeing lamps being worked out of tomato tins and every kind of object made from paraffin tins; seeing men sitting out in the street at a sort of loom weaving coloured borders on to pieces of silk; and finally buying every sort of spice in a little box of a shop where women come to make unguents for their hair—

"smeared with dull nard an Indian wipes
From out her hair":

I got eleven different kinds, chiefly plants and mosses from these hills, and the yellow stuff they put on their faces.

You will be pleased to hear that the exam this week shows no dysentery germs inside me, so I hope that may have been got rid of, and I am certainly feeling better now.

8 January, 1935.

Dearest Venetia,

Shabwa is not going to be a small matter as it appears to mean seven long days (of 15 hrs.) with no water, and an unknown quantity on the other side owing to the impossibility of knowing where one will go and to the fact that the Imam's people take you straight to prison. Your cousin Colonel Boscawen gave Shabwa up because they shot his servant through the shoulder, and the only other man who tried was a German who got nearly looted at the gates and hurried past. But they neither of them had a Shabwa guide, so I still have hopes.

We have been living in a perpetual chaos of what sounded like pistol shots these two days—really only small boys pouring gun-powder out of their fireworks, covering it with a small stone, and making a concussion by flinging boulders on top in honour of the end of Ramadhan. You can't imagine anything gayer than this feast. The broad straight street runs up from the sea to my flat and the mosque opposite, and groups and processions have been going up at intervals, sometimes with flags and singing, sometimes Somali or tribesmen dancing, sometimes just family parties, the little girls with new veils and flowered chiffon or silver skull caps. The tribes-men, Zaidis and Yafa'is, come along dancing in the afternoon, all in a mass, every kilt and turban a different colour and the knives stuck in their sashes at an angle out and upward, so as to be quite handy. A man in the middle with an oblong drum like a barrel, and an old man beside him with a reed flute led the procession, running forward, stooping, running back, while the groups behind danced to and fro, singing with a rhythm very like the drums of Leja [Jebel Druse in Syria] but friendly and gay, and quite pleased to be photographed. The sight of all that colour, those proud quick pleasant faces, the easy beautiful brown limbs moving so freely and unshackled in the white

[52]

street, was worth coming to Aden for all by itself. I wandered about the suqs afterwards and saw them all feasting, and smoking, wasting their money on deceivers who spread old and greasy cards on little tables—even a roulette, a sort of tin wheel with white divisions painted on it (with numbers) which never stopped on any of their poor little pennies. My teacher came with me, and took me to the Young Men's Club, a dingy little room up a staircase where about twelve young Adenites were lying about on cushions, with photographs of Arab celebrities above them on the walls and a few hubble-bubbles and bundles of Kat before them: the Kat is the Yemen drug—five little bundles cost a rupee, as the Government gets a lot of duty on it: it comes from the hills round Taiz and looks a harmless little shrub rather like laurel: the little top shoots are the best, but I thought it unpleasantly bitter: the young men told me that it keeps them awake and is not an opiate.

After sitting there (and being promised a letter for the Imam) my teacher took me up a back street to a very tidy little room where a charming young Muslim from Italian Tripoli received me and showed me the plan of a history of Hadhramaut which he is writing: he was so delightful, dressed in a smart brown European suit with an astrakhan colbak on his head, and greenish very quick eyes, and a mouth that had a little smile always lurking at its corners. He travels round the world like Ibn Batuta, learning, stopping where he finds new things, and then going on. The MS. of the book is at Mukalla and will be shown in secret: he is afraid the Government there may burn it if they get sight of it! He loathes the Italians and has very good words for the British: we only seem to shine when people have to put up with someone else!

I practised my rangefinder on the roof this morning lying on my tummy, as it is most difficult to make it steady. When I got up, two hideous bald-headed white and brown vultures were sitting there in the sun; at least I suppose they were vultures.

The Residency shows signs of being fussy about my journey. If there is any hitch I shall cable to Henry and he will just have to *make* Sir John Maffey send instructions: anything more half-hearted than his letters about me to the people here you can't imagine. I sometimes feel that the real type of the Moral Coward is the average Civil Servant!

8 January, 1935.

Dearest B,

M. Besse spoke to Captain Hamilton who was dining here, about me, and said that of all the people he knew, men or women, I was the most likely to reach my objective, as I had all the necessary assets. He thinks I should get through with no difficulty at all.

He took me and Mrs. Ingrams for a longish walk yesterday, over the crater edge and down to the sea on the other side where there are rocks lined with a thick covering of barnacles, so many that the rock is *made* of them, and below there ought to be parrot fish, which he says are more beautiful than any fish in the world and every colour of the rainbow. However they were nowhere in sight, but there was a beautiful water garden of bright emerald green in a pool: I thought it moss and tried to pick it, when all its little green shoots began to draw themselves in and only little grey jelly discs remained, most unpleasant to touch. Then we came round the corner and found the launch, and M. Besse and I bathed regardless of sharks, of which he denies the existence in these particular bays though there seem to be two opinions about it. It was delicious in that buoyant water, just cool enough to be pleasant, with the sun sinking into it over the spires of Little Aden. Then we came back and he read Monna Vanna out to us and so to bed, and this morning, alas, I am packing.

13 January, 1935.

Dearest Venetia,

My little steamer sails at midnight to-night. She is called *El Amin* (The Safe One) and belongs to M. Besse, who is really making her go with half a cargo for my sake—I am so spoilt by my friends. On the way we are stopping at a roadstead called Bir Ali where one of his dhows has run aground and the cargo—worth about £2,000 —has been pinched by the local Sultan, who won't let it go for less than half its value. Though it is in our sphere of influence we can do nothing but write mild remonstrances which have very little effect on a South Arabian Sultan: so M. Besse is sending an independent negotiator and we will see what happens. I am glad to land at Bir Ali: it was probably the old port of Cana, the chief harbour along the coast and the outlet for Shabwa and the Western trade.

I am spending these last three days in the Residency and have enjoyed talking to Sir Bernard Reilly. Everyone as pleasant as possible everywhere and I leave Aden with a feeling of pulling up roots already. From the Residency headland, where they have built a little trellis-work breakfast room with openings on all sides, you look across to Little Aden in outlines, and to the white mounds of the Salt pans, and the sands beyond, and the Yemen hills, all across the blue, green and purple water of the bay, where forms of ships ever so old sail across. The kites, brown ones and white bald-headed ones with brown-tipped wings, come hovering and screaming, and stand on the tip of the gun-wheel or sun themselves in the dust: it is impossible to work there—one sits and looks and the hours slide by.

It is an interesting moment here in Aden now. We are just altering our policy, chiefly by reason of the taking over by the R.A.F., and instead of narrowing our interests and shutting out all the hinterland we have got two more political officers and are taking an interest in the tribes behind us. Perhaps soon we may have them as well policed as the Imam has his people: he says he cannot encourage trade because the British Protectorate is so unsafe.

off BIR ALI on S. Arabian coast, 15 *January*, 1935.

Darling B,

We sailed at 2 a.m. on Monday morning. I had a last rush up the hill with M. Besse and looked on Aden Crater, its straight rows of houses pink, blue, grey, and cream-coloured in the ruins of the volcano—then dined quietly at the Residency. Colonel Lake came before dinner and we arranged the best policy for the route I am to take: when I get to his borders I will write and ask the Imam's permission to enter, and meanwhile Sir Bernard is writing a personal friendly letter to Raghib Pasha, his wazir (who looks a charming old man). I think that everything that could be thought of has been done, and no one in the world could have thought of so many things as M. Besse. He and Meryem took me over with the A.D.C. (Captain Cotton) at the pier and we went in the launch to M. Besse's ships in harbour—first to the *Hakk,* which is the bigger and newer of the two, a handsome creature with shining oil engines and comfortable little cabins. It cost £55,000 and carries M. Besse's drums of petrol all over these eastern seas. It was going to Africa, while we on the *Amin* were for Mukalla.

Well, I was left on the *Amin.* I was so sad to leave the dear

[55]

Besses—what they have been to me is quite impossible to say. I went to sleep and woke up with the lights of Aden slipping by: slept again and woke with the lighthouse streaming in, lifting and lowering its mask and bobbing wildly up and down, and I thought of how I went below it on Christmas night, wondering where M. Besse was taking me. The sea was horrid, we had deluges of rain in the morning, and the wind was in the wrong direction. Everyone was ill next day, including the chief and 2nd officer and the engineer, and the Sayyid Abd-er-Rahman Jifree who is being sent as M. Besse's ambassador. We were too ill to see each other all yesterday, and this morning I feel none too grand, but got up, as we slowed down, to see the Arabian coast. We are east of Bir Ali, near where the dhow foundered: her cargo is lying shining in the sun on a little sandy rise, and the Arabs were all on the look-out, waving their mantles to us from the roof of their little square white fort. A friendly Kuwait dhow is anchored in the bay, waiting to carry off her sister in bits and put her together again in Kuwait: the disaster happened just round the eastern headland out of sight.

It is a rather pleasant landscape in the sun: a flattish plain of scrub and sand; through the sand come sudden little rocky hills, whose blackness shows the lava; then higher hills, flattened at the top; all reddish and yellow, even the black rock is as it were dusted over. There are innumerable wrinkles and smooth sunny patches, but no sign of cultivation or habitation except the white watch tower and the piled up wrecked cargo on the shore.

The Sultan at Bir Ali must have seen us passing: he has sent a messenger and is hurrying here on a camel: so we are waiting and that is why I can write (still feeling rather sick).

9.45 a.m.

The wretched Sultan is *walking* to us round the bay, so we may have hours to wait.

He is just arriving in a little boat with a square sail.

SHIHR, 15 January, 1935.

This is a place I had no thought of coming to, and as a matter of fact we have not landed, only unloaded rice into rather beautiful boats which they make here—the planks sewn together with coco

[56]

FREYA STARK IN ASOLO

MUKALLA FROM THE SEA

WOMEN WATER-SELLERS: MUKALLA

THE BEDUIN OF THE JŌL

fibre and no nails, and sharp at each end and wide in the middle, with
a long point to the prow to ride through the surf which beats high
against the little white and sand-coloured town in the monsoon.
These boats have been described in Marco Polo, and before him by
the Greeks; they have green, white and black patterns, and white
fishes painted on them, and other signs: and the crew seem mostly
negroes, an unpleasant lot of inhabitants to fall among, not so fierce
perhaps but more stupid than the graceful curly-haired tribesmen of
Bir Ali.

I am so demoralized by this roll of the Indian Ocean that I don't
undress so as not to have to face dressing again: and this morning
we have been rocking gently but unpleasantly off Shihr and are now
off again to Mukalla. The coast here is quite flat with a long ridge
looking like limestone some miles inland—none of the volcanic
spiky fringe which juts up from the Mukalla land and makes it the
wildest rocky coast I have seen except in Scotland.

MUKALLA, 3 p.m.

Anything more picturesque than its approach you cannot imagine
—tall houses, every shade of white and grey, piled together against
the red cliff—bare hill behind them rising straight to a long ridge on
which are four small white square forts. The houses have a kind of
false stucco splendour which looks well from a distance: a little
round minaret in the centre, steps to the water, a naked crowd with
brilliant loin cloths, turbans or curls; dhows riding at anchor, beautifully grouped and coloured, their rigging very fragile against the
solid rock behind.

The police inspector, who has been in the levies and speaks
devotedly of Colonel Lake, took my twelve packages in charge. They
were hoicked over the side while the police and the Amir al Bahr
(the harbour master), he in a yellow turban and green gown, were
hurling billingsgate at each other: sleek and snakelike curly heads
were appearing and disappearing—brown arms and legs: the water
green like paint, the little wooden huris running in and out with their
round oars—while the captain looked down on me and all this tumult
with an expression of the sincerest pity—quite wasted for I was almost
quivering with joy and felt quite at home especially with the policeman. A motor car received us: the streets are full of débris: an
esplanade is being made but so far has only got to the state of huge

[57]

blocks and holes on the sea front: the colour of the whitewash and brown figures is delightful everywhere. The Sultan's palace is west of the town, new and with horrid bits of coloured glass: the guest house is dazzling white in a garden with green plants (the only ones I have yet seen in the landscape). Here we entered in procession: a blue plush sitting-room with mirrors: a dining-room with long table and eight chairs, six varnished and two covered with pink plush roses— a bedroom with mattress and mosquito net and chest of drawers complete, and bath and W.C. all European. A handsome princely old Arab from Khuraiba in Wadi Amd is in charge: a motor at my disposal. They have got over the shock of my having no servant, and now at 4 o'clock the Governor is coming to call. I hope I shall do credit to Lord Halifax, but I shall soon long to be away and in the hills.

Meanwhile here I am, the adventure has started. I feel I am such a small speck on this large map of Arabia—but such fun to be on it!

18 January, 1935.

I think of you locking up carefully every night in peaceful Asolo. Here I am I suppose, the only white woman on the Arabian coast between Aden and Muscat—how many hundred miles—and no one locks any doors. Awiz, the servant, leaves after dinner. When I feel sleepy I wander out into the little court and the verandah and put out the two lanterns, and go to bed: the royal compound has only one gate where a few tribesmen, all in bright but different costumes, lounge about with guns: and in the different palaces inside (there seem to be three) no one bothers to shut doors. I am enjoying this: it is comfortable and I have a hot bath every evening: mice eat the ribbons off my frocks at night, but I have a mosquito net, simple but innocuous food, and I have seen where the water comes from a spring in the hills, brought in pipes to a little open channel which seems to produce nothing more dubious than green weeds. What is best of all is the view from my window west over Mukalla beach to the great sweep of the descending hills, to Ras Burum far out to sea. The long beach stretches away into the sunset mountains: it has two delicate lines of ripples broken by an almost invisible headland, just enough to give a Japanese unexpectedness to the lines of the breaking waves. I have been sitting so still that Awiz comes in with the lamp

[58]

without seeing me and is concerned because the Sultan's Emir came and was told I was out.

He came again just now after dinner and has been sitting here for the last hour, an Italian-looking man with nice little features completely squashed under a black waxed moustache that would extinguish anyone: rather heavy and self-indulgent, grey stockinette vest with zip front, European white coat, turban, ivory twisted cane, slim little hands and narrow fingers with henna nails and aquamarine ring; very feminine, and looking upon me with some suspicion. By the end of the hour, however, I hope he thinks I am best left to myself: I have told my plans exactly and suggested that the last and more troublesome bit had best be arranged later on. I hope I may be able to start in two or three days' time. Meanwhile I think we got on quite nicely. I am the first woman alone in this country and the Sultan and his family are not *Alpinisti* anyway: the Sultan fell ill after riding up to Wadi Hadhramaut, and the Emir here opened his eyes like berries when I said I liked to walk three hours a day. He really thought I must be able to face anything when, on asking me whom I had here at night, I told him I had been sleeping quite happily alone. He was very pleasant and obliging and promises to do all the necessary to get me to Shibam: step by step we get along.[1]

This morning I went over the suq again, the one High Street of Mukalla: everyone crowds round, but quite politely, though the children have a horrid way of shouting "Nasrani" (christian). About 50 followed Ali and me this afternoon when we went out walking and started up the cliff at the back; they thinned down and only the more sporting followed: we got in 50 minutes to one of the four forts and a small cannon. They are little square towers at the top, with a heavy carved door half-way up the wall, and all stand in a row on the edge of a plateau ledge which must have been quite recently inhabited as one sees plain traces of little square fields. The top of the hill was another half-hour up: Ali said there was no road and it would take us till dark. With persistence and tact and two rests he was got up however, and eleven of the most enterprising children: then we

[1] The Hadhramaut is roughly divided between the two reigning dynasties of the Qu'aiti and Kathiri, of whom the former ruled the sea-board and western, while the latter held the inland eastern half. This uncomfortable situation had been a cause of warfare until the year of my arrival.

looked everywhere, to the flat mound-like hill near Shihr and Wadi Bo'ash and Rukub between it and us: to the valleys that lead north over long ridges to Du'an; to the villages in palms, Dis, Naggera (castle) Bagrain, etc., below us, and west to Fuwa: it was a fine but barren view, a rust-coloured landscape. The top of the hills has a cemetery, but quite modern I think and probably belonging to the time of the fields just below. The children were all very pleased and friendly: not one of them had ever been up the hill before, though the whole expedition only took us 2½ hours. As we came back I photographed two nice tribesmen by the gate and another came forward with two kids in his hands to be taken: they are all friendly and pleased to be taken. This morning I went to see the smith who was sharpening knives and a fine variety were handed to me for inspection—they all have a razor-like edge which it seems is frequently needed.

19 January, 1935.

My dear John [Murray],

This is a charming little town to look at, rather like a picture by Carpaccio, only white: a little harbour with eight or nine dhows; a minaret in the centre; the indigo tribesmen strolling about among the markets, and nobody (except the Sultan myself and the chauffeur) wearing shoes or stockings, not even the Army on Parade. From my window westward is the most lovely view of beach and mountains, range after range and the sunset behind them: only one village in sight, 13 miles away. It is terrible to think how one gets accustomed to this emptiness of Asia and feels that one needs an almost completely deserted landscape to breathe in freely: there is a luxury of solitude here, and looking out on it makes up for the fact that I am always the centre of about 60 children when I walk about in the town.

19 January, 1935.

Dearest B,

I saw lots of things to-day, beginning with Army manœuvres this morning at dawn: I got up and watched the Regulars, 150 men about, with a band, march in fine style out of the gate, all their bare brown legs keeping time and everyone with something bright and varied in the matter of costume, so that one felt like quoting "C'est

[60]

magnifique mais ce n'est pas la guerre"—in fact it was much more like a Lark. Two cannons and their four padded camel saddles were carefully brought out and dusted under the eye of a portly old man with a green wool turban and a watch chain—and that settled them: but the army, and I behind it, walked out among the camels and drilled down by the ponds (which smell much worse than they look). It was an amusing sight, and rather pathetic to see the four officers (who must all have been in the Aden Levies) saying "Lef, Righ," so ardently and trying to apply their military rules: they looked so smart and soldier-like themselves (and I believe they make excellent soldiers), and here they are battling with odds which a giant couldn't tackle. However we were all very happy on the drill ground, till my morning was spoilt by discovering that I had been winding a cinema with no film inside it! The black bodyguard marched in little groups and the tribal 'Askeri', the real army, did quite difficult ins and outs; I then retired and sat in the gate to watch them file back: it is an amusing place to sit in and one feels one is in the Bible times, for all the life of the place goes in and out here.

After breakfast Afzal Khan took me 13 miles along the beach to Fuwa: this is the only village (he says) till you get to Bir Ali, an incredible stretch of loneliness; there was only one house in the 13 miles, and hills and hills and hills, rolling up like waves, reddish brown, no blade of grass or earth visible, but all just rock and stones. Women from Mukalla come all this way to gather thorns—they carry back the bundles on their heads, their eyes shining over the thick cloth which masks them, while their legs are bare and kilted to the thigh. When we got to Fuwa there on a wide clear space was an R.A.F. Landing Ground; they have three now in this district and mark them with little white-washed cairns which will soon I suppose take the place of shrines.

20 January, 1935.

It really looks as if I am to go to-morrow and to-day has been hectic with luggage, everything having to be redistributed for donkeys and in view of the fact that one goes over more or less desert country for four to five days before getting back into the comforts of Wadi Du'an: this is a perfectly safe route, but, as Awiz said to me with an air of giving information, "There are no hotels as you find on the sea coast." Considering that the only place I know of along this coast is Bir Ali where the Sultan is just trying to pinch M. Besse's wreck, Awiz's comparison is rather funny.

I have got my luggage all straight now—the warm things all handy, the cameras close by, and I hope all I need ready. The two little men and their small brother Muhammad are not nearly as unprepossessing as a complete coating of indigo (lips, hair and all) would make you suppose, and look at me with smiles which flash their eyes and teeth out of the general blueness. We shake hands at each meeting. We parted a little sad, as they were getting only 50 rupees instead of 70 for their four donkeys for four or five days to Du'an; after that a new arrangement is made. I think this is more than one should pay but not unreasonably so. It is all a cut-and-dried route up to Shibam, and no need to take bearings as several parties (and two women, though not alone and husbandless) have been so far before, so I shall be just a tourist enjoying myself and not think it serious travel till after Shibam.

This morning I visited the two schools, one Arab and one 'English' run by an Indian missionary. It is always rather a pathetic sight to see people struggling so hard against such terrific forces of inertia. One of the Arab masters, Sayyid 'Omar, had such a nice face and was obviously proud of his job and the children, and they looked *so* stupid, and the learning by rote cannot give them very much: they were proud of their course, which consists of about five different sorts of Quran (including one course on the laws of inheritance and the ways of making a will—all for quite small children of 10 to 12). The little classes sit on the floor, the older ones have benches. The learning does not lead to anything in particular, and the masters complain that instead of five years their pupils are hardly ever left for more than four. It would take a great ardour to keep on for these very poor boys, when there is no particular material advantage in doing so; and one feels that Mukalla is very far indeed from the rest of the world: a few books come from Egypt. The great treasure of the school was a globe on a stand: it is kept in a bag, and evidently only pulled out on great occasions; they have two big maps on the entrance walls and a few readers—and over 300 pupils. There was a rather nice feeling about the place, the work being done for its own sake in however poor a manner. The Indian missionary was also a nice man with yellow teeth and spectacles. He in his upper lodging has two poor little shelves of books, a thin little brown Indian wife who makes the best of things, and 60 rupees a month from the Sultan with which he must run his school, provide all the stationery, and keep himself and his family alive. He has 55 scholars, and they are all much cleaner and better dressed, though with a certain smugness of which there was no trace in the Arabic school. What a lot of obscure heroisms there are in the world—and all those people, struggling in this remote little corner, have a share. The culmination of Education both in the Arab and the Missionary school, seems to be Signalling: this is what you only reach in the last year, after so many terms devoted to Qurans and grammar: then you are allowed to take a flag and learn the Morse code in Arabic, and I sat and watched while four words were flagged from one side of the court to the other, a triumph of Education! Such curious crumbs of the Western life come floating in this East: football in the camel camp; "Lef, Righ" and "Form Fours" among the soldiers in their skirts and turbans: "God Save the King" in English and then in Arabic in the Indian missionary's school.

21 *January*, 1935.

It is 3 o'clock and all my luggage has gone trotting away on the four donkeys. I shall follow by car in an hour or so and meet it up the valley. It looked very amusing, a series of curious little baskets of food being added at the last. It is five days to Du'an and there seem to be different ideas as to whether or no one finds food en route. At the last the Government has insisted on giving me a Somali soldier of the Bodyguard. I think it was because I gave a ring to old Ali Hakim—they think that I must be somebody after all, and I feel sorry not to be left alone with my Beduin. They are almost incomprehensible but I shall pick up their language very soon. J is pronounced y for one thing, which makes things difficult at first.

Everyone has been very kind here and I believe I am quite popular in spite of this strangeness of my behaviour. I gave 5 rupees for the prisoners; this is a proper object of charity, and far better I am sure than showering presents on the wretched little street boys merely because they see a guest.

To-day I visited the third school and heard the first poem or so: they were all massed in front of me and enjoyed themselves and did it very well. Twice a year, the teachers told me, they have a reception—once in the school and once in the mosque or somewhere, with

[63]

all the learned bodies to attend, so that the scholars may learn 'how to behave': they also have a class for learning how to behave. I suggested that it might teach them not to crowd round strangers in the street, but my Arabic was not clear enough to convey this. The little boys sang the Quran very well.

Did I tell you, by the way, what M. Besse said to me when I told him I had been out of charity to call on a dreary German's dreary wife? He said my philanthropy was like the Morse code, only dots and dashes! I do wish he were here. I miss him so much!

I have quite an idea now of the working of this little Arab town. This morning I called on the Governor to say good-bye, and then went and saw the sort of Government office by the port—the Sultan's divan going on in one room, three Qadhis sitting on a case in another (the appeal is to the Sultan, the law is Muslim Shar'ia); a quarrel between soldiers being settled in another room; the Treasury up-stairs: three or four clerks sit along the wall on mats on the floor, bending their turbans over low desks—and the whole business of state is a little local affair very much like Tarascon, I should say.

It is a lovely feeling to be off again—the donkeys' nice familiar noise munching corn out of a bit of sacking on the ground. I am on a sort of ledge inside a cave and looking down on all the camp operations. They have given me coffee with ginger (I am trying to get to like it as I shall have to live on it). The four chickens destined for my food are being fed by Salim Nasir, the escort, and rice is being cooked in a black pot with various songs and flute tunes round it.

The valley must be limestone; its sides are eaten away in holes and caves, and at one time, a little below here, was water-worked in huge columns, just sketched in and left, and flat faces one would never think made by nature. Its stream of clear water comes up in pools here and there, and lets green trees and bushes grow. *Nathib, 'Ashir, Galaigula, Harmal*—all kinds I don't know.

<pre>
                                          ta
The Beduin are singing songs, ta ta   ta
                             ta   ta   ta ta
                                 ta   ta   taa
                                 ta ta
</pre>

the last note sinking away and down, not as good but not unlike

[64]

Aziz's songs in Elburz—and one of them is just pouring masses of fat into the rice. We shall stay here till 2 o'clock, they say; it is already 11 : I am going to sleep.

On the JŌL, BEIN AL JEBLAIN, 24 January, 1935.

Yesterday I did not write and to-day I am doing so instead of sleeping after lunch and that is a great effort. I have only had time to scribble necessary notes in my notebook; as it is I have not yet much to do, as I am not doing any geography: this route as far as Shibam has been mapped out by Wissmann, and though there are blanks on either side it would take me far too long to fill them. I am getting on very nicely with my people and I should not have any difficulty in mapping, etc., if I could keep them with me: but having to get quite a new set in Shibam will complicate things a lot.

Sa'id has just come up with the best bit of a thing they called Wabar[1] which they shot among the boulders this morning: it did look very like a large rat, but tasted quite harmless and good, only very tough: they said it was "bil marra hallal", that is to say lawful food, and was much nicer than the rotted fish they like: that is a real drawback here, as every donkey has a little of it ready for his owner's lunch, so that the clean pure air of solitary places is apt to get sudden and unpleasant whiffs of it.

We have been coming up wonderful country: up and up, following the length of the Wadi Himem and changing temperature every day—following as it were the work of water through millions of years, for when one comes into these landscapes one is brought face to face with the history of the earth—and what a ravaged history: even knowing nothing, one feels that here have been immeasurable ruins and convulsions; one can still see the forces at work and knows by the relief that comes with every small oasis of palms or little emerald field of maize, how much too big for the human this immensity is. Where there is water among the white boulders and green things on their slopes, some of these rock-imprisoned valleys must be a paradise: one can see it, for the structure is all there, and delicate little grey thorny shapes ever ready to burst out with the rain: an enormous diversity of trees too, and incense trees, they tell me, in side valleys, far from passers-by who destroy them (though I can't

[1] Coney.

F   [65]

think why). The most charming is the sumr tree, a little feathery acacia, with thorns longer than its leaves and a flat top twisted this way and that, like some very graceful figure holding a tray above its head; all the branches and leaves lie flat so that it looks like a Japanese Invention against the flat but not ethereal background of these great terraces.

Evidently what one sees there are not originally mountains, but only the lower stages of which the higher tiers have long been washed away. As one breaks at last through the narrowing, greener, tumbled boulder bed of Wadi Himem and out into the jōl, one is on a great tableland tilted seaward, undulating, with the wadis cut into it like oubliettes, and with a series of wide and shallow terraces which we would think of as downs if they were not completely covered with very hard stones scarce rounded at all. It makes an immense and shallow catchment area, and when the rainstorms are pouring down, the water must collect and find the weakest place and swirl down, and one can see here on the top the beginning of all the ruin down below, the surface stone eaten into and cut away bit by bit, the sudden round whirlpool of earth which forms a valley head, and the terraces worn away among the trees so that they look like stones carefully cut for dry walls. At the first step below the limestone fortress tops there are no houses, only the open spaces, the low mounds which are going to be mountains, and the caravan tracks through the loose stone on every hand which have made a shiny line of polished rock on which beduin scribble their names. The little sumr tree still stands up in this nakedness, but chiefly other smaller shrubs, a green bush called dhodar which looks as if it had been varnished, and was still sticky, and a grey round bush called deni. I collect as much as I can and will send back specimens (including the head of our lunch-rat): but wherever there is more shade and probably water in the wadi underground a mass of various trees and shrubs comes up, and it is difficult to get them all: they look very attractive, like a Romantic Landscape, with the columns and flat walls, and wind-pecked wind-swirled sides of the valley above them. Anywhere here below the surface of the jōl you can find a cave if you want one, and it would be the easiest thing in the world to wait for travellers and kill them: it says a great deal for Mukalla that it is able to guarantee a safe journey from border to border. They do it apparently by keeping two hostages from each tribe except my Murshidi, who are liege to the Sultan—the same prisoners I saw down below in the dark court in Mukalla and sent five rupees to.

I like all my men, even Salim Nasir the negro soldier is very good, though I resent being looked after so much and would be happier without him. They are always ready to stop my donkey for a snapshot, and now try to keep him from breathing by holding his nose because it makes him wobble while I photograph—and they are all nice to me and tell me I am a 'Bedawin'; Said II has been at a war between his own tribe and the next: I asked if there was peace now: "No," said he, "there is fear between us: but we carry on trade with safe conducts."

We slept last night at Hisi at the top of Wadi Himem, where their relations live. They have little square houses, very poor, with nothing in the way of carpets, mattresses, etc. Their riches are the gun (£3 10s.) and dagger of which a really good one costs about 75/- and the girls' silver ornaments. In the house beside which we slept was Mariam with her little first baby, sister of Salim who is with us: you can hardly imagine how pretty she was all in black, clothes and skin being pervaded by the same indigo, with only the silver at waist, arms, and nose to relieve it; one felt that we are altogether too much divided into different colours for the same graceful general effect. What these people give one is the sense of beauty in *movement*; a boy with a cloth round his curls, and a loin cloth, catching his donkey yesterday as it rubbed against ours on the path, was a thing to make one catch one's breath, like a Greek statue come to life.

These people are all as cheerful and good-natured as can be— one's difficulties with them are when they cannot understand what one is driving at, and I am sure that keeping aloof and dealing with them through third parties is the great mistake. Anyway we will see if my tactics get me to Shabwa. I am sure they ought, if only as a reward for eating their fish!

SARAB on the JŌL, 25 January, 1935.

I have just been looking sadly over my instruments—they are not in a satisfactory state: rolling off the donkey did no good to the aneroid and it has got its needle stuck to the roof so that it has to be coaxed to a place that does not stick before anything can be done with it. The compass also has five air bubbles in it and sticks: the rangefinder and clinometer I haven't tackled yet and I think I shall have very little chance of doing anything with them—but one might do quite a lot here getting the names of the wadis and where they join up. I have collected a few.

We had a good evening last night; at least I enjoyed it though it was perishingly cold and the wind went round and round fanning us, as it were, with the smoke of the fire. The wind came rushing over those barren stones and seemed to play sadly up and down the notes which the young Beduin touched with his indigo fingers, the white of the nails showing up in the firelight, and the huge curved silver daggers in their belts, with the cornelian bosses.

To-day we continue to ride over this upland: I love it, and like to see the wadis dropping down, as it were, at my feet: the earth opens and a valley is born, and Sa'id tells me where it goes to sea: usually he gives the name but sometimes he just says "Oh, that goes to sea", as if this were unusual in a valley.

I am having a little struggle with them now as they all want to hurry me on and I *won't*, and they are all sitting very bored and wondering how long I shall be (and I haven't slept at all yet).

We have left all the flies behind. I like this hard and open land, and the distances are lovely, though nothing has any very particular shape. As we came over the low terraces that divide one of these sunk wadis from the next, we suddenly reached the edge of the upper jōl plateau and looked down on the lower, far out of sight. It is not flat: it is all hollows, but planed off in flat shelves and with little plantations of dhodar, duweila, qaradh, etc., coming up according to what there is underneath.

I can't *see* for sleepiness. I must rest.

25 January, 1935.

I am lying in comfort on a little stony rise under a qaradh tree whose smallness of shade keeps on moving me round, but there is a long long view of our three days' journey—the opposite side of Kor Saiban on whose fortress edge we travelled: it looks soft as an undulating ridge in Wales or Dartmoor, with mauve shadows of clouds. The horseshoe shape of concentric terraces that makes a wadi slopes away below: a little outpost empty tower stands there, almost invisible as it is only the mountain stone put to a shape: a little black slit shows where the wadi itself drops suddenly into its canyon.

We slept last night in a village, Burayira: I had one end of the room and the rest of the party the other. I got annoyed with Nasir Salim because I found him sleeping just at my side below my bed, in a mistaken wish to guard me, and sent him off to his half of the apartment.

These little villages have only about ten houses at most and the high undulating jōl all round them. I like its open spaces and sense of height, all the valley world tucked in dark winding alleys out of sight below. When there are clouds it is lovely: when the sun shines in an almost white sky and you see nothing but the hard edges of small stones everywhere—you get rather oppressed by its inhospitableness; but the qaradh tree which grows here and there is a graceful umbrella shape, with twisted varied trunk, and always ready to place itself in the best position against any available background.

MASNA'A in DU'AN, 27 January, 1935.

I am sitting in the Government house at Masna'a in Wadi Du'an, and a kind man is just chasing away all the female inhabitants and children, and leaving only a comparatively harmless half-dozen.

Any artist would go wild over a roomful of Hadhramaut women: the pretty ones have very long regular faces, charming big mouths, and the eyes, with a deep black line under them, almond shaped and extraordinarily brilliant. When to this you add a very pure mustard yellow complexion, made shiny over brows and nose on great occasions with a mixture of oil, wax, and the yellow colour, you get an extraordinarily 'fin de siècle' decorative effect. The length of face made longer by the orange and red kerchief tied under the chin: the barbaric effect greater by the great silver and gold-plaited or striped and brocaded breastplates in front (usually crooked over one shoulder,) the gold belt with little bells, dozens of bracelets in groups above and below the elbow, and all the gold beads and torques they can put round their neck. The black hair cut short adds to it all: it looks like a lacquer work extraordinarily fascinating. The Governor's daughter has really amazingly beautiful eyes and would be lovely anywhere: she is very pleasant too and all are cordial: they came and ate with me a thing called *harisa* of meat and flour like porridge with a cup of melted butter in the middle—and very good. We all ate out of the dish, before I heard that one of the children has measles: there is no doctor—everything, they say, is done by God.

[69]

28 January, 1935.

I am luckily in a comfortable room and everyone being nice to me, which is just as well, as I suddenly developed a temperature, and aches all over—probably a touch of 'flu. I hope not measles as they seem wandering around. It is very horrid, but I hope will go in a day or two, and I found a lovely little clear spring of water falling into a cistern out of the uninhabited cliff and sent the doorkeeper to get me a jug of my own: it is only 100 yards or so away, but the people never trouble to get anything but well water from close under the sewage. It is curious how differently one looks on matters of hygiene according to how one feels. I now feel that everything I touch has measles, especially all the children who sit in a close and grubby little circle round me.

I went down into the divan this morning and met two people for whom I had letters from Aden. It is always amusing to sit and see the business of government being carried on in a friendly way. It is the medieval life, just as it must have been all over Europe 500 years ago or more. The beduin and the valley people, quite distinct, come and sit round the whitewashed walls and pillars, the beduin rifles making a sort of frieze. The two old men I had letters to, Ba Obaid and Abu Yasin, had charming faces. What one notices is that nearly everyone here looks good-tempered. I think it must be because they are never in a hurry, and always have to live together seeing each other all day long.

The children are rather nice and not a bit shy after the first day. There was an awful tragedy to-day, for as I was going up the narrow little alley to my own carved door with a curved wooden peg-key in my pocket, there was a small baby with an embroidered cap and a tassel on the top of his head, swinging a bird by a string round its wing. I rescued the bird and promised something better, and the little wretch, howling, was brought up and presented with a little metal bird that whistles—but repudiated it with fury, and was finally taken away with the real bird in the hands of the doorkeeper under promise to let it go—still furious at the offence to his masculine dignity: I suppose he was three years old.

4 February, 1935.

It was measles as I expected, and I hope the worst is over. I had a high fever all these days, and at last this morning am back to normal.

Everyone has been so kind; Khadija, the Governor's daughter, comes in first thing in the morning, all rustling with bangles and girdles, and provides breakfast—everybody rather takes it in turn with meals, which has disadvantages as one's efforts at explaining what one would like have usually been directed to the wrong person —the eggs have been hard-boiled instead of being raw, the soup filled with red pepper and chilis (which is hard on a lacerated throat) and little things like the sight of one's hostess taking a lick out of the sugar basin are apt to upset one if one is feeling rather ill anyway. The effort to keep anything clean is very great, and if you could see the general surroundings for half a day you would not find it strange that when I am in Europe I love to be in places where I don't need to think of how and what my food is made of. Milk seems to be very difficult to get hold of: it goes funny when boiled because the cow is having a calf. Nobody eats vegetables except raw carrots, and though they have lovely water straight out of the uninhabited cliff, they prefer the yellow stuff out of the well. I have just succeeded in getting it brought me at the end of a week.

Every afternoon the two brother governors come to see me. They have such nice kind faces, so alike, only one with a little black whisker all round his face and the other with only a tuft under his chin. They run things here as they like, and the Mukalla Government has very little say. The Sultan came up here from the coast for the first time this autumn, and was still suffering from pains in his legs from the riding.

The harem sees all the events from its rooms: when we hear a noise, a scream, or anything exciting, we rush to the window and look out right over the valley. It must have been very exciting when every little citadel had its own war: the shots are so loud— they flatten themselves out against these cliff walls. One would either become incapable of initiative as are the women, or else break away and do great things like the men—the two effects of living in this sort of cage in the middle of great spaces.

The Governor's aunt came with another ancient lady to see me to-day: hair dyed *brilliant* orange, exactly matched her kerchief: one tooth; very benevolent. The Governor's mother has given me ten lovely gold beads, and Khadija a local dress: I shall try and get all the valley costumes I can. Another lady has sent me honey.

I am longing unspeakably for a wash! *Nothing* can persuade

[71]

them to give me water till to-morrow—the 7th day; they are kind but firm about it, and I have been so uncomfortable, but find that one doesn't get *much* dirtier after the first two days. Anyway, I know all about life in the Middle Ages. Little details one would never think of, such as one's hostess stopping in the middle of dinner to see if there is vaseline on your knife, as it has just come out of someone's waistband.

It is not at all true that these people are so very hardy. We have had a hot sea wind and everyone has gone down just like ninepins.

6 February, 1935.

The harim all thought it a great joke to-day when I told them that flies bring you disease; it seems curious how uncivilized minds *despise* one for thinking of things beforehand; they seem to think it much superior to go blundering into perfectly avoidable trouble, and then they are not a bit heroic about it—they collapse twice as readily as we do.

Salim Nasir comes up every day to see me, and burbles away like a fussy old Nanny. In his woollen cap with a tassel on top and with his little three-cornered eyes he looks just like the pictures of the villain in the *Chanson de Roland*.

I am getting into the habit of retaliating, and when people come to me with their impossible diseases, I tell them "This is from Allah" and everyone in chorus agrees: I don't see why I should be the only victim of this sort of piety.

Nur and her mother have just come back after two days' weeping at a funeral. It goes on for four days; the men don't take part.

There are quite a number of mosquitoes here and collections of peculiar but harmless little things in the bathroom next door. It could all be very nice if it was kept properly clean: but what can one do? Pretty Khadija has just been interrupting her little song to lift the edge of the rug and spit under it—and they always use the carpet instead of a handkerchief!

SIF, 8 February, 1935.

This is Sif, where former travellers had such a bad time. The Ingrams found it friendly, and so do I: it is like a clustered fortress

THE JŌL
FIRST SIGHT OF WADI DU'AN

ARRIVAL AT MASNA'A IN DU'AN

IN DU'AN

HAJAREIN

against an amphitheatre of rock—a grim place, and the houses like towers.

There are far fewer towns up this end of the wadi, and all looks more desert-like: the earth is hard clods, light and bleached of all colour, and people just as dusty are turning it over to about two feet or so with sharp little hoes and a basket nearby; and when the flood comes they sow millet and it comes up.

We had 1½ hours ride up the valley last night to the village of the man from Java who came to see me. He has a lovely new house of which he is very proud, and it is really beautifully clean, and all painted in bright colours. One feels as if one were inside a *fondant*. The ceiling pink, yellow, on a pale blue ground outlined in red, and the woodwork to match. A red velvet dais with red satin quilt for me to rest on: a samovar and tinned milk for tea (the grass here is so dried up it produces no milk). Clean towel, clean soap, no dust on the furniture, your tea glasses *wiped* with a clean towel (not just one black finger)—a W.C. really charming, the little hole arranged in a wavy stucco pattern with sea-green lid and a lot of clods of earth instead of toilet paper: even the beetles looked clean. We had a white tablecloth to eat off, and excellent food including tinned fish and fruit. I am nearly speechless with my cough (one of the consequences of measles is pneumonia, says my little book), so I wasn't much of a guest, but I think anyone was welcome. And yet he prefers his valley to the splendours of Java. The great preserving force in the country is the women: I haven't met one who wants to leave the valley to go with her husband, and as they keep the children the feeling of home remains. This man has a son and daughter in Java and one little girl here. He was a nice man, with a curious mixture of type—the little delicate hand of Java, so different from the huge bony intelligent fingers of Ahmed the Masna's governor. A yellowy skin and little dark imperial, but the nice good-tempered huge mouth of Hadhramaut.

HAJAREIN, 8 February, 1935.

I had a bad night and don't feel really happy here.

Now the arrival of a car for me has given a new excitement: we looked down on the meeting of the camels and the car by the water reservoirs which are built like beehives at the bottom of the hill (just out of range of the sewage, I hope; the water is turned in here in

[73]

good time and then kept). Our chauffeur came up the hill—a very hearty stout civilized and friendly young man who has been to Baghdad, and whose one fault is that he will talk halting English: he said better come away at once: this of course could not happen, especially as he discovered that I had too much luggage for the car. My flower press, medicines and books, beside the poor little Sayyid and his bundle, were put in charge of two beduin, who are bringing them along by camel. Everyone swears at the beduin and complains of them, but I have found that they are the only people who really do their own job in a competent way, so long as they are doing it their own way!

The charming old Mansab of Meshed came in the morning with a red and green ribbon over a green velvet gown, a yellow turban, and a silver-headed stick in his hand.

MESHED, Evening, 8 *February,* 1935.

We stopped to look at ruins and were late, and found the Mansab without his velvet gown but in what looked a nice white nighty having a sleep with all his faithful round him in a big white room with open door and eight open windows. He came rolling down his stairs, which just contain him, so cordial and welcoming, gave us coffee, and turned everyone out to give me the large room: I am sitting in it now by the light of what they call a '*trik*',[1] as comfortable as anyone can be with unfinished measles in a draught.

After lunch it was too late to rest. A beating of drums and sudden shrill noise of women next door told of another wedding and I went out to see it. All the Meshed ladies were there, wonderful to look at: all sorts of innovations in paint, green chins, green round spots on their cheeks, hair plastered down the forehead in a wave over one eye; masses of silver and sequins and heavy anklets; tassels of many colours on the head or under the chin to hold the little veil (*meqba*); and one girl with a coral band from back to front of her head over the parting and heavy silver collars. They danced with their heads as at Mukalla, holding one hand just below their breasts, the other stiff, full of rings, in front of it; their faces like masks, especially when seen slantwise with their eyes rigid from the strain of tossing their

---

[1] i.e. "electric" because, although it is a petrol vapour lamp, it is the desert equivalent of urban light.

heads up and down; the innumerable pigtails whirling like wheels; and a low rising and falling drone accompanying the monotonous drum, with occasional wild noises with their tongues and clapping of hands. They put their hand up modestly when they make the noise, so as to hide the tongue which beats from side to side in their mouth like a clapper.

It is a charming little open village altogether quite treeless in the desert waste with only the mounds of old buildings around it: a little mosque and minaret all sand colour, and two deep cisterns white and turned pink with dust, and a large *saqaya* and trough for animals to drink above: and a few of the box-like houses round about. It was a charming sight this evening after sunset; a herd of black and white speckly goats and a woman or two by the steps, while a few beduin sat with their guns on the long bench.

SEIYUN, WADI HADHRAMAUT, Evening, 8 February, 1935.

You needn't worry over me any more. I am safely arrived in Seiyun, and lapped in comfort—a bed with mosquito nets, a warm and a cold bathing pool, and everyone ready to look after me. I shall spend a fortnight resting so as to be perfectly fit for Shabwa— which is only three days' journey away anyway.

When I left this morning the dear old Mansab pressed two Himyar seals and a little alabaster stand into my hands, and a collection of chewing gum, cloves and peppermints, into my pocket for my cough. He was so cheerful and nice—like a capable and busy mother of a large family.

We are in the magnificent wide Hadhramaut valley proper. The old style of fortress-house in the valley seems to have corner round towers and the newer goes up straight: at least that is what I judge from present appearances. We passed an old fortified village in the plain; wells and people working them with the drowsy creaking of wheels; the broad empty R.A.F. landing ground; a little domed saqaya here and there, a camel or two; the fringe of palms almost continuous on the south bank, but the valley itself empty, full of sunlight, the ridges of cliff running out into it. And there in the distance of the valley, in the middle of it, was a little bit of mountain ridge all by itself, like a slice of one of the upper ledges deposited in the valley. The top of it was white, a thin splash as if done by a

[75]

Minaret of Qatn

Titanic brush of whitewash. As we got nearer its sides showed the same little beehive holes, the same vertical fissures, as the ancient cliff sides. But it wasn't cliff—it was Shibam, 500 houses all crowded together in a narrow space in the middle of the valley, with a huge graveyard in a hollow beside it. We got near it into bumpy ground, with palms and ditches; the long cliffs of the side valleys open away from it, we saw it through lace-top of palms, the houses rising seven stories or so, their narrowing white decorated tops giving them a look as if they leant back away from us; a little mosque is clustered in their shadows, squashed up amongst them, its minaret and cupola reaching shoulder high, another little white mosque in front like lace —it is all delicate work of trellis and wave in mud, white and made smooth and shiny, and then pink with dust. The houses have long straight shafts let into their sides for drainage, which makes them even taller and more like skyscrapers; we went round the outer ditch and came to a sloping earthy space, a well and saqaya with rows of earthen water jars beside it; women in trailing blue carrying skins of water, and on a rise of about 6 metres, up a cobbly way, the white gate of the town, low among the houses, with camels laden with timber lifting their hoofs as they step out one after the other over the threshold. I was busy taking snapshots; the people came running out, soldiers, beduin, citizens in turbans, women carrying the city rubbish in baskets on their heads (the women seem to do the municipal jobs all over this country).

Then there was trouble with Salim, who took it on himself to say we must sleep here with the Qu'aiti government, and not go on to Seiyun to the Kathiri: he must have been arguing with Hasan and I only heard when they were both hard at it, and was annoyed at being dictated to by Salim. He was really anxious not to take a public leave of me as he was out for lots of bakshish. However, I went on serene, brushing arguments aside, and finally, when all the camels had come out, we took the cobble slope, bumped over the threshold into a little outer court, through another gate, a steep little square with white minaret and the towering houses overhanging all round, a crowd gathering rapidly—walked along to the house of M. Besse's agent Ba Obaid, welcomed by a nice neat quick little man and taken up little steps and passages to his office where my packet of letters was handed to me. It was a strange mixed feeling to see them there and the room rapidly filling and Salim, instead of letting Ba Obaid attend to me, murmuring a long oration so that I had to put a stop to him and it. The governor came in, portly with a stick, and a hennaed beard round a huge round face: no sort of authority. Another nice man in turban was introduced, with gold teeth. I had to explain that I was making straight for a chemist in Seiyun and would go back and stay in Shibam in a few days. It is always a dreadful mistake to hurry people in the East, and is the best way of taking away any friendly feeling: however, they are really all as friendly as can be, and understood the reason for not staying, and only the wretched Salim made trouble by buzzing like a fly over his bakshish. I handed him 6 dollars (one month's pay) and that wasn't enough and at the last as I got into the car I handed him two more, though it was not necessary, and was altogether annoying—and we were off again out of the heart of a crowd with a feeling that somehow I had got into a Russian ballet and everything was unreal, especially as I looked through your letters while going out into the wadi again.

And here I am.

The Sultan and his brother came to call. He is round-faced—not fond of Europeans, I believe: his brother rather saturnine. They did not seem very pleased to see me: but after a while, when we talked of Islamic things and Arab poets, and the indiscretions of Ayesha and origin of women being veiled, things improved. I felt, as I nearly always do, that the way to get on *is not* to be western, even if they want to be so, they are not grateful at being made to feel that they are here to learn—who would be? My hosts, two Al Kaf brothers, soon arrived, very pleasant and friendly. It must be a great bore to have to entertain everyone who comes, and especially in a European way —but they do it beautifully and one has the *luxury* of the east here— cleanliness: it is the keeping things clean which is so rare. Usually just one effort is made and then the dust settles on you rapidly through the rest of your stay. But here Sayyid Hasan is looking after me: I have meals at a table with zinnias in a pot, looking out on the lovely pool and white walls; and a hot bath in the morning.

The chemist's assistant, a frightened little Malay, has just come with cough mixture and injections. He pushed the injection into my arm and then, with a sigh of relief, said "It is all as God wills". As a matter of fact I am only doing all this out of fussiness and to be as quick as I can, as I am quite all right, *no* temperature, and just in need of two days' rest. It is only 15 days since the measles started, and an 8-hour day on a donkey was rather an effort.

This is leaving to-night, and I hope to send again before I leave for Shabwa—but the date of reaching you all depends on when a boat calls from Aden—it may be anything within three or four weeks from arrival on the coast.

11 *February, 1935.*

Dearest Venetia,

I got your letter, January 8th, yesterday at Shibam: this should encourage you to write into the blue, for it was a joy to get. It was very strange too, a packet of familiar things in that medieval town. I won't even begin to describe as this must go at sunset across its mountainous way to Shihr, and the next boat for Aden will take it.

I am glad to have got here, as after six days crossing the desert and jōl from Mukalla I landed in Wadi Du'an with measles! There is an epidemic just now: wherever I go they tell me that 25 children have died. I was quite ill. For three nights delirious, and wisely refrained from taking my temperature. I thought I had been told the secret of the universe and had forgotten it—it was very worrying. I pursued it all night: it seemed to be something large and undulating, but I never got to it: towards dawn however I would feel that all was all

[78]

right and the fever dropped for a few hours. The third day was better and I discovered my thermometer and found it 103 : in six days it dropped and all the measles came out. I spent another six days trying to pull myself together under difficulties in a harem crowded at all hours by ladies drinking coffee and ginger, and people with strange and mostly catching diseases. They were all so kind to me and a lot of it was great fun. The journey up with the beduin delightful, one of them playing to us on his pipe, and war dances to cheer the little donkeys on. As soon as I could I got up and rode two days up to Hajarein where a motor came to meet me. There are 80 cars in this valley, and every luxury once you get here: I am in the guest house of rich Java merchants—thermos to keep my water cool, and an ice machine—two bathing pools, one cold, one warm, and hot bath in the morning; two gardens: outside is a pure Arabian medieval town, ladies trailing in strange beautiful blue gowns and Welsh high hats; and on all sides the cliffs that hem us in with days of desert steppe between us and anywhere else. Five years ago people were potted at as they rode from one little town to the next, and ruins are still about: but now there is peace and soon no doubt there will be tourists. Now it is still one of the unique places in the world.

I am lying in bed to try and finish off the measles which have left a bad cough. I shall probably be ten days or so before attempting Shabwa. Every hope for that venture and a promise of good beduin.

12 February, 1935.

Dearest B,

Hasan is an excellent bodyguard, always thinking of what I really want to do and making no difficulties, and I am sure it is he who has created the pleasant atmosphere around me. He is one of those bull-necked practical Arabs who must, I think, have been the original fighting business men of Mecca: he is so keen for civilization and so proud, anxious to have 'the Arab' thought well of—and is treating me to a hospitality which it would be rare to find in most places. He is just now trotting about with his portly blue and red check skirt stuck out in front, developing my films. We got quite a lot of women without their knowing it, but of course never in the trailing house-dress.

In the afternoon we went again to the market and tried the cinema

—great good humour all round, except that I thought the black slaves got too venomous with the crowd. They are uncertain people, and suddenly go off the deep end, so that one never has the same feeling of safety as with an Arab.

When I came back the old Sultan came to tea and I showed him my Hamdani, and he was enthralled and sat reading it, and told me of a place whose site was not known, which still exists: this will be a great find for me and it is not far off my route. He also said he is going to give me a dress and a dagger. I shall have to send him his photo in a lovely frame. He is not really old: his hair is black in little curls round a completely round head, and he has a pleasant sociable mouth, comfortable: he likes his garden and to see what is being planted, and to drink tea with his friends under a palm tree. To-day his telephone is being installed: I have a premonition that it may not work. But as no one here can draw the wires very tight, they buzz like organs in the wind, and I woke up at intervals in the night wondering what the noise was!

Evening, 14 February, 1935.

I am writing in the intervals of fixing and developing films: each one takes me an hour, so it is rather a labour and this and Tarim are probably my last chances of doing them.

We went for a drive this afternoon, with about 100 or 150 children sprinting after and catching up just in time to get into my foreground. They were all very friendly, and very vague as to what I was taking so I hope to have got a few women at street corners, standing lifting their hands to their veils so as to get a look at me. After wandering through the little streets, we went out to where the old city wall runs up the hill by a ruined fort: it was very fine and rugged in the last red sunlight, wall, fort and hill all one colour; the dilapidated gate and wall broken through all over its length show what a peaceful time it now is: I am rather sorry no longer to have the sensation of being potted at outside the gates!

On our way back we met some Sayyids and walked into their garden and were presented with three beetroots growing there like rarities in a bed filled with something else.

I am to go to Tarim on Saturday, as there is a wedding on. They say I will be even more comfortable than here, but I hate to change. My voice is not yet back but all fever has gone so it is just a matter of

ENTRANCE TO THE GREAT WADI. DIAR BUQRI HOUSES
THE MANSAB OF MESHED

WALL OF SEIYUN

MY HOME IN TARIM

THE CHEMIST'S SHOP: SEIYUN

THE RAFIQ: TRIBAL ESCORT BETWEEN SEIYUN AND TARIM

time: the ladies here say 41 days without washing—and it is only 19 since the fever began! However, I have been washing!

TARIM, 16 February, 1935.

I have got to Tarim and am writing in a very gorgeous guest room all cut out in glass and wood and stucco, all painted like the worst sort of church, with an equally cut out and painted gallery all round it, blue W.C. and green bathroom, standing by itself with a little raised court to connect it with the main building of the house, the whole thing enclosed in a shabby court and mud wall.

We came into this big house, and were welcomed by various Al Kafs; they are all very rich: those that don't wear gold sovereigns as coat-buttons have an *enormous* diamond on their finger. They began all in one house, and now there are about 40 different families. Last year the Sultan's slaves here (there are about 500 negroes in Tarim, more than elsewhere in the Wadi) quarrelled with them and the whole clan moved to Seiyun. They are the all-powerful and doers of all that is done here, and keep dispensaries, schools, etc. I had to translate a German letter to one brother, from a young German who said he was young and energetic (but did not say what in) and wanted a job to see the world: and that God says, "I give, do thou give also": I advised not to give in this case.

The first Angel who appeared to me in this house was the chemist —a pleasant man, of Afghan descent, Abyssinian birth, trained in Aden, and practising here for the last six months: he banged my chest, and there is no more disease, only a little weak—and he has given me so many medicines that I shall certainly either be killed or cured.

Afternoon, 17 February, 1935.

I had a visit from about four learned lights in Tarim this morning and a discussion as to the real boundaries of Hadhramaut, which have been given so variously by different authors that one says it is the valley between Tarim and Shibam and the other puts it as the whole land between Aden and Oman. The two most learned were nice little people, one an ex-editor from Singapore, who did all the talking and is no doubt a thorn in the flesh to local governors; the other a shrivelled up little man of learning with features all pinched together,

G [81]

but amiable, who is translating the Dutch book and wrote a little travel book of his own when two Al Kaf brothers and about 20 Tarim citizens rode to Mukalla to meet the third brother. They all joined in chorus to say things about Aden and her dilatory policy, and begged me to speak about it and their poor road.

We stopped at one of the Kaf houses with beautifully worked doors all carved in mud and painted over, a complicated tracery of branches: this is no longer done now as it costs too much. It is really stucco work, only in mud. My W.C. has a very elaborate design of storks kissing each other in a blue shiny room very gothic, so that the carved and stained glass windows make me feel as if I were in church whenever I go.

This morning we drove about the streets and had millions of small black boys all round, a perfect pest, and much worse than Seiyun, so that I longed for the black slave with the stick: but here the Sultans are weak and helpless, and the 500 slaves have it all their own way, and are a curse, as there is no other force to balance them except sometimes the bedu, whom the Al Kaf set on against them. Hasan told me all this. He tried to train boy scouts and make soldiers out of the peasantry, but he says they cannot buy guns, the Qu'aiti won't let them through and the British are no help and gave only 60 mausers; and what can they do without guns? They have an old cannon which goes off with great *éclat*; we saw and greeted it with cheers at a wedding scene in the Cinema. As a matter of fact I think the only useful government in these lands is one that is strong with the beduin, and that is what is wanting in Tarim. The Seiyun Sultan apparently has much more authority.

Hasan tells me all this gossip, and also the bad treatment by the Qu'aiti of Sultan Ali Ibn Salah at Qatn who was governor of Shibam. The beduin killed two of his soldiers at the town gate, and when he got up troops and guns to punish them, he was stopped and made to give them money by Mukalla, who then turned and blamed him. Now in Ramadhan these same bedu killed one man and two camels of a Shabwa caravan. He is a strong man and has great influence, and probably therefore is suspected. Anyway *he* is the man I am going to for my beduin, as his word is law, and the Slave put into power in Shibam carries no weight at all.

SEIYUN, 19 February, 1935.

I have just got back to my little palace in the garden, so sunny and white and quiet after the grandeur and coloured glass of Tarim where one is always being caught up between the Middle Ages and the style of Monte Carlo! It was quite home-like to come back among the garden walls: they are mud and have dusty outlines; otherwise they would be very like Italy.

We stopped to photo beduin with their bales camping on their way up from the sea. The Tamini bedu live round Tarim, and another tribe, Awamis, run from Urfa to near here; but these were Kathiri, the Sultan's own tribe, and very boisterous and friendly, and Hasan's feelings were outraged while I let them look through my camera. It is no good—the bedu and townsmen speak languages so opposite, they cannot meet; and I always feel one of the bedu! All their sacks were lying in the sun, and the camels grazing on the coarse grass in the broad flat wadi, and they sitting about round a little saqaya, not caring for anyone or anything.

It is nice to be back in Seiyun and away from the feeling of wealth: all the houses are still homogeneous here, and brown—and whole streets of beautiful fancies without any casino intrusions. And the Sultan quoted early Arab poets on the unnecessariness of riches. It was all very pleasant. And the Sultan's little son Hasan has a much better time I am sure running about and bossing the town, than the little boys who each have a small slave of their own.

When I came back here after sunset, with great flutterings and announcements, three of the Sultan's harim ladies came to call— very friendly and anxious to see all my things, drink sips of my cough mixture, take away a dose of Eno's, and wonder at me for daring to use soap on top of measles. "The smell says nothing to you?" they asked; as if the smell of soap could have any effect against so many other smells—though as a matter of fact Seiyun is very clean and all its drains nicely covered and really ornamental.

I meant to leave to-morrow morning but I am to be given an old Hadhramaut dress and I think it is not quite ready—so I shall not start for Shibam till the afternoon or day after and then go to the ancient cities of Huraidha and Andal, and back for three days to Shibam—and then I hope make for Shabwa.

I hope my letters are not as dull to read as they seem to me—I can just jot down in a great hurry and I still feel stupid and with no well of energy inside me.

Hasan has been telling me his story. He has a wife here and a baby died; and all his people are in Mecca: he does not dare to go back as he fought for Husain against Ibn Sa'ūd and dropped bombs on them by air—and worked the "seven tanks of which two were good" against them. All this civilization is dreadfully pathetic.

SHIBAM, 22 February, 1935.

Dearest Venetia,

I am writing this now that I have just got here (in that long long interval before any food appears) as I may not have time again before I leave. I am going to-morrow by car to Huraidha, an old old town, and on to another town mentioned by the old geographers but so far not on the map: this should take two days, and then I come back here and get ready for Shabwa if I am well enough. These measles have been the devil, and I seem unable to get any strength back: the 'elasticity of youth', alas where is it? I began to feel as if Destiny were playing ninepins with me, and only yesterday succeeded (I hope) in stopping a bout of dysentery with emetine. I feel the good desert air may be the best thing and so hope to set off if at all fit. (Also it is getting rapidly hot, 88 in shade.)

Here I am in a charming little bungalow which is always lent to the R.A.F. who now come to a landing ground in Shibam. If the worst comes and I fail of Shabwa, I shall retire here and wait for an aeroplane. It is delightful, the valley all open round it and the sky-scrapers of Shibam to the N.W.; a little pool of water in a built-up colonnade, pomegranates and palms, and a well which is reassuringly far from every drainage but our own. The dining-room has green shutters and palm branches rustling outside. What one likes here about the green and growing things is that they are *clean*: I can't tell you what a strain it is always to be bothering about the dirtiness of objects: I almost wish I knew nothing about microbes and put it all down to God as they do. They say that if you smell any scent when you have measles you just die that very day: the scent rushes to your head, and because of the dryness of the air, it expands and bursts! A woman snatched her child away from me in the fields to-day for fear of my being scented.

[84]

P.S. I recommend to you *Zarathustra*. It is not a book for the weak or sentimental but a great book. I have been fortifying myself with it in moments of weakness. I have come to the conclusion that I am poor in courage really—all I have is a certain obstinacy, but not that serene cheerfulness which one should have to face death if it comes.

A Shibam Siqaya

25 February, 1935.

Dearest B,

Ali did brilliantly to get us to Andal, as it is on the far side of the wadi and a lot of sand dunes to get in and out of in the middle. The whole place turned out and rows of black veiled females saying "Is it a woman? Tell her to come and let us look at her". One girl got an awful shock as she saw her own reflexion in the varnish of the car and thought it a veiled woman.

There is nothing left except stones and a few traces of mortar of old Andal, but it covers a big bit of ground (about five acres I should say) and I collected pottery bits—about 13th and 14th centuries, I should say. Anyway it proves the site and is something achieved. I took its bearings and we gave two rupees to the children, postponed the old headman's invitation to settle there, and came racing away, Ali thinking the risks he took the greatest joke, with his loaded Lewis gun beside him ready to go off if we did collapse.

It is much easier going along the wadi side than in the middle,

[85]

and this way brought us near the lawless little row of towns where the Dyar Buqri wars are. The present peace was only made for eight months in honour of the Sultan's visit and they are all working hard to prepare for war in two months' time. Here you see nothing but watch towers and trenches among the dunes, and walls with covered ways and towers behind the towns on the cliff side. One lives in the Middle Ages absolutely. No wonder the car felt out of place, lurched on two wheels on the sand slope, opened one door and spilled me gently: I was sure the rest of it was following and got nimbly and quite unruffled out of the way, and found Hasan clutching me in his arms (which I promptly stopped) and the two Sayyids climbing out of the dicky. I had a tiny pearl in my hand, found at Andal and held for safety, and that was lost: we groped about but couldn't find it. Sayyid Alawi called it a 'ransom'.

We then went on right across the valley about four miles—a new way, across a waste of dunes to Henin where the bride from Hajarein was taken to: I saw her and she seemed very happy and gay, only fourteen years. This is still in lawless country though supposed to be under Qu'aiti rule! Four rich young brothers from Batavia have a house there, surrounded on all sides by Nahd beduin, who sit in their semi-nakedness in their divan and are much too powerful neighbours to a solitary rich household to be really pleasant: the house however has electric light and wireless and in the evening the beduin came up to the roof terrace to listen to London. It happened to be Sunday, and suddenly I heard some clergyman saying "The Lord keep and preserve you body and soul" and the thing went off into appalling noises, a caricature of sound and no sense but with a religious intonation, until I could bear it no longer and said I preferred the flute and made them stop. But it was a comforting message to get.

I slept in a little painted room, curves and waves of all colours— and a draught in every corner—but otherwise gay. I called on the Harim and saw the bride, but they were not interesting, and the only real charm of the house was the sense of doom of its solitude, and the surrounding beduin and the encroaching sands, and the careless jovial cordiality of the two brothers now at home there. The sand dunes come very near, and an old fort we passed close by this morning is buried up to the shot holes of its walls: the 'ilb trees are dying and stand up like contorted bodies against the clean yellow ribbed sand hills. The sand is finer than any I have ever seen, reddish. Further

[86]

on it began to solidify: rāk bushes grew up, and a dune has collected
by every bush, so that it is all little mounds crowned with green.
This was a robberish bit and things happen even now they say (not
officially).

28 *February*, 1935.

I have given up Shabwa, because I am not really strong enough to
face such an arduous waterless journey before the heat—so am sadly
renouncing it. It doesn't seem worth so great a risk: I am spending
another week or so here, perhaps a fortnight to see more of the valley
and then back to Aden so that you will hear from me in a month or so.
Anyway you will not be anxious after this reaches you as I am in the
arms of civilization again.

Everyone so kind here. I am awfully sad at my failure.

9 *March*, 1935.

Dearest Venetia,

I don't know when or what I wrote last. I have been very ill
but am better now—heart went and for three nights was on the edge
of stopping. Now only a slight dysentery (or liver) left, and I am
getting over it in a few days *I hope*. In what I thought my last moment
I wrote to Aden and don't know what if anything they will do about
it. They will think me a nuisance anyway.

You can imagine my sorrow at this illness, my beduin and all
waiting ready. And now a last dramatic touch has added itself to
my bitterness—a horrid stunting German who has already written a
cheap book about this country, is here again, making for *Shabwa*!
I am helpless. I think I may be able to go there in ten days or so but
not before, and meanwhile he is getting beduin and all. No one
here likes him and everyone is trying to stop him (and I am meanly
letting them do so—but he does not deserve any sympathy: he has
told such lies all in self-boasting).

Anyway, Shabwa or no Shabwa, I am glad to think I may yet be
seeing you again.

I am being fed on milk and hope to begin to get up in a day or
two. So lovely here now and I have a lovely room which can open
doors and windows on three sides, according to the sun. A cool
breeze comes in; and the sleepy noise of the water pulleys soothes my
(very jagged) nerves.

[87]

My kind friends here took it upon themselves to wire to Aden from any ship passing Mukalla—to say "please send aeroplane—Stark"! I fear to think what the R.A.F. will say if they get this! P.S. I am all right now—no need to worry. Damn the German.

10 March, 1935.

The German drama is getting very acute. The German and his beduin got to the starting point at El Qatn yesterday. The same afternoon and without telling me till afterwards, my host here wrote to the local Sultan to stop him if possible: the letter will have reached him last night—and so now goodness knows what will happen. If the German were not such an outsider I would feel these efforts of my friends to be unjustified, but he has been trying to sneak by and I feel it is open warfare—in fact my blood is thoroughly up. Meanwhile I can't do anything myself, being still in bed with dysentery. I wrote a mild reproach to the traitor Hasan, who writes back denying all (not very convincingly) and apparently almost had a fight with my chemist. So there threaten to be a German and an English party in Hadhramaut if this goes on. I will write again to-morrow when the news from the Sultan comes.

11 March, 1935.

A letter came yesterday from the Sultan to my host saying the German had arrived there with some quite useless bedu who would certainly not penetrate Shabwa—and that he would not go. So we now wait and see. I am to have beduin whenever I am ready. I am only waiting for this wretched dysentery to stop. I rather think it has produced inflammation of the liver and perhaps a week's joggling will do it good. I am going to try to get up to-day. Such lovely weather, it is wretched to be ill.

I was thinking about war last night and how good it is for the individual to have to face danger; these beduin are a splendid type. It seems to me that the only thing for a pacifist to do is to find a *substitute* for war: mountains and seafaring are the only ones I know. But it must be something sufficiently serious not to be a game and sufficiently dangerous to exercise those virtues which otherwise get no chance. There must be something *heroic* in life, and no amount of enthusiasm over material things like good drainage and infant welfare,

[88]

TARIM

GATE OF SHIBAM

WOMAN'S STREET DRESS: SHIBAM

SHIBAM

etc., will give this heroic life to more than a very few people. In fact there *must* be danger. The problem is to find a sufficiently dangerous alternative for war, and then half the jingoism of the world would vanish.

Evening.

That horrid German has gone: he and a Sheikh (they say), i.e. a man who is not allowed to carry arms, and they say that he cannot get into Shabwa proper but only to the outskirts—but I am rather sad about it all.[1] I got down into the garden to-day but nearly had another heart attack when I got back and dysentery still continues, though I am dealing with it with yatren.

Meanwhile my chemist and the (traitor?) Hasan have quarrelled over the Shabwa business and the result seems to be that I shall see neither again which is tragic as far as the chemist is concerned.

12 *March,* 1935.

It was lovely to get down among the pomegranate trees, putting out buds, blossom and fruit all at once.

To-day I had a visit from the Governor—he is a kind, ugly and incompetent old slave, so anxious to be helpful. He has a short hennaed beard and a wart on his nose and carries a cane by way of authority: it seems to be a symbol of rank. He asks me my plans: how I wish I could know them myself!

13 *March,* 1935.

If I should die before I get back (I hope not but it is always best to prepare) will you see that £100 of mine are sent to this valley to go towards a *doctor* in Shibam: it might encourage them to institute one. You can't think how many people die for no reason at all—and there are quite a number of rich people here who might afford a doctor. And I should like Meryem Besse to have a nice jewel. I can't write this to Mamma as it would worry her so.

Luckily I have Virgil with me—I read him on my terrace in the afternoon when the sun has gone off. Nothing could be more comforting, more serenely strong; he has more beautiful descriptions

[1] The German reached Shabwa and did in fact make a very good journey.

of the quiet night than any poet I know. And perhaps the pagan poet is more of a help when one is near death, for he hopes nothing and faces it with so calm a courage.

To-day is the second day of the feast and my two attendants have both neglected me leaving only an amiable but invisible negro soldier on guard; Salim is busy butchering numerous sheep and Yuslim is just enjoying himself and rifles are being shot off in every direction: it is very expensive, every four shots one dollar.

15 March, 1935.

I thought I was better yesterday and that a little walk would improve matters and went and sketched by the old wall—came back for lunch, lay on my terrace reading the Aeneid and rather melancholy over the slowness of it all—and suddenly a buzzing came from far away: it crept into my ears so gradually I hardly noticed its strangeness in the desert valley—and four Bomber planes came skimming from the direction of Tarim. Out of the planes came a doctor. They landed, all the city notables went like a row of ants in flowing gowns to meet them; and finally the doctor came up to me and squashes any hope of Shabwa for a long time. It seems my heart muscle has just stopped work and the rest period (dy-as-tole?) of the poor little pump is non-existent. They have all been awfully nice, but I believe they are cursing me in Aden (though after all it isn't the fault of a woman traveller in particular to develop measles). They are carrying me off on a stretcher to-morrow, as it seems I could not possibly do the litter journey to the coast; it is very good of them and I believe against all regulations.

I would have given I don't know what to avoid all this and it will make them much more fussy for ever after—and if it had only happened *after* Shabwa. It seems incredible that to-morrow night I shall be in an English hospital in Aden.

Anyway it will I hope soon bring me to a sight of you and that is a comfort.

Everyone here so nice to me. I think they are really fond of me and I feel I have many friends in the valley.

P.S. The commander of the flight that is rescuing me is called Flight Lieutenant D'Aeth!

Darling B,

Damn the papers! I did hope this business could have been kept quiet and am dreadfully sorry it should have come to you before my news came. I asked for a telegram to be sent you the moment I touched ground here yesterday—at least *I* did not even touch ground, as I was packed in a R.A.F. stretcher and lifted out of the plane. It is all a dreadful disappointment, but not final I hope, and nothing is really wrong with me except absolute exhaustion due to the measles and the fact that I was unable to diagnose the symptoms that followed them and did all the wrong things. I kept on feeling ill from Tarim onwards, got a touch of dysentery and tried to stop it with emetine: this seemed all right till a day or two later, when most peculiar and unpleasant pains and shivers began—I never thought of my heart, whose solidity I take for granted, but decided it must be malaria—took masses of 'atebrin' and thought the sooner I get into dry desert air the better. Luckily, having ordered the beduin a few days ahead, I thought I would first make a little expedition by car to try my strength, and went into the Wadi Amd and found my medieval town (the only discovery I have been able to make). This brought on the crisis and when I got back to Shibam the heart gave out unmistakably and so I wrote to Aden and asked, if aeroplanes were coming (as the Shibam people told me they were on March 12th), would they send a doctor. If nothing came before the 12th, I would make my way to the coast. I got a little better, and in fact hoped to be well enough just to go to Shabwa and back before I returned, and therefore waited till after the big holiday to see—luckily, for on the 14th four bomber planes appeared sailing up the valley from Tarim, a sight more blessed than I can tell you. They were coming up on a practice flight anyway and Sir Bernard had got a special permission from the Air Ministry and sent a doctor who looked me over, and found that the heart muscle had just given up work completely and the poor little engine was going on no reserve at all and threatening to stop at any moment. He said that if I wished to die I could stay or go to the coast in a litter, but if I preferred to live they would take me by air! They were so kind to me: I was so miserable at the failure there on the very threshold and at the thought of my having made such a nuisance of myself. Of course there was nothing for it but to go, and as it was they had to get permission to wait a day for the doctor to make me fit for the journey.

So I left the Wadi Hadhramaut at 6.30 the day before yesterday. The three airmen, and the mechanics, and half the coolies of Shibam hoisted me up, strapped like a mummy in the stretcher, into the cockpit of the little bomber and we flew down to Mukalla in two hours, refuelled, flew at terrific speed 2½ hours more (the whole distance is about 500 miles) and landed in Aden at 12: there was a dreadful ordeal as half the R.A.F. were on the landing ground to watch me being lifted out and put into a car and they brought me straight here to hospital. To-day I am already much better, and there is nothing wanted but rest and nursing, owing to my 'peculiarly resilient constitution!'

I can't tell you how good everyone has been, the care with which they flew me down to avoid bumps and excessive heat: Sir Bernard coming to see me this morning and Mrs. Portal, and no one has rubbed in the nuisance that it must have been. They are keeping me very quiet and not allowing many visitors—but they did allow the Ludlow Hewitts who pass through Aden to-day. It was so nice to see them and it was providential too, for I thought the R.A.F. here would never let me travel in their districts again and Ludlow's first words were: "This is all a good preparation for next time" and when I told him how I should *never* know how to thank the R.A.F. he said: "Oh! that is what we are there for"; this was comforting and reassuring and makes me feel a little less unhappy over all the fuss. I feel when I think of this that I ought to have died quietly without saying anything to anyone—but I am glad I didn't.

It is all wonderfully arranged for the wounded on a plane. The stretcher is made of flexible bamboo, strapped across you at intervals, in a wool and windproof casing and can at a pinch be slung on to the outside of the plane in a hurry. I, however, was lowered with much trouble into the cockpit, just big enough for me and the doctor. Even my head was strapped down, so I saw nothing but a bit of sky and all the little knick-knacks around me, all clean and silvery aluminium, beautifully made and thought out. Flight-Lieutenant Guest was out of sight in front, and the other three were round and above us in the sky. The doctor described the country as we went, shouting down through a tube the wadis and little camel tracks I could see in my mind so well, and the plateau desert and then the

[92]

blank volcanic mountains and the sea. At Mukalla the fat little Ali Hakim came climbing over the edge to see. After that they raced me through the air: I was counting the minutes as my feet were too tightly tied and I was in agony, and no one could get at them.

Will add a line before this goes on Wednesday.

20 March, 1935.

P.S. Mail just going. I am doing splendidly. Hope to sit up to-morrow. The doctor says the heart is remarkably strong and will soon be as good as new—just a case of strain.

2

Iraq Revisited, 1935–37

A FEELING of happiness lay over the spring of 1935.
It escorted my chair from Aden hospital up the side of the steamship *Orontes,* and hovered in the privacy and quiet of the ship's hospital, for I was still too weak to travel in the ordinary way; and it stayed through the spring and summer in Asolo. It was partly the peace of renunciation: Shabwa and all other Arabian travel were over for the moment, and life flowed as it does for animals, filled only with what trickles into it from day to day. I was surrounded by affection, a kindliness which makes one's curled-up petals unfold; and for an all-too-short period I was in love with no one. Looking back now over my life, I realize how pleasant these vacant periods were; they gave leisure for all sorts of small and unexacting friendship.

These ingredients of happiness are negative in a way, but they do what is done by the cutting of a tree in a clearing—they allow the delicate, the unnoticed, the incidental little plants and grasses to come into their own. From love one can only escape at the price of life itself; and no lessening of sorrow is worth exile from that stream of all things human and divine: but, if one has taken the buffets of the current even to the verge of drowning, a reach now and then—stagnant perhaps but smooth—may be welcomed. It gives a pause of detachment. I see that these intervals have been the richest in their reward: they rise to no peak, but keep a level of contentment whose total perhaps surpasses the other; so that one would wish them to last for ever, forgetting that their very serenity is due to the sharpness of what was before them, and that—like all harvests—they garner what has come through the pains of growth, the darkness of earth. These intervals, shorter than I could wish, I now recognize as delight and liberation.

The kindness of Anton Besse and his family made the summer of this year. His daughter Meryem travelled with me in the *Orontes* and brought to my bedside the small ship-gossip that wound itself round her vitality and youth: the genius of life seemed to enter with her, surrounded by reflections of light from the water, the peaceful chug of the engines, the patter of footsteps on deck like wind among leaves. We made for Naples and reached Asolo overland; the elder Besses arrived soon after; and in the summer, A.B. came to fetch me, drove me across the Lombard plain, over the western Alps that dip to the pass of Argentera, by Barcelonette and the Montagnes des Maures to their summer home of Paradou near St. Tropez.

Everything mechanic was against us on this drive; we lost our way among the lesser roads of the plain where dusty ox-carts with creaking axles are hidden in the maize and no garage is in sight; and we broke down at irregular intervals as we climbed to the passes. But no one could be more cheerful than A.B. to break down with; so exacting with human nature, he was prepared to take anything from a machine. We reached Barcelonette late at night and slept there, and next day wound down among the lonely woods of ilex and mimosa, the hills where the Saracen pirates raided away the vestiges of Rome.

I now came back into the light and shade of living. Three months in Asolo had passed in a sort of dream, a little harassed by the floods of people my mother poured over me in my enfeebled state. I had spent long days embroidering in the warm garden, had talked with old friends and met and made new ones, and went—when Asolo grew hot—to a mountain inn with Herbert, who read *Middlemarch* aloud to me through the afternoons; and when I began to be able to walk up steps again and to go out, Jock Murray came and we drove to Grappa where the wild narcissus blooms in mountain meadows, and drank our vermouth in the high square of Feltre at the end of a long street of palaces, derelict and neglected above the busy market town below.

This mirror of Shalott existence came gradually to an end at Paradou. The Besses' house stood on a slope of pines with broom and pungent maquis all around, where a stony, water-wrinkled track up the hill served for the game of boule—bowls without the bowling green, with all the accidents and pleasures of the unpredictable; this was a sport in which everybody joined.

Rich earth grown with vine-rows stretched below, until the sands began under a flatter sort of pine. The house enlarged itself over the hillside in a crop of small pavilions where guests, parked independently, could work in peace through the morning till A.B. collected his team for the beach. He ran his family like a charioteer, his wife steady but unobtrusive beside him at the reins: he seemed to be made, like the brilliance of the landscape and the sky, out of the sane, extrovert, unhesitating air of Provence, and even now a hard, bright, unclouded day on the European side of the Mediterranean will make me think of Anton Besse without apparent cause. In Aden, for all the vastness of the Asiatic background, he was the conqueror of his world: but here he seemed rather the embodiment of something more enduring than himself. His Scottish wife Hilda has these qualities of vitality as it were in a different mood, chastened by the struggle with which we make room in our careful northern natures for the southern certainties. Somewhere, in this meeting of spiritual climates, the norm of civilization was reached; perhaps when the Dorian invaders came down upon the plain of Argos. I think of the Besses at Paradou as an embodiment of it, a late and quiet example of what, beginning in turbulence and confusion and opening out into the Grand Tour and the ages of refinement, has gone on uninterrupted, ever since tall northerners crossed the first rivers of Europe and saw the unforgettable waters shining against the beaches of the south.

I now began *The Southern Gates of Arabia*, laboriously, with a fatigue that has hung about me ever since. A usury of fate obliges me to write nearly all my books with a chorus of doctors

[96]

prescribing total rest, so that a white sheet of paper waiting to be filled now produces automatic exhaustion. But at Paradou my friends took me to the beach before I could wear myself out in the morning: we bathed and lay on the sands and watched the sparkle of the wave as it turned over; and came back to Provençal dishes in huge *terrines* of earthenware, followed by figs and grapes and peaches hidden in their leaves, eaten at a shadow-sprinkled table under vines.

I met here some charming people from Alsace called Schlumberger, whom I became fond of and visited on my way to England in October. By this time I could walk again and thought myself strong. I had spent a month in Asolo. The King of Italy had come to our mountain, the Grappa, to open a mausoleum for the 1914-18 war: not only the bones of Grappa—where the youngest soldiers had stopped the Austrian armies on the brow of the descent to the Lombard plain—but many others from the neighbourhood had been brought. A sort of tunnel was arranged for their reception, with glass-fronted cubicle and name-plaque for each set. Happening to go up there a day or two before the opening ceremony, we saw ribs and skulls, femurs and tibias promiscuously shovelled above any name that came handy. It was done better at Marathon where they made a common mound of all the dead, or on the Vosges, where the memorial was beautiful, free of the fascist swagger which in those years made God appear as an afterthought in the places dedicated to His name; the French angels of gold, their bare altar, low crosses and empty trenches, gathered in the eyes of Mulhouse and the plain, still found a voice in the silence, and crowned their hill-top with humility.

Apart from my hosts, the French I met in Alsace were more against the British over the Abyssinian affair than any of the Italians we knew. No inkling of its implications seemed to touch them; they spoke of it as a move in a colonial game, with Britain an unsporting loser. It was a time when Sir Samuel Hoare's speech in Geneva (on Sept. 11th) had given its last flicker of life to the League of Nations, and we hoped that

Britain might lead the small people of the world out of that ignoble morass of 'safety first' of Mr. Baldwin. It was a false hope, but it lay like a ray of light on all the autumn journey— on the little towns, Ricquevilier, Keyserberg, Kainzberg, Colmar, Freiburg, Strasbourg, Bitche, Saarbruck and Trier: I think of them illuminated, warm and tender, in a cloud-threatened sunset of peace.

In England everything pleasant awaited me. Venetia's care and gentle welcome at Penbedw; Port Meirion with Jock Murray; the Methuens at Corsham; the Chinese exhibition; new or familiar faces—Goodenoughs, Peter Flemings, Michael and Julian Huxley, Osbert Lancasters, Hector Bolitho, the Leonard Woolleys and a charming frail ghost of civilization— old Mr. Eumorphopoulos. I met for the first time Lord Goschen and Lady Goschen, an old lady as vivid and young-hearted as a fountain, with the same kind of refreshing sparkle, whom everybody loved. In their house in Kent Phyllis and Frank Balfour, their daughter and son-in-law, came to be my friends.

The great houses of England were still open and parties at Petworth were reported in *The Times*. Lady Leconfield, whose friendship also came through my book, invited me for a week-end in that waning English splendour, where in a beautiful room carved by Grinling Gibbons hung the portraits of men and women who once had lived in it—people with bold faces and no fears for their future, and an obvious conviction (in the women) that even the absence of beauty mattered little when cushioned on the Whig opulence of their day. In the kind glow from lamps and sconces and firelight, above the mellowed carpets and brocades, they looked down with careless eyes and delicate white hands with pointed fingers, on the descendants who had taken their places, who moved in a world of less reliable daylight, with assurance subdued to modesty, and a wish— perhaps—to serve more than to enjoy. This seemed to be the difference, as one looked at the two sets of human pictures, the upper painted tier so vivid with life, so much less questioning than the living crowd that moved below. What I liked, in spite of my shyness, in the great week-end, was its freedom; one could break away and make acquaintance that turns to friendship, as I did with several people and particularly with the David Cecils, who walked about in their own atmosphere wherever they went—*A Midsummer Night's Dream* atmosphere, so that one met them and always does so, with a feeling of exploration. And I liked the quiet hour before dinner in the tapestried bedroom with a fire burning, luxury blossoming quietly out of its centuries, gleaming like the firelight on surfaces of dark presses and carved bed-posts and embroidered chairs. Outside in the park, the fallow deer followed the same sort of life, elaborate in ritual: I watched two stags walk side by side with slow composure, till they reached a suitable place, turned as if at a dancing class, and fought with antlers interlocked; while the doe, slim and graceful as a Gainsborough, with the same delicate wrists and ankles, looked on, hesitating but not perturbed, with perfect refinement.

In the midst of this social existence I lectured on 16 December to the Royal Geographical Society. It meant a desperate effort, as usual, comforted by the most endearing welcome from the audience. However often I lecture, I shall never cease to be surprised by the humane quality which succeeds in making a bond in a public place: the explanation is, I suppose, that the lecturer sees a crowd of people before him while the public can develop personal feelings by seeing only one. I know now that my happiness consists in dealing with individuals by themselves: I like small parties better than large, and a tête-à-tête better than a party; I dislike philanthropy because it deals with groups and like charity because it can concentrate on individuals; and I can write, or speak over the air, merely because the solitude of these two processes enables me to forget that they are directed towards numbers. For this reason, too, among others, I prefer the country to the town; even in the garden I prefer flowers to stand by themselves, each on its earth and not in a tangle; and the happiest days are those that go by with one person, and certainly not more than three at most, in pleasantly empty surroundings.

The Christmas of 1935 was such—spent at Sidmouth with Jock Murray and his father—with the tide racing against red cliffs in yellow eddies, grey gulls against it lop-sided in the wind, and happy walks in the soft, south-western air. And such were the succeeding months of Penbedw, filled with good talk and good hours, in spite of the fact that I collapsed again and—having finished *The Southern Gates* with much pain and effort—was unable for weeks either to write or read. When the book came out in May I was in a nursing home in London enjoying the detail of life as one does in sickness, when not only the wish, but even the conception of activity deserts one.

As I recovered and the summer passed, and the beauty of England returned with its gentleness to my heart—Gloucestershire and the Cotswolds, the gardens and delicate stone of Corsham, the downs of Avebury, Dartmoor and Haslemere, the valley of the Wye and Kent, places known before or unknown, seen in a light of friendship from the houses of friends—in this pleasant atmosphere a shock darkened my world as nothing had been able to do since the breaking of my engagement long ago.

A love had come into the interval of quiet. It had not entered my life, but stood on the threshold, frightening—for there was no permanence about it; and I was still young enough to think that human permanence exists. While I hesitated, my friend and lover met, an old story. I was rather unattractive and fat from illness, and the unstable masculine horizon was instantly filled with my friend's grace and charm. I knew that love was dying, and as a child to whom I once offered a toy bird in exchange for a live one wept and knew the living from the dead, so did I. I withdrew, with sorrow and longing; but before doing so, spoke to my friend. Her own heart, she said, was free; I asked her to be generous and eclipse herself from my overshadowed little orbit for a while.

[100]

I think a man might have said this to another man and been understood: with a woman, one collides with the elemental, the glitter in its shadows of the jungle. I tell the story not only because it shattered me for a long time, but because it also showed that I was blind to the mechanism of communication between men and women. Emotion, beauty, the art of words, even the daily things of the house, come to me with an abstract light, as if a planet shone on them from far; they all appear, and in my heart I think they are, universal. My friend looked on the question as particular. She rejected my appeal, and my whole world drowned. So much so that for many years I never trusted a woman again in any intimate matter—and now when, with hesitation and doubt, I have made more happy trial, I still think that the general rule of women is the jungle rule, only to be mitigated, and that imperfectly, by advancing years, hopeless plainness, or the total elimination of men.

Out of the destruction left by this emotion, a lightness rescued me, gay, temporary and spontaneous, without possible permanence, unpossessive and free, a butterfly in the sun. It was an alms in my loneliness and I let myself slide into it with full consciousness, with a childish gratitude, for a warm friendly hand in the dark. For it demanded nothing: nor did it reach or bruise those wounds that heal slowly.

I think of this time with tenderness, and of the small happy things that belonged to it, the hours that came slowly and went fast, the little shock of meeting as if, every time, the memory and the reality had to be re-introduced, as strangers. I walked along Knightsbridge to buy a chiffon and lace nightdress, wondering strangely, as one might if one had lived all one's life by the sea and never gone in to bathe; and thought as I brought it home that I must be someone else and could never be myself any longer. I was pleased to find that I was myself more than ever, with life added, and no bite of conscience or regret—which appeared, strangely, to surprise my lover, who thought it 'a-moral'. For myself, I would not have welcomed him if I had held it wrong. I would, I believe, be faithful even in

[101]

prolonged absence, from the mere fear of hurting what is beyond myself: but at that time I felt free of all claims, with liberty in my heart. It was delightful to be desired, to give pleasure, to be a partner in the mystery of life, which now and then, in a look, in a touch, seemed to open out away from both of us in an abyss of its own where shining wheels of the universe revolved.

For a year or two this happiness flickered along, doing no one any harm, till the darkening circumstances of the world swallowed it up. On its sweet and smooth undercurrent my London year passed; friends came and went; week-ends, lectures, interrupted; I was given a medal, the Mungo Park medal, by the Royal Scottish Geographical Society; the outer world came pressing in; in February 1937 I left by way of Asolo for Iraq.

Because of the lightness of our union, no sorrow attended this departure. Unlike most women, I prefer love without matrimony; if a man does not wish to remain, I had rather lose him, even if I care for him, and would keep marriage for the Christian union only, so deep that death is temporary beside it. This comes inevitably, I suppose, from an inability to live with a façade; what comes out of the ground has to be in harmony with its roots, or die; and this gives a desperate need for sincerity, an uncomfortable and solitary desire, which I am far from recommending as a general rule. I would indeed often be glad to be more conformable myself.

In February the road of the Levant opened out again with pale seas and islands round the steamship *Galitea*: from Brindisi to Athens: from Athens to Alexandria: from Cairo by Egyptian airways to Baghdad, and thence in a day or two to Basra and Kuwait. The charm of that sun-washed oasis between earth and water was greater even than I remembered. It was in Gerald de Gaury's care, and I was his guest there for a month, and much of its pleasantness was made by his suitability and contentment with the background of tribes and tents and deserts, pearl-fishers, gossip, intrigue, and little wars, spicery of the east diluted by distances and delays that make it humanly tolerable, which most European communities, when they have it at close quarters, seek to exclude or ignore. The only way to be happy in the East is to accept, to modify or provide intervals of rest from what is too exacting for our constitutions, but to live with the remainder: and this Gerald did in his big ugly box of a political agency, with the sea of Alexander before him and the deserts of Muhammad behind, legendary expanses both in space and time which he made to contribute to the daily pleasures of his guests. He was the most thoughtful agreeable host and the month slid by almost as swiftly as the small wild iris that blossomed and died under our horses' feet.

In April I was in Baghdad again, in the kind and happy Sinderson house, watching the Tigris rise day by day till its yellow earth-encumbered waves lapped at the sand-bag dykes that protected the city. I fell ill and at last discovered what the trouble was—the sun and dust inflamed and poisoned my head, still weak no doubt from its operation three years before. Another operation, for sinus this time, was inflicted upon it, by an excellent surgeon who looked after the R.A.F. in the cantonments of Hinaidi between the Tigris and Diyala. This pleasant camp, shaded by oleanders and filled with gardens, was even then being handed over to the Iraqi government and has now, I believe, almost melted away under repeated floods. I was told that I was mad to be operated on in a country where every particle of dust is liable to poison—but I was tired of travelling home to be cured, kept the microbes at bay by inhaling menthol, and within a fortnight dined on a terrace over the Tigris with Hamid Khan. He was a dear and true man, a cousin of the Aga Khan, and he brought two of his Shi'a friends and sat talking with that timelessness which is like the Persian pictures: an absence of perspective makes everything equally important and days and distance cease to be. One of the guests was Salih Jabr; he later became the first Shi'a Prime Minister of Iraq, and even then I recognized his directness, capacity, and modesty. Like Nuri Pasha and others, he became my friend during the

war, but the foundation was laid in the soft spring evening of
1937, with Hamid Khan as host and the great river rolling under
reflected lights like a scaly snake whose every movement might
destroy.

They gave me advice for my stay in the holy cities of Nejf
and Kerbela, to which I travelled in a few days' time. Dark
walls still girdled Nejf on her hill, and no European woman that
I know of—or man either for that matter—had yet thought to
spend a week only for pleasure within her religious enclosure.
The new moon above the golden dome shone on a world
familiar but infinitely remote and aloof; the life of Nejf was an
echo of medieval history in Europe—the craftsmen's guilds,
the copiers of manuscripts in the scarcity of books, the hostels
and pilgrims, the holy men with their schools of disciples, the
young men's timid dreams under the heavy hand of authority
and age. It was difficult indeed for a woman to get in touch
with the Shi'a teachers of religion, and Gertrude Bell met only
two of them as far as I know: I was admitted to visit one among
the wittiest and most amusing, and found an almost French
quality in him, cynical, sensible and astringent. During the
war I think I met them all and came to know the holy cities well,
as I could never have done but for this week of introduction.
Although on this occasion I was not (much) dissuaded by anyone from my venture, it continues to surprise me that British
authorities neglect the *encouragement* of suitable visitors for
difficult places, their only means—just because it is unceremonial
and done at odd and accidental times—of preparing knowledge
and friendship for any coming strain.

At Kerbela I spent a more secular time with the Mustafa
Khans: their family, through the Aga Khan, lived in a curious
blend of the international world and the mystic East. From
their hospitable house, where you could choose any degree you
liked of summer coolness in cellars that descended one below
the other into the depths of earth, I drove to Ukhaidhr and
Shithatha. I had seen Samarra and Tekrit with Stefana and
Peggy Drower; and Kadhimain I knew well. When I left

Iraq at the end of May for Damascus a gallery of new pictures was in my mind—desert ruins where the wind eats the bricks with a continual whisper even on the stillest day; the middle ages of Islam, in porticoed courts with painted pillars, in small towns where manners are unchanged; the elegant river-silhouettes of Basra. Even more than before, I had come to see the variety of Iraq, built in depth as it were, for every surface difference goes down into unimaginable antiquity, founded perhaps on life before the Sumerian deluge, whose story is the beginning of history for peoples in Europe.

Westward across the Euphrates, the Hellenistic atmosphere of Syria seems strangely modern as one returns from the farther lands. I stayed in Damascus with Guy and Cynthia Fain, who were running the country in the absence of the High Commissioner, M. de Martel: they had driven across the desert to Kuwait during my stay there, and invited me on my way home, showing me a new Damascus from their cool, welcoming, beautiful old Turkish house on the slope of Salhiye.

For many years now, in one country or another south and east of the Mediterranean, I have watched people striving for their freedom—freedom from other nations, British, French, Italian, whose civilization they desired and whose capacity they recognized. This very struggle, perpetually recurring, gives its ancient-modern colour to the Greco-Roman Levant. And I have come to the conclusion that there is a fallacy at the bottom of the discord, a single conception which, by its essential wrongness, renders futile every effort at reconcilement or peace. This is the fallacy that the most civilized nation should *rule*. The methods of power are barbaric, and civilization becomes corrupted as it seeks for power: direction, advice, service are its road, and along that unobtrusive highway it will meet with nothing but reverence and welcome. The recognition of this limitation is the secret of the long success of churches and—when they forget it—the explanation of their fall; and in the chain of Arab countries from Tunis to the Levant one can see European failure becoming sharper in the measure in which this

[105]

basic secret is forgotten, until it ends in those hideous blas-
phemies against the very gods they quote which fascist inscriptions in north Africa perpetuate to their shame. The
French and British efforts on the other hand both seem to me
to have erred, the former by adulterating their teaching by the
pursuit of power, the latter by too often forgetting that they are
there to teach: these two defects, I discovered, shut me off almost
equally from the Arab world as soon as I entered an official
atmosphere, whether in Damascus or Baghdad.

My Damascus stay was nevertheless enchanting, the third
delightful visit of this year. The Irish and French in my host
and hostess went together as lightly as a good soufflé; they were
kind and gay, and shuffled society and sight-seeing with tact:
we drove to Homs and Hama and Aleppo, where the memories
of St. Simeon Stylites have involved themselves with a cabaret
and dance given by the general, in a hall decorated with black
and white cubes, like dominos, subduing the lights. Dress
also was only white and black, and as the dancers passed over
pieces of illuminated floor shining through glass from below, a
curious illusion divested the women of all their clothing—the
white gown and everything else disappeared and only the
female silhouette remained, happily unconscious. This was
unintentional, and the officers circled round their general in
fascinated perturbation. "Il faut bien faire quelque chose,"
they said at intervals, with eyes glued to the spectacle, and not
the slightest sign of action to follow.

In Beirut I found Gerald de Gaury and went with him to
Beit ed-Din where the blood of Christians massacred by Druses
in 1860 is shown splashed on stone walls; the old pleasure palace
of the Amirs is just above, in a common Eastern juxtaposition.
All these were places new to me. Other friends, the Seyriqs,
took me to Palmyra, forbidden without an escorting car when I
was in Syria before. We drove to Qasr-el-Hair whose painted
floors and Byzantine carved doorways, just excavated, were too
unlike the present nakedness even to raise a ghost in the valley,
until we turned aside and found a ruined dam in a cup of the

hills, built with gigantic stones to last for ever, with no water left to hold in the neglected land; but still it stood there and explained the old prosperity. Water in landscape is like eyes in a face, when the lids close, the expression of life departs; and so it has departed from the lands round Palmyra, whose fields, I am told, can still be seen from the air, under a dead skin of sand. As we drove in the twilight towards a low pass flanked by tombs, whence the city appears with its quiet streets of columns, we were made anxious by a row of boulders across our road; the driver got out in the solitude to remove them, and nothing happened: but it was still a time sufficiently disturbed and a country sufficiently deserted for such an obstacle to be a sign of bandits now and then. On the next day we made by a yet more lonely and far less easy track for Aleppo, slope after slope descending in yellow expanses of hard earth cracked with summer, with edges blurred and trembling in the sun: and in the midst of this fierce emptiness found a small Hellenistic temple, with the edges of its cut stone sharp and delicate, tawny as the land and quite alone.

I reached Trieste and Asolo and spent the middle summer with my mother at L'Arma; and when Jock Murray came to visit us, took him for a day to Monte Carlo where he watched me with anxiety while I gambled away thirty gold sovereigns. The mere sight of them had caused a small sensation in the Rooms. I lost gently but steadily, while Jock registered this new trait in his author's character with evident distress. The explanation was that I had just discovered the thirty pounds; packed in a belt I had carried to Arabia, and left among my things during my illness, they had been forgotten. For years I had been anxious to try out the very unsound theory of doubling one's stakes, which had never been successful with me because funds always ran out; and now both money and Monte Carlo were there. By the afternoon, with only one sovereign left, I felt that I had given the system a fair trial; we drank the remaining sovereign, and I have never gambled at roulette again.

The summer ended with the Paris Exhibition, where the

German and Soviet buildings opposed each other, gaunt and rectangular; the air of Europe was darkening. A sort of anguish oppressed me when I went to England now, for the war, obviously coming on the continent of Europe, seemed to be the very last thing people thought of. It was a fashionable thing to go to be petted by the German authorities at the Nüremberg rally, and Mussolini was still considered a pillar of the Conservative party; in Italy my mother still included fascists in her love for Italians in general, regardless of the fact that every Italian we thought well of loathed them: the issue was becoming so acute that it affected the relations of everyday life.

We now had in Asolo a fascinating neighbour with dark purple finger-nails and tiny Russian boots and high heels— Marina Ruspoli, the daughter of the finance minister Volpi who has bought Maser. That beautiful Palladian villa was being arranged and furnished to make her home, and a friendship began which has continued, strengthening through good days and bad, year by year. One can walk in two hours over the hills from Asolo to Maser, its pediments and statues and long wings cream-coloured against the hill; and find its mistress inside it, clear-cut as a gem in person and mind, and so spontaneously and definitely alive that even her Veronese background is subdued at her approach. This new friendship, which was to be my mother's refuge and comfort in the years that followed, made little impression on me at that time, for I was on the edge of another Arabian journey. I spent three weeks of preparation in England and a last week-end with Jock at Chiddingfold enjoying the autumn loveliness, the mists that curl over tiny streams, the silence of hedgerows settling into winter, the smallness and dearness of the dwindling winter life of earth. Each year these things came closer to me, enhanced by absence, and by the precariousness of everything that mattered: two thousand years and more of our civilization were balanced on the edge of chaos. From the Abyssinian war onwards I was never unaware of that precariousness: like the knowledge of the presence of death, it gave a supernatural beauty to all good moments—and this in itself is the one great compensation in time of insecurity. The other compensation, the knowledge of the indestructible immortality of our foundation, we were not yet braced to recognize.

* * *

S.S. ORONTES, 10 April, 1935.

Dearest Venetia,

I am on the way to Asolo and should get there from Naples on Thursday (15th). I was carried on board yesterday and put in the hospital, and am being looked after by a charming sister and the doctor who was with Shackleton when he died and spent 14 months without washing! It was like a night coming into daylight to emerge into the world again—and I could not help feeling very melancholy, as I looked out at Aden, its jagged crater peaks and the harbour stretched out and orange lighters in the sun, and felt I was leaving it all with nothing accomplished. And that horrid German I hear has got to Shabwa after all (but he cannot have seen anything of the old city as he was fired out by the beduin in 3 hours and the ancient site is a day's ride inland). However, it is no good thinking of it, for the present, and we will have a long time to talk it over before the next attempt.

Meryem Besse is on board with me and a young American has changed over on to our boat at a cost of £16 to himself—and so I am being chaperone and enjoying it: I am rather a nice chaperone I think, and a much nicer one than I ever had the luck to possess (with the exception of Minnie Granville!): of course a chaperone confined to one place is also a great advantage. There is a certain brutal roughness in modern love affairs, but I rather like it and it seems to me quite a good beginning to show oneself as much like one's ordinary self as possible in good time.

I am carried up on deck in the afternoon and can sit out watching dolphins, flying fish and the dark blue sea: to-morrow night we may see the mountains of Sinai, and that will be my last sight of Asia for this time: I am sad to be leaving it so soon.

[109]

ASOLO, 1 May, 1935.

One's family is not the one for nursing, and it depresses me because I become so *disgusting* and my temper is just nowhere. I think the amount of self-control needed to die decently in Arabia has just permanently damaged it.

I am not supposed to write yet, but am much better—pulse down to 90 again, from 110.

7 May, 1935.

Elizabeth Pollock, who is a charming young neighbour for a few weeks, has just been quoting Austin Dobson to me:

"The dark days of winter are over:
  The lilacs get mauver and mauver"

—which pleases me by its idiocy.

They also have a nice story of the hunting man who came up from Ireland and saw "Holman Hunt Masterpiece" written up in a Bond Street shop. "Holman Hunt?" said he: "I never heard of it. Thought I knew all the hunts." And he went in and saw . . . Christ riding on a donkey!

The brother and family, who are diplomats in Vienna, have just joined the party—so we will hear some news. I feel more and more that it is only from people on the spot that one can learn *anything* now: what is published is so wrong always.

Even my little *Oriente Moderno,* the best paper on current Eastern affairs I know, is now becoming propagandist in a disguised way. The Abyssinian business makes me sick: if they bring it off I really don't think I can *bear* to live here: it is all very well to shut oneself away from politics, but if one feels that a real crime is being done, it does not seem right to just turn away and think of something else. However, I am doing my little bit by telling everyone who asks me about things that the Abyssinians always mutilate their prisoners, which rather damps the enthusiasm: as a matter of fact almost everyone hates the idea of war here.

25 May, 1935.

I can't remember whether I wrote last week or not. I meant to, but when one is allowed to do nothing but embroidery, the days are so much alike that it is difficult to keep count of their passing. It is quite untrue to say that monotony makes time pass slowly: I think it goes ever so much more imperceptibly, and then one suddenly notices how much has gone.

Now your letter has just come and it is such a dear one. I too had been thinking over our good friendship, one of the best things I believe in both of our lives. I was tidying up photographs and came on those of the Pyrenees, the Lake of Soularet and Seo: what a delight it all was. Do you remember bathing by the wayside, and coming down in the evening on those two old people, and the night in the hayloft?

The making of your will is academic, I hope and feel, as far as I am concerned: but if you are sorting out things for fun, put me down for the pink roses we drink our breakfast out of, or one of the pictures we pass going up and down stairs: I hope I shall not enjoy them anywhere except at Penbedw and that I shall have the pleasure of making you spend your money in riots together and not all alone. Do you know, I am still in my heart a little shaken by my so *very* near approach to death: it was so near and took so long—four days, or nights rather (they are so much worse) on the very edge: I think I had got over the worst of it, but I know that I was sorry to leave, and regretted not the big things, not leaving you for instance for that I felt was not a real parting, but little things like fire-lit rooms, or flowers in the garden, all the ordinary pleasantness of life: so much that I felt it was a disaster to be losing all that of my own will, so to say. That is why I cannot help feeling sad over [T.E.] Lawrence's death (though merciful he did not recover with brain impaired)—but he had so much still in him to get out of life: he would have been less of a legend if he had reached old age, but so rich a past might have developed into a happy harvest after all.

I am still weak in the brain and tired if I do anything at all, and unable to let things slip over me quietly enough. Such as the fact that I have no word yet of my luggage (and all the photos) in Aden, and Mama has lost the few negatives I sent home.

The garden here is lovely, all roses and iris—almost blatant after the austere tropics! I am allowed to walk about a little now on the level ground and hope to get on without any more set-backs.

14 June, 1935.

The war too is hanging like a black cloud. Boots and clothes are being given out to the local people to make for the army. If there are fiends in Hell how they must laugh. I am just reading Benson's life of Queen Victoria and can't help feeling that if we had old Lord Palmerston now he would probably close the canal and have done with it: after all why should one sit still and watch a big man knock a little one down and never move a finger?

CASTEL TESINO, 22 *June*, 1935.

This is a quiet remote little gentle valley, a wide green basin filled with hay and small potato patches over which women with stout legs grown enormously muscular by climbing up and down, stoop and hoe all day long while their men try to make money in Johannesburg or Portuguese Africa. It was the last township of Austria and taken without a fight by the Italians in the first days of the war, but there was fighting later and Col Bricon just out of sight north of us was always being mentioned in despatches. Now it is a motor highway for summer tourists, but this is still the off season; the cinema has not started; the village is full only of old men and boys and women in black skirts with red or yellow borders according as they are married or not—and yesterday we had a procession and finery, and they made an altar outside the hotel and the Host was elevated to the bugles of the Fire Brigade who all flanked it in uniform. I am able to walk along the level road *two miles*: I hope this long weariness is drawing to an end. But I do not yet feel up to anything in the least intellectual and unable to do more than just keep the head of my correspondence above water.

Yes, it would be lovely some day to retire together and look on at the world as it goes by and have few possessions (but beautiful) and live in the cottage and come to Asolo when we want the Continental air. Only do have one really *big* room in the cottage: I think what is wrong with cottages generally is that *all* the rooms are small, whereas what one wants is few but spacious: I used to notice that in Baghdad where my one beautiful room with five windows made me feel palatial, though it was all I had.

As we walked along the road here we came to an unfinished house all by itself in the valley. A man was working at it, and he told us that he is building it for himself in his spare time: he began in 1932 and it will take another three years. It must be rather fun, and the man seemed so quietly and solitarily happy. These hard-working

[112]

easily contented people seem very wasted in the sensational deliriums of the present. I don't think I had better write more of this.

LE PARADOU, 22 July, 1935.

I am happy to be down here—the light air and sun, the scent of everything growing on the slopes which have been soaked in sunlight ever since the ice age left them—and the Besses, so full of a good sort of life—it is all a restful harmony pouring peacefully into one's soul. I am much better and begin work on the strength of it: but what a hard labour it is—every word seeming to have to be squeezed out of my brain like grape juice out of a wine press, by a painful crushing process. M. Besse told me he once came on a man sitting over the débris of his car which had just been smashed to smithereens by a lorry: a countryman coming up, contemplated the ruins and said: "Hé, les morceaux sont encore bons." That is just what I am beginning to feel again about myself, body and soul.

13 August, 1935.

I have done five chapters of my book, and that takes it out of me. I seem to have a substratum of fatigue, and it is like walking on hard snow, if one presses ever so little more than usual one goes through into it. You must know this far better than I. But I am really better, and lead quite a normal life now, and even row the canoe! It is the head which is still soft.

I am so delighted to have *The Seven Pillars*. I read the poem again, which I liked, and am keeping the rest for a little as all the household here are enjoying the book. I think the Arab portraits are among the finest things I have ever seen—but as for the British—do you think they were chosen purposely to look feeble-minded? Only Lord Allenby and my friend Hubert Young come out tolerably—and the latter was done by his wife.

25 August, 1935.

I am glad to hear good news of your head. That is really the important news. One's head and heart must be more or less intact to let one get on satisfactorily with the business of living, and you and I are rather deficient just now in those two points between us.

I am going back to Asolo next Saturday. I don't want to be

caught there by any sort of a war, and so you *may* get an S.O.S. and me arriving after any time. I will write from there at all events and tell you how things are. I imagine an Italian must feel like an ancient Roman when Caligula or Nero was ruling—a helpless feeling when one madman has all the power. But what a *flock* to let it come to this! We dined with some delightful Alsatians yesterday and they told us they know Mussolini. What a sad difference he shows now and years ago: from a really great personality to an evident lunatic. I only hope we will call Italy's bluff and stamp on it. I feel that it would bring the whole thing down like Alice's dream with the pack of cards.

I have got to Chapter IX, but now feel tired and *shock*: it is horrid to have no sort of elasticity to draw on and writing is a gruelling business. I have just done a review of a charming book on the Libyan desert by a man called Bagnold who first proved that one can motor up sand dunes. Did you know that the Libyan desert is bigger than the whole of India? He gives very vivid pictures of its loveliness, and the old slave route from Kordofan to Cairo, marked by *millions* of camel skeletons. Nothing ever disappears there, and you find palæolithic camps with the shells of their ostrich omelette still beside them, together with last year's car tracks or the things left over in the Dervish war.

We had a *terrific* storm last night: pink and yellow thunder bolts falling all round us.

9 September, 1935.

Here one just sits horrified, watching a nation gone mad—all the young that is, who don't remember what we do. The peasants and all the nice and humble people just groan and bear it—so poor and prices rising. I hope we are not going to be cowards and will lead as we ought to do. What is the good of all our power and wealth if we can't face the responsibility in a crisis when every principle is at stake? I am not so much of a pacifist that I would not fight for Peace! Anyway I had better not write too much about it all.

I am reading *The Seven Pillars*. The chapter about the Arab character is very true and finely put.

ASOLO, 20 September, 1935.

Things look bad here. How it will all end goodness knows. I hope we will not falter.

[114]

26 September, 1935.

It is surprising how charming everyone is to us—even strangers going out of their way to be nice. One can't help feeling that lots of them look on us as their saviours from themselves!

I do hope we are going to be stiff at Geneva: all our future hanging on it as I see it—not to mention saving the wretched Italians from themselves.

CAMPDEN HILL, 15 October, 1935.

Darling B,

It was nice to get letters at midnight yesterday; that is when we arrived, as we drove slowly through a white fog and moonlight from Dover—I don't think I can tell you all about the journey (as I found about 20 letters waiting here!). It was all very pleasant and Anne such a dear, always ready for anything, never fussy, a perfect gem to travel with. S. is a tiresome little pedant, but no doubt will mature, youth being an acute and not a chronic disease, and it was nice to see him enjoying it all, though I did get tired of his being so intelligent. It is dreadful to feel that one must be intelligent on a motor tour. We saw lovely things. The Grande Place at Brussels, the castle of Ghent, and the buildings at Bruges were well worth the journey—and now I feel that I have seen sights enough for six months at least.

PENBEDW, FLINTSHIRE, 6 November, 1935.

My dear Jock [Murray],

Do you think the 4th line of the poem would be improved by saying "To watch the daylight and the town". I like watching the town myself, but it may not be a poetical thing to do.

WIMBLEDON, 21 December, 1935.

Dearest B,

This should reach you for Christmas and bring my love. I am going to try to send a book which you and Herbert may like, but have no idea if it will get through as it is not by either Shakespeare or G.B.S.

I am terribly worried at your not yet having gone to Treviso [to sell out Italian investments]. Don't make Mr. Smith's [Mussolini's] mistake of thinking that advice, when quietly given, is not urgent. Please go at once.

[115]

Venetia has put her foot down. The doctor spoke seriously to her and told her that I *must* have three months absolute rest and nursing, so I have cancelled everything and go to Penbedw from Dorsetshire after the New Year. I have had to cancel the B.B.C. and the Scotch lectures and all my week-end visits.

The country here has risen like one man and shown that a principle is still something which counts. It has all been very exciting and everyone a little more comforted after the first horror and dismay— I had no idea the feeling was so strong.

It is bitterly cold: I can only get warm in bed or bath! I hope Sidmouth will be milder—Jock has reserved a seat for me and is lunching here to-morrow. He sent me a huge bunch of flowers after the lecture with the word Magnificent printed in a neat hand.

PENBEDW, FLINTSHIRE, 7 January, 1936.

My dear Jock,

If there is one thing I really dislike it is this horrid American fashion of dropping away the Parts of Speech. Please may I have "*A* South Arabian Journey" and not just "South Arabian Journey"? Apart from my own prejudices, it is a fact that other people have travelled in South Arabia too, and if you take away the *A* you make it sound as if I consider mine the one and only Journey, which will not do. I hope this may be accepted?

I am sending you ever so many chapters—eight in all, so that should make a good beginning: but have you got a *very* intelligent printer, because the corrections seem rather intricate? And do you think he can deal with such things as dots under the h's and s's where I have put them, and lines over long vowels, like jōl? I hope he will be very careful with the corrections, because it means fearful agonies of mind to settle them all over again.

10 January, 1936.

When would you like to have the next instalment? I will not send till you are ready for it, as I get ideas to add now and then. I hope I have improved it a lot. I spend *hours* over it.

Five trees have been blown down during the night—such a tragedy. Beeches are so silly, they let their roots lie carelessly at the top of the ground: you would think they would have learnt to do better after living so long in this climate.

[116]

28 February, 1936.

A problem has arisen as to the height of the Kor Saiban, which I see I have put as 8,700 feet in the proofs. The Geographic proof has just come and makes it 3,400 feet—which is absurd. But would you just glance at Von Wissmann's map and tell me what he says in metres? I know there is a discrepancy between him and the English map which says 8,700, but if it is not too big I will take his rendering as being more recent: I know however from my own aneroid heights which you kindly translated that 8,700 is not far out—how almost impossible it is to be fairly accurate in this world! As for the Zoo—Mr. Ingrams had a dead ibex—shot at his feet so to say—so that settles Mr. Pocock!

The answer to an enquiry I made as to the length of Wadi Hadhramaut was not so satisfactory: it was sent by M. Besse's Arab interpreter: "after careful enquiry" he made it to be the "length a donkey can cover, going fast, in twelve hours . . . about 120 miles." A case for the S.P.C.A. !

19 March, 1936.

How *horrid* of me! I feel conscience-stricken; and the thought of a cold bath at this time of year—It wasn't really, was it? Just a little cool refreshing sprinkle?!! Anyway *please* forgive me!

As to the Preface, I am so glad it can be done without. I have nothing to say except that the list of thanks has to be much longer on the left-hand page to cover the whole story. I have written it out and also a little footnote about the plants which can be shoved in wherever you like.

I am consuming so much iron that I'm sure it simply can't help entering my soul wherever that may be, and the headache has nearly gone—but I still do nothing. Such a *lovely* feeling to wake up and feel there is nothing in the world that *has* to be done this day.

Yes, do come and protest as much as you like.

Yours remorsefully!

P.S.   *So* nice to see a chink in the armour now and then!

23 April, 1936.

The Abyssinian business is too sad for words—and I feel sure that if Italy does succeed we shall be fighting her on our own account within the next few years.

[117]

Venetia has filled in my life history for you: and you can add any fancy touches your imagination suggests—and eyes whatever colour you like!

COLNE ST. DENIS, COTSWOLDS, *April*, 1936.

Dearest Venetia,

This is a village so beautiful you would think you were in a dream —all grey stone, houses just simply *grown* up out of the needs of their dwellers, and all enclosed in a small remote valley in whose long grass a stream meanders. An absolute remoteness and peace. It seemed a pity to have to listen here to Baldwin's speech—filling one with shame. How can it be that words as cowardly come from an English minister? I can't tell you what I felt like listening—but you were no doubt listening too. Peace at any price: what a thing to live for. And what a misery that, because of their insane policy on defence, we have no other policy to support. Why doesn't some Labour man see that a Labour policy based on defence would carry the whole country? Why can't we stand up for what we believe like the Soviet, and make our ideas *live*. Well, one can't do anything much about it except to resolve *never* in one's own case to compromise on these fundamental things—and perhaps we may yet live to see a more virile generation come along.

PENBEDW, FLINTSHIRE, 1 *May*, 1936.

My dear Jock,

I have been for two motor drives, so you see I am getting on: and I am reading a book called 'Tadpoles and God' which pleases me by talking of Mr. Wells who "in his wordy rush misses all but the obvious and trivial".

We concocted a letter to Venetia's M.P. asking to be reassured about Abyssinia and threatening to vote Labour, and got a most unsatisfactory reply: it appeared that they will do *anything* to keep out of war for the next two years. By that time our name in Asia and Africa may well be mud. I am beginning to hate pacifism if it means seeing all one's ideas of decency trampled on, all round one. It seems to me that we might start a corps of volunteers something on the line of the Boy Scouts: every nation to have its own independently but with the obligation to join and fight when a decision of the League calls them up. I am sure they would find plenty of volunteers.

Dearest Venetia,

V. came to see me. You would have been amused. First she said that if she had known I was looking so well she would not have bothered to come. Then she said that my legs were very fat but if I wore long skirts it would not matter so much. Then she said that Admiral Goodenough had talked to her at the R.A. private view about nothing except my book and added that "it is a pity to over-praise it so, as it is apt to put people off". By this time it was time for her to go and I went down and saw her gratefully into a bus!

I have just written a long letter to Miss T. to justify the making of poison gas in our case. I suggest that the same principle be applied as to alcohol and sex: one need not be a total abstainer or a monk, so long as one makes fit use of the gifts of nature (in this case a use of modern weapons *only* in a just and peaceful cause). Whether my argument will appeal to an elderly maiden lady who neither drinks nor makes love I don't know.

17 May, 1936.

I went and sat in the Park yesterday. An old gentleman walked by complaining to an elderly woman about the birds: "The starlings build in the chimneys and the sparrows sit on the spouts, and one gets no rest anywhere," he said. Poor old man! I took my embroidery and sat there under a tree and had occasion to try my Arab tactics— for a party of hooligans came up and surrounded me—"Soothing, that knitting there" one of them said: I looked up quite slowly and straight in his eyes and smiled, and then he smiled back rather apologetic and quite nice and they all went quietly away—which shows that a soft answer is useful anywhere.

29 May, 1936.

My head is swelling so (in spite of *Morning Post*) that yesterday I went and bought two hats. I feel very dubious: a little black one, like a rather gay widow which is what I always feel I should like to be, is all right: but Henry and the letter inveigled me into a white Breton with a blue band which I feel resembles a halo too much to suit my style.

Henry looked in and talked of Roman Deep and I talked about it to Mr. V. who was painfully unsympathetic, but I got him to promise to look up the Secretary, and it will be up to him to turn him into a believer. Women when they talk of gold mines are never believed: it is one of those subconscious masculine reactions which are simply unconquerable.

The Daily Telegraph interview with Mussolini makes me sick. What *fools* they are. Every word M. said was just vague nonsense: *anyone* who knows Italians can see how he just thinks us fools to be diddled till Sanctions are got rid of and then he has a clear hand—and one can read it in every line: and the *D.T.* distorts it into all sorts of peaceful promises. One is tempted to despair.

All sorts of people come to see me—three or four every day so that matron begins to look serious. Dr. A. came . . . but I was invisible. I know now what is the matter with him. "Commonplaces patter from his mind"—just that!

BOSBURY, 14 June, 1936.

Dearest B,

I had a charming letter from Sir John Murray, saying how nice it is to publish a "great book". I wonder if it is great: I have my doubts myself, and will be dead before the matter can be ascertained.

CORSHAM COURT, 2 July, 1936.

Dearest Venetia,

I dined last night with some nice diplomatic people—Victor Mallets—and felt *so* stupid, gauche, untidy, and dowdy: and she was so *chic* with hair all rolled back in golden waves and sylph-like figure and roses in her bodice. A most fascinating creature, with a sort of cosmopolitan brilliance about her. I am sorry to leave my Chinese room and these kind people, but glad to be seeing MacDonald on Saturday, as the head is being stupid. I really think it is just worry, and hope now to have come to the end of that and to put it out of my system. Most of the bitterness of things is gone if one can only eliminate *vanity* from one's system: it is not easy to do so, but I think it is the secret of contentment. That, and the knowledge that nothing, nothing in this world can betray one except oneself: one always has the power to be master of one's own soul.

24 July, 1936.

Darling B,

I am enclosing a cheque for £20. You can tear it up if you *really* don't want to use it; otherwise send a telegram to Dorothy and come back with Jock—I think you would enjoy a little time on the moor and it would be lovely for me and I really *can* afford it: I have just told Chris to invest £200, so I feel I have done my duty by economy for this year—and I have bought *no* new clothes at all and the book continues to sell. I shall not be able to reach Asolo till Christmas and then not for very long—so that it does seem a chance.

I have had an interesting time these last days, but much too strenuous—an evening party at the Huxleys, listening to Kathleen Long, a beautiful pianist—Mozart and Bach, and Schumann sounding rather shallow in between. I went to the W's party the same afternoon where everyone had a title but was otherwise rather dull, and it was curious to notice the different atmosphere—one just social and the other really enjoying itself—Ruth Draper was at the Huxleys, and Jelli d'Aranyi (if that is right) and a most charming old couple, Lady Ottoline and Mr. Philip Morrell looking just as if they had stepped out of Walpole's letters. Mr. Morrell and I fell in love with each other at sight and talked about music, poetry, and the 18th century, and he told me he hated books with a lot of nature descriptions in them. I said I did too, but that it is worse to have to write them. No one there had read my book: I can't tell you how nice it felt to be happy and friendly and liked without the assistance of a label. I *know* now that I don't enjoy the limelight: it is not of course that one is not pleased to have one's efforts made more of than they deserve, but it is oppressive to be *ticketed*: it is bad enough to feel like a mechanism expected to work in a certain way, and worse when you know that it simply *don't* work that way at all! Ruth Draper has a very intelligent face which looks as if it had suffered by being sensitive: I should think she must be a good and true friend to those she likes. She gave me a lift in her car and, as I told her I had never been able to see her as the theatre was always full, said she would see that I got in if ever I wrote to her.

Yesterday I went to Gertrude Caton Thompson to lunch and there met Lady Rhondda, a powerful person with a really beautiful face, with kind and amused mouth and strong broad forehead and square hands—all square and small and strong she is. She runs *Time and Tide* and tries to raise the standard of literature: I meant to ask her how much it costs to do so, as I am sure it cannot be a paying proposition, but we talked of so many different things that I forgot. She lives with a Miss Bosanquet, who is quite different, fastidious and amusing and they go very well together, and I have promised to see them in the autumn and help raise the standard of literature too in the paper. Gertrude is toying with the idea of digging in the Hadhramaut with me: she would be an excellent person and knows as much as anyone about prehistoric flints. She has looked through all my Meshed stones and found two insignificant little obsidian things that are probably the teeth of a saw, and about 4,000 or 5,000 years old—and interesting enough to be published in the autumn. I wish now I had collected more.

Yesterday I talked a little Persian with the A.D.C. of the Maharaja of Mysore at the Goschens: he comes from Kermanshah and it is rather remarkable that the Maharaja, one of the holiest of the Hindus, has only Moslem or Christian advisers. He was a slim clever immaculately shirt-fronted little man and knew the Goschens well as he had always been taken on their camping tours, but he never lost the sort of reserve which they put on with Europeans—no glimmer of the friendly easiness I am accustomed to: one has really a great pull if one travels like the poor! I didn't talk much to the A.D.C. as Phyllis' husband, Frank Balfour, was there and we had such a lot to say about Baghdad that when I left they induced me to finish the evening at their own house in St. Leonard's Terrace. He was political officer in Nejf all through the worst time, a friend of Hubert Young and Lionel Smith. He had to lay siege to Nejf when they murdered one of his colleagues, and refused to have any artillery but spent 45 days in a proper medieval siege with a truce every morning to get out the pilgrims: and at the end of the 45 days the town surrendered with no bloodshed at all. He told me about Leachman, the most reckless man I imagine the war produced, who introduced himself by bouncing into the office at Nejf and saying "Are you in a bloody funk or aren't you?" Mr. Balfour, looking so nice and tidy, as if he had never been outside a London drawing-room, with a monocle in one eye, explained to me: "Of course I was in a funk" (he was quite alone in Nejf with none but his native police in very small numbers to rely on)—"but I told Leachman that if he had not sent his bloody robbers to take rice from my people when they hadn't enough for themselves, I shouldn't have any reason to be in a bloody funk." He managed to keep the town quiet, but it must have been an almost superhuman task.

Mr. Guest is ever so much better. We are doing great propaganda for the Arabs, but I don't know if it will be very effective—though people seem to begin to realize that it is not just a casual disorder which can be put down.

THORNWORTHY, DEVON, 15 August, 1936.

Dearest Venetia,

I am reading some Yemeni legends and tales. One nice one about two rival doctors, a good and a bad one: the King said he would take as his family physician the one who succeeded in poisoning the other. The good doctor every day found a new poison in his food and took a new antidote: he did nothing to his rival, but always, when he saw him at court, said: "To-morrow I will poison you." The wretched man, unable to detect any poison in his food, was reduced to milk which he watched as it was taken from the cow. One day his rival saw him with the cup of milk, half finished, in his hand: "Ah, now you are poisoned," he said: and the wicked doctor fell down, dead with fright, while the good one became Court Physician.

LONDON, 5 October, 1936.

I have been studying the little pamphlet [on the Arabs] in the train and feel that, though you have improved the language, the whole thing is so ineffective that it is not worth bothering about. I gave Miss N. £1 which is a lot for me—and that is all I have done about it beyond asking Mr. R. at the F.O. if he thought it any use—and he seemed to think not. I am sick of these women! I think the Parliamentary Committee is the useful one—because it is little good to bother about *general* public opinion: there is too little time and the Jews are too strong. On the other hand a lot could be done for more instructed opinion: my advice was to get *personally* at M.P.s, editors and such, and I am talking to anyone who comes my way—but the committee do not see it in this light! How it will go eventually is very doubtful. There are too few people in the Cabinet who know the East and its conditions. On the other hand, it is obvious to anyone that 600 miles of pipe line in an open and hostile desert with things as they are in the East Mediterranean is too uncomfortable to be thought of —and I hope that this, if not ordinary decency, may have some effect. On the lowest grounds—we will not lose the Jews who have only us to turn to just now, even if we limit them in Palestine— while there are plenty of people ready to lure the Moslems away. I

[123]

am told that Italian intrigue is at the bottom of a great deal of the Palestine trouble. The Spanish business is pretty bad too.

I had a lovely week-end quietly with the Goodenoughs—a lovely autumn day and sun on the Michaelmas daisies—and harvest festival in church and a dreary sermon on the necessity of "investing" in good works—revolting.

27 October, 1936.

Darling B,

We had a great party at Mr. Murray's—all sorts of friends and new people. I met Robert Byron—he is author of that nice remark that Persia (or any other country for that matter) is busy looking "to see when the British Empire, disguised as a worm, is going to turn".

After the Murray party Frank Balfour took me out. He had a table at the Savoy because he feared the London Casino might be too low—but I said the lower the better, so we cancelled the Savoy and sat and dined at the Casino, all little tables in semi-circles round the stage: it was a most amusing subject as one entered, the people's backs, and waiters moving about, and the lit stage beyond—a sort of Degas picture. The least improper ladies on the stage were those who had nothing on and I suggested now and then to Frank that he might drop his monocle.

DUKE'S HOTEL, S.W.I, 23 December, 1936.

A *dreadful* contretemps. I was just going down here to telegraph my arrival on the 26th when Anne's doctor rang up. They have *found* the microbe, they say—right at the back of my nose—streptococci—and the choice was to go away and trust to the sun in Egypt or to stay here for *weeks* and make a vaccine: and I have chosen the latter as I *must* be quite fit next autumn. All this *year* wasted, two years nearly and now to hear only when my sleeper is actually taken! and I am so heartbroken to think of your and Herbert's disappointment too. I will write details when I see the doctor to-morrow—this just in haste to break the news—I don't even know where I shall go or anything.

I came away from Minnie to-day not to fuss her with luggage, departure, etc., and also because I have a bad cold. . . .

The projects for the Hadhramaut dig go well. Gertrude hopes for £400 from Museums but £1,000 still to find! And for my part I think the government offices will be kind.

[124]

LONDON

Christmas Day.

How dreary this is! All the time I am thinking of you. Poor little Moysii is sitting wrapped in waterproof outside my window, and I have asked Lady I. if she can face taking her and the Records—the rest will come later with me. I *hope* to get to you by the 20th, but can't be sure till the vaccine is tried: the microbes are busy being *grown* at present. Dear Jock came as usual to the rescue and took me and Hector Bolitho (also a waif) to eat delicious lobster at Prunier's— and last night just as I got into bed, a breathless little page boy came running—so excited that he would have burst in without a knock if the door hadn't been locked: and he bore a stocking almost larger than himself, with crackers bursting like a cornucopia from it and all sorts of excitements inside. It was a really lovely thought and cheered me up marvellously, and my right and left hands pulled a cracker between them to celebrate the occasion.

It does seem rather sad that my only clothes bought for this Season are a white dress, a big straw hat and a bathing costume! However I shall just be shabby till I leave.

WIMBLEDON, 30 December, 1936.

My dear Lionel,

I have just been reading a rather nice version of Genesis in Arabic. It says that Gabriel was sent to the Earth to bring a bit of clay for the making of Adam: but the Earth refused to give any: and then Michael was sent, with the same result: then Allah sent the angel of death who snatched the clay without asking, and brought it back in three different colours from which the human races are derived.

DUKE'S HOTEL, S.W.1, 14 January, 1937.

Darling B,

All being well I reach Padova on Monday and will send a wire with the time. I hope the Simplon Express won't collapse under my excess luggage.

Now I must tell you what has happened to me! Some weeks ago I told Charles Ker that Miss C. Thompson was looking round for grants to finance our expedition next autumn. He said: "Why don't you write to Lord Wakefield and I will add a word to say you are not bogus." So I wrote and on Tuesday was asked to go to his

[125]

office in Cheapside. I got there punctually (for which he compli-
mented me!) and climbed up through rooms full of typewriters to a
genial little old white-haired man behind a big desk who asked me
what it was all about. He wasn't the least interested in archaeology,
but looked very shrewdly at me; then he said that I had found a
wonderful advocate in Mr. Ker, that he thought I could be trusted
to make good use of his money, and handed me a cheque for £1,500
which I had suggested as the total cost of the expedition. I came
away in a sort of dream after being taken round to see all the photographs of Lord Wakefield with various Kings of England, Boy
Scouts, Mussolini, and d'Annunzio, "a picture they want me to buy",
etc. I said it seemed rather hard that he gave the money and we got
all the fun. He was such a dear, and took me out to the lift, and did
it all so charmingly and *nicely*, and I walked back through Cheapside
in an intoxicated sort of condition thinking that I had just been spending the morning wondering whether I should buy cotton or leather
gloves at Evans' Sale, and now had all this wealth at my disposal.
Of course it has a fearful responsibility and means keeping accounts.
I think it will be enough to allow us to add a member to the expedition
—a geologist who would be very useful. But that is not my affair,
and Gertrude will settle all the details.

Train near MILAN, 18 January, 1937.

My dear Jock,

I meant to send a card from Paris, but we only stopped in far off
places among sheds and when we did just look in at the Gare de
Lyon, I was *so* busy doing these proofs that I never noticed: this is
quite *true*!

I can't tell you how depressed I should have been if you had not
been so nice and found such supporting things to supply me with on
the way to the station—and it is nice to think that you are coming
out any time (quite soon!) so that it is not quite like tearing oneself
away like Byron from his native land. I have never done this
in the Orient Express, and it is really incredibly easy and would
have been as comfortable as any bed anywhere if I had not had an
awful Russian woman and a singer at that who became temperamental
at 2.30 and rang for the conductor to say she was too hot—"Qu'y
puis-je faire, Madame?" They had a grand scene and I got no sleep
till she left at Sière and the man as he was doing my bed said this

[126]

morning: "On comprend qu'une dame comme celle-là ne voyage pas avec son mari." I saw Monte Rosa just for a minute in full glory in mist and snow.

ASOLO, 6 February, 1937.

It was fun to hear your voice last night: I could not get over the extraordinariness of it—it does seem like magic and I am not quite sure that it is not black magic: one heard all the voices of all the telephone exchanges between us answering each other till at last one said "London wants you". I mustn't go on into these abstractions, but thank you first of all for all this enormous lot of trouble you have been at: I had no idea I was letting you in for such a colossal job. Imperial Airways are very tiresome, as one can't be expected to fly away at four days' notice into Asia—but I suppose they naturally do prefer people who like to go to Australia. Do you think they will be more accommodating when I go to Rhodesia in the autumn?

It is a pity one can't travel as easily as one's voice. You might come to dinner and that would be very nice. Perhaps in time one will just be able to send one's Voice out to dinner, and stay at home oneself. How awful! I think I should enjoy being disembodied myself, but should hate it in my friends.

12 *February,* 1937.

I have been waiting to write in the hope of receiving your letter and ticket, but I believe my things are being opened and they come with great delay. I don't mind the Italian censor reading all my letters, but I wish he would send them on a little less slowly.

The Baghdad Sketches agreement has just come and I have been studying it and see with sorrow that you are making it *less* than *The Southern Gates,* and as I only had a deficit of £2 on the edition published in Baghdad I don't think I can *bear* this. You will have to give me the same royalty as the Southern Gates and you needn't give me *any* advance royalties as that always makes me feel as if I were getting into debt. I hope this isn't going to ruin you—and if it is I will have to put up with what you suggest: but I will always remind you that the nice man I met at dinner and whose name I can't remember offered me more, and I'm sure this will give you pain. However if you think it is really all that can be done, I will bear it, my dear Jock. I only tell you so that there may be no hidden wound rankling in my heart (not that that is the place where my accounts are kept!)

[127]

ALEXANDRIA, 25 *February*, 1937.

Dearest B,

Too choppy for writing. We had a lovely day in Athens, sitting about on the Acropolis all afternoon—then another good morning in Rhodes, just as beautiful as ever—but beginning to be too smart. I have a nice Englishwoman to talk to, who knows less geography than anyone I have ever met and was very interested to hear that the Mediterranean and Adriatic are all one. Our acquaintance began when she told me she had come from Venice to Brindisi by way of the Corinth canal.

BAGHDAD, 26 *February*, 1937.

It seems very strange and yet oddly familiar to be here. The old bridge of boats is to be pulled down and a stone one built, and I am glad to have seen it again, and waited 40 minutes while it opened to let a steamer through, and watched the crowd, *incredibly* dingy and just the same as ever. The flight from Cairo was very successful and I enjoyed it in spite of the incipient qualms I always feel in a closed plane. The sight of the desert below is an impressive thing, and as we flew 6,000 feet high we saw the whole of it as it were—first Egypt with friendly sands, soft as snow cornices with their sharp but gentle ridges curving away, the paths trodden over the dunes lying like seaweed patterns on the sea bottom. We travelled above little separate white loose clouds that drifted along just like sheep, showing the yellow world speckled with shade below. "Like flocks to feed in air"—I thought of Shelley's line. Then the canal looking unnecessarily devious, but I suppose it isn't—then the flat coasts of Sinai, its inner mountains hidden in a frothing foam of cloud—then sudden bits of green, very pale and the yellow sand coming through, just like a bit of very ancient green brocade showing the coarser warp (or is it woof?). Then the fields of Lud, brown soft and ribbed and variegated like old corduroy velvet, and all the world in "Novecento" rectangular patterns, so that one infers that modern art is just the world seen from above (the Padre Eterno no doubt being far enough off to get a better blended effect). Lud is very tidy: little orange trees in rows, probably Jewish, and every little square of cultivation with a tiny grey square of building inside it, like a cell and its protoplasm. Then up again, only three of us now left as two rich Jews swanking seven heavy leather suitcases had got out, and also the bishop of

Jerusalem's sister. We went on to Haifa over the stones and russet hollows of Carmel: saw Haifa's new roads planned white on the green plain, and 24 petrol tanks, and turned away over the hills of Moab across the Jordan rift all green now, flowing with water in a pale and treeless solitude and Galilee half lost in cloud like a dream to the north.

Moab is a wild and lonely country, heaved up in round and stony ridges, red with small poor nomad scratchings of its barren soils, and every ridge embraced in what look like white paths, but are only dry and wasteful torrent ways: the seamings of what looks like so many human paths and no houses in sight make it more lonely than anything. But here and there are little lichen-coloured olive trees, and villages of square insect-like buildings, and black tents on the shallower valley dips: and then we came into the open roll of the North Arabian desert, all brown, seamed also with innumerable paths—some made by camel feet, some by trickle of waters—and all over that immensity little black circles thickly strewn: at first I thought them painted outlines of rock to mark the pipe line, which the aeroplanes follow—a thin straight smear only visible by its straightness: but finally I saw that these were all little enclosures, to keep the cattle I suppose, or shelter from the wind—something infinitely pathetic to see those tiny human markings alone in that immensity and to realize how little here, how much elsewhere in a landscape is made by the hand of man: there was *nothing* alive for hours on that land. Far on our left, very small, a zebra stripe of snow on Lebanon. Across that immense waste the pipe line runs, quite straight and alone in and out of the shallow hollows curled by the wind. In the middle there is a little square garden and a pumping station. The desert tilted a little eastward: shallow outlines of hollows ran that way, waved with ridges where thin green showed on the damper side: and there were the little black tents, living in nothingness; an animal life almost, so that one wonders at the same species producing an aeroplane. We looked down on Rutbah; saw shadows thrown by invisible camels and men: came over the completely lifeless lost waste—not even brown, mere reddish non-entity—and finally saw green again mixing faintly like shoal-water, and crossed the Euphrates: put the clock on over a peculiarly barren point where Iraq begins—saw Kadhimain domes shining in palm groves, and swung down over the Tigris into the new landing enclosure which was only just in use when I left: that was seven hours from leaving Cairo. We crossed Imperial Airways

K

crawling below, keeping near as it could to the earth to avoid the wind that was helping us. We had Egyptian officials, but English pilots—such a good type and, my goodness, *how* different from the other young men about. I don't think we need worry about our future!

Whiffey met me at the boat in Alexandria, just as engaging as ever and full of theories and plans and asked could I get him a stone from Mecca for his mosque. He told me lots of things which will not be repeated. He brought the parcel and took me to lunch on caviar sand-wiches and saw me to my train—a lovely but fatiguing hurly-burly. Stations all decorated with arches and cotton curtains and flags for the King who was going to Europe: dozens of triumphal arches. Polite effendi very pleased when I admired them and helped me with my luggage.

Must stop this, I am *so* tired. It felt rather melancholy all alone here, with no friendly greeting only a C.I.D. message to ask *why* I came: now, however, a little waiter has rushed up full of smiles, shaken hands, and said: "Did I remember he had picked me up when I fell off a horse" and the hotel man has remembered me and come up to ask about Captain and Mrs. Bamfield's twins—so all is fine and friendly.

KUWAIT, 3 March, 1937.

This is a lovely place to be in: the weather delicious, hot at mid-day, but too cold to sit in the shade without a *very* warm coat—I got here with a little difficulty: slept in the train from Baghdad and woke up just in time for Basra. It used to take 24 hours last time: then people said: "Can't it be hurried up?" and with a stroke of the pen 12 hours were knocked off the time-table, and no visible difference in the comfort of the line.

Basra was rather uninspiring, but I asked for the post office: an inspector happened to be at the station and offered to come along, and hoisted himself and small son into a taxi with me: at the P.O. I found a polite effendi, young and fat with no chin and a rosebud mouth who had just had a telegram about me from Bill Bailey in Baghdad. I left them to deal with the motor company for Kuwait and went to try and get my hair curled. Mansur was the man, they told me. He was an old shambling Turk, very tall, with one black lock, oily and smooth across his bald head and a trembling hand with which he gingerly ran hot irons through my hair. I had to wait a long time, since he had not yet come, and another Englishwoman was waiting too, and a native lady then came in. The Englishwoman never made a move, but I bowed and handed the newcomer one of the illustrated papers, regretting as usual our insular rudeness.

When I got back to the post, the effendi told me that a car had been sent for and would get back to Zobair at 6 and leave again at 6.30: this seemed very dubious, as it is a 4 hours' run, and Zobair is a comfortless little walled town half an hour from Basra. I sent Gerald a telegram to say "possibly to-night, probably to-morrow" and was taken to rest at an awful hotel called the Alhambra: the effendi came later and showed me the new airport (Basra will soon be the greatest airport between Europe and the Far East)—gave me tea, and altogether depressed me so much by his kindness and quite hopeless inner self that I was delighted to let him see me along a dark deserty road to Zobair at 6.30. We passed an old ruin where the battle between Ali and Ayesha is said to have taken place (Mesjid Ali al-Jemal) and we got into the dark streets of Zobair, heard of course that the car would not leave till to-morrow, and I was settled in with the postmaster of Zobair's family for the night and said good-bye to the effendi with relief.

The ladies of the family were all dressed in knitted cardigans, but otherwise un-European, and they had a Persian guest who was also on her way back to Kuwait and had just had eight days' pilgrimage at all the holy cities. She told us that at Kerbela a woman had been picking the pilgrims' pockets when the hand of Abbas stuck out from his tomb and struck her dead. There were ten ladies altogether, all very cheerful. My hostess was an ugly young thing with untidy elf locks; but she dressed herself up like a man with a long brown gown, a blue serge European coat, a keffiah and 'ighal on her head, and looked the most engaging young boy with a very glad eye indeed, and came along pretending to make love in a quite unmistakable way to one of the visitors from Amarah. They asked me which of the ladies I should like to have as a bedfellow, a trying question. Two of them shared the same husband, and they told me they were very good friends and that "it all depends if it is a nice man and treats them fairly, night and night about".

I was very tired, and having eaten eggs, bread, celery leaves and very scented sweet stuff made of fat, flour and sugar, I at last went to bed: it was a big four-poster affair with quilts and velvet covers but a very trying odour; the Persian pilgrim lay on a mattress on the floor, and there was one other guest; the lamp was left to burn itself out. The room was a mixture—photographs in frames, glass pink vases, cushions made of little triangles of gold chocolate papers all put together by a sewing machine.

Next morning I just had time to wander through the little arcaded market and then found the company's car ready to start. The "company" was an old old man in a yellow keffiah: I paid 5 rupees for my seat: the Persian lady beside me and three men behind: and the doors and mud-guards all buried in bundles. We raced along, the desert faintly green and with many tents, and sheep and donkeys near them: we had an early lunch off a saucepan filled with habisa, a mixture of dates, bread and fat which they quite naturally asked me to share, and so I did: and finally drove up to Gerald's gorgeous new palace and had to be lifted over the door and out by his rather surprised *cawasses*. He was very pleasant and gave no outward sign of pain at this method of arriving, though he mentioned it later. It seems that it isn't proper for me to stay with him, but I rather hope he may get me a room out, and meanwhile I am with the Dicksons while he has gone for four days to Bahrain. I lunched with him, and heard a lot of interesting news; and this morning saw him off in Imperial Airways, a huge gigantic monster which stops twice a week outside the old medieval wall.

The Dicksons know more than anyone about the desert. They know all the stories. Yesterday the maid, Hamda, a plump little semi-African, was sitting in a corner of the room having her glass of tea (they always have her in as she is the only woman servant in the house) and we were talking of the danger of being buried alive.

"Only one man", said Hamda, "came from the dead, and he was called Salim at-Turab (Saved from the Dust) and married my husband's brother's divorced wife. His mother died while she was pregnant with him, and they took her to bury her and forgot to make a sign over her body with a sword: they make as if they were cutting her open, and that kills the child inside her. But they forgot this, and the child was born in the little hollow of the grave, and it grew till it was strong enough to crawl about, and at last it began to leave the grave, and the men who go out early for milk or firewood would see it playing about and try to get near, but it always rushed back into its hole: until one day they got to the grave hole and stopped it up and caught the little boy and took him to the village. And they knew the grave and went and opened it to see how the child had lived, and they found the woman dead inside, all but one eye and one hand and one breast, with which she had nourished her son."

Mr. Dickson said, "Is this true, Hamda?" and she said: "Would I lie to you?" and we left it at that.[1]

Mrs. D. has another quite recent grave story from across the Gulf. An old man was found in a mosque and he was doing the pilgrimage to Nejf: and the Mulla of the mosque asked if he had any money, was told he had 150 rupees, and strangled him and stole them in the night. Next morning the dead body was found and the people of the village washed it and set out to bury it: the Mulla joined them and helped and finally got into the grave and arranged the body there: and when the earth was thrown on and he stood over it, the grave suddenly opened and swallowed him up to the shoulders, so that he could not get out. The people of the village built a little tent of palm leaves over him and bring him food and water, and that is the latest news of this interesting contemporary event. Mrs. D. didn't ask why they didn't dig him out with pickaxes! Mr. D. capped this with the story of a man who buried a holy venerated old dervish and dropped his purse in the grave while doing so: he only noticed it when he got back and told his mulla. The mulla gave him leave to open the grave and look for his purse: when he did so he saw that the holy man, instead of facing Mecca as he had done when he was laid there, was now turning his back on the holy city. He went to his mulla, much perturbed, and told him, and they came to the conclusion that the holy man must have been leading a double life. So they went to his house and hunted and hunted for evidence of crime and at last they found it—in a little cranny of a wall, a small pouch of tobacco and a pipe! This was in the wahabi days. . . .

6 March, 1937.

My dear Jock,

I seem to have travelled a long way—and here the sea is shining, and the old boats are all drawn up behind their shallow tide-filled

[1] For many such excellent stories and all the lore of the Syrian desert see *The Arab of the Desert* by H. R. P. Dickson.

walls, a little shabbier than they were five years ago, since Kuwait is
suffering from the slump in pearls. They are going to find oil
instead, and there is an Anglo-American company starting, but not
yet in force sufficient to bring the blessings of civilization too closely
home to one. I have just been out, pottering by myself among the
boats, with friendly Arabs in long gowns ready to put in their pockets
the rosaries with which they pass the time, and come with me to explain the mysteries. I climbed up the side of an unfinished 'Sambuq',
built to carry water from Basra to Kuwait, and took photos of the
carpenters and the old foreman. I stopped and chatted to the maker
of nets, and the old Persian who collects all the odd bits of string and
makes new (and I should say very unreliable) ropes out of them: and
found out that a big new boat, all carved, costs 1,000 rupees. And
this morning I went at 10.30 to lunch with the widow of the Sheikh
of Muhammerah, who lives in poverty alone with her mother in a
huge four-square palace. I wish you could see it all. Dear Jock, you
would enjoy it so!

Your letter came last night, with no visible post to bring it: it was
nice to get, as I have so far outstripped all my mails.

Mrs. D. has been telling me about Gertrude Bell and her rudeness
to women. When Colonel D. introduced his newly arrived bride,
Gertrude did not even shake hands, but said: "It is such a pity you all
marry and bring out incapable young wives."

7 *March,* 1937.

Dearest B,

D. G. got an invitation for us to go to lunch with the widow of
the Sheikh of Muhammerah in a dilapidated old square palace yesterday,
and never told us: I thought it was to be just a morning call with Mrs.
Greenway, the doctor's wife; went off to pick her up, and found this
invitation of which I knew nothing. We sent a hasty messenger to
ask Mrs. D., but of course it was too late and she was inclined to feel
huffy, and it has added one more nail to D. G's coffin in her estimation.
We two, however, had a pleasant time. The ladies are all Persian,
the little widow 26 or so, from Isfahan, with a piquant little face. A
dreary life—the old Sheikh married, and then dumped her here to
live in seclusion on a tiny pittance. The palace is huge, with open
loggias on a square, two storeys, and cool 'sirdabs' underground for
summer with the Persian 'bad-girs', towers with open shafts down

them to catch whatever wind may blow from any quarter. The rooms are mostly unfurnished, the grand room, with panelled walls and ceilings, shows signs of collapse: there is only one kept in order for visitors, and D. G. describes it rather aptly by saying it is like the bad dream of a Goanese cook: it has green columns with corinthian capitals in stucco decorated pink like Edinburgh rock: under the arches, red and green glass balls are stuck for ornament, showing dust. The wall is covered with brown and green flecks of paint and a geometric frieze of varied colours, pink predominating: and a few hideous glass objects are stood about in niches. There are handsome curtains of wool embroidered with Persian figures in chain-stitch—Solomon, or the story of Joseph, or Jesus in swaddling clothes held at an unscientific angle by Miriam with a halo. The ladies were very pleasant. There was a cousin called Shankat, now a grandmother of 35 or so, but she must have been a lovely girl and is still very handsome, exactly like a Persian miniature with very low broad forehead, and the eyebrows low and very regular over the eyes, and the nose exactly like those one sees only in the Persian pictures. They had a table completely covered with food and when we complained it was too much, said: "You should have brought more people to eat it," as here the guest is supposed to bring as many as he likes. I could have arranged to sleep there in one corner of the old palace, but I am not feeling strong enough for harem life and D. G. will jolly well have to find me something more comfortable. He is expected back to-day.

8 *March,* 1937.

Yesterday afternoon we drove out of the southern gate across the desert now pleasantly green over its yellow earth—with a few patches of corn. Mrs. D. told me that for the first three years after they came the people sowed this corn and the locusts ate it all: the fourth and fifth year there was no rain, so they did not sow (they sow after the first rain), and the sixth year at last they had a good harvest. Only the townspeople sow, the beduin never do here. When we left the green patches we came to a camp of the Mutair and went and had coffee in three of their tents: such a nice welcome. Mrs. D. had brought a white gown with blue flowers for one of the little girls: the women sat with us all, but of course with their black face cloths so I only saw their eyes and dark hands with tattoo marks and amber bracelets.

[135]

There was a spoilt fierce little boy who was playing with a miserable lizard, or rather gecko—a thing with webby feet and white tummy and a scaly tail. It tried to lie still, till the wretched little boy scratched its tail to make it move and finally the poor little beast was dead in the most lingering way—made me feel quite ill. Mrs. D. tried to rescue it, but the small boy flew into a tearing rage, snatched it, and threw it at her. The men all have the long nice faces of the Northern proper Arab, with pleasant humorous eyes and very nice mouths: just a little more distinction in them than the typical Hadhramis. They are very aristocratic, their pedigrees going back for centuries unmixed. We called on a bride yesterday, a widow who came as a small girl from Central Nejd and is now marrying an elderly man who is taking her to Riyadh—a long journey into Central Arabia by camel. He asked his daughter to find him a wife, and they were all very friendly together.

The Scotts took us out in a launch to an island, the "Mother of Ants", uninhabited except for a little camp belonging to a very holy old sayyid who cures one of snake bites. He can cure by proxy, which is very useful, and he gives one charms which enable one to handle scorpions. He wasn't there, which was a pity, but they gave us coffee in his tent. We came back with a swell behind us, and saw the tide slowly oozing away, leaving the little harbours of Kuwait in mud flats and their fish traps all exposed: they are elaborate sort of palisades made of reeds, and the fish get in at high water and remain stranded when the water ebbs. Yesterday we came back through the loveliest sunset—a shiny fiery sky, so strong that the desert earth reflected it, the light catching on all its tiny blades of grass: and under it the sea, in the narrow visible shaft of bay, a cold and luminous blue, cut by sails here and there. As it got dark we stopped to leave a message with a dark long-faced Beduin with black tuft of beard just like the statuettes of Egyptian tombs: he came rushing out from a little tent he keeps as a sort of hotel at the gate of the town, where travellers can get a night's lodging and food in return for a little cheese or wool or whatever they may have to spare. He came rushing out with three cups in one hand and his coffee pot in the other and gave it us as we sat in the car. It is nice to go round with the Dicksons, because all the people are so genuinely friendly.

11 *March,* 1937.

I celebrated my arrival here by going down with 'flu—poor D. G.
very distressed. I am installed in a little annexe—bed and sitting
room: a referendum among the women here pronounced that all
is proper so long as one does not sleep under the same roof. Haila,
the maid, likes this arrangement, as she has to veil herself whenever a
'*farrash*' appears, and here she knows their arrival because they first
have to negotiate an outer grill: Haila says this is just like a harem, and
I do feel rather as if D. G. ought to bring a padlock when he sees me
home at night! I can't remember what I wrote about to you last.
I left the Dicksons with many kind feelings, though rather glad to be
here talking to Gerald.

He drove me out to see his two horses camping out about 10 miles
away with some bedu in two little tents: they were the same group
of bedu as I went to with the Dicksons and it was amusing to see
their difference of manner, the D's being genuine friends and D. G.
just 'government'. The Dicksons adore the beduin, and now that
he is no longer the representative here they go on pathetically giving
all the little presents they can afford and indeed far more, to their old
friends. The beduin are fond of them, but whether these presents
have not something to do with it is hard to say. It is a difficult
question altogether and I am glad that, as a woman, it does not much
affect me. I am much happier to have my friends without the financial
basis—but then they are *so* poor, one cannot blame them for thinking of
money. Before I left an old old sheikh came with his nephew, all
the way from Qatar down south, hundreds of miles, and sat and
chatted about the desert news, looking so nice with his abba and
'ighal, and two little envelopes with 20 and 15 rupees were pressed in
to their hands as they departed—then they can buy presents for their
wives. Once a year they come in to "town" and visit their friends
and the Sheikh, who presents them with a few cloaks and 100 rupees
or so—and so they return to their desert with no loss. That is Arab
hospitality!

15 *March,* 1937.

My dear Jock,
    It is such fun to be out here. I spent the morning calling on
Persian ladies—my Persian quite gone!—and this evening the whole

[137]

British Colony dined with the Sheikh. It was not too exciting to me, as I like my Arab society more undiluted and the Sheikh stopped being Arabic at the neck, where his black beard and white drapery ended and European grey flannels began. We walked from the drawing- to the dining-room floors across a short open space where two close ranks of slaves and servants stood with ewers and basins and towels alternately to wash our hands as we passed: and their black and brown faces, gowns and cartridge belts made the best of the show in the flickering light. It was an excellent dinner and fun to see the Sheikh's hand digging energetically in the roast lambs to give us succulent bits while the missionary and oil concessionaire ladies ate refinedly with their fingers. But other times when I have eaten so by myself in a beduin party the peculiarity of it never struck me, and one realizes how one can't combine the East and West.

Meanwhile I am getting ever so much better. You can't even *imagine* this sun and light, a sort of quivering gaiety: and the sunsets on the bay and its mauve edges and the shadow pools of the receding tide.

20 March, 1937.

Dearest B,

We have just come back from such a perfect holiday—an Arabian island called Failichah, all low but undulating, with one little town on it which the people call Failichah and the maps call Zor, and it grows, where it does grow anything but many-coloured pebbles and long-eared grasses, patches of barley corn, sparse and small, but very green now, with masses of blue lilies and red gladioli wild in it, all heaving very gentle over old and invisible sites. D. G. thought it might be an island called Icarus which once had a temple to Apollo—so I spent some days looking up as much literature as we could lay our hands on, and there is a mound called Sa'd and Sa'id, where the Sheikh now has a little belvedere of mud, which looks as if it might be the place.

We rode on donkeys. D. G. rather worried over decorum and we simply couldn't face jodhpurs and woollen long skirts, so he asked for some 'covering' and two very ancient torn black abbas were produced and carefully draped down to our ankles. The donkeys were small and two of them almost indecently in a family way, and enormous ears furry and very pretty but more like a rabbit than a donkey. We had seven altogether. Jusuf's two sons, two nice boys, came, and it was pleasant being jogged along once more in the sunshine—larks singing, a little cool breeze under the heat, and the island so flat in the sea with its lonely bays scarce emerging, and women and boys about in the growing barley: it grows so thin that one does not hurt it by riding through—and only ripens in the years when it rains. We were invited to lunch by Sheikh Fahd, a cousin of the ruler here by a slave woman, and found him camped in a tent all open on one side in a grassy place, with cows and ducks, goats and donkeys, and two tiny mud hovels with the Kuwait flag floating on one and a radio battery windmill going round and round on the other. He speaks quite good English and is an intelligent nice man with rather African features and a quick sense of humour. He took us to see his wife, whom he must have bought, as she is a Turkish or Armenian refugee with aquiline features and blue marks on her cheeks, chin and forearms, and was brought down from the North as a child too small to remember. She wore a magenta dress like mine over her head, and a cotton printed thing underneath of very crude blue and it looked quite lovely. Her little girl looks African like the father, with a tight curly pigtail and they call her 'Abd al-Latif', which is a boy's name, because she wants to be a boy.

We came trotting back in the dusk, a little sore (only sackcloth and a rug to sit on) but lovely and all the grasses catching the sunset.

We had rain and thunder in the night and a rough sea in the morning and Colonel Dickson champing to be off. He wouldn't let us stay on, and you know how D. G. wavers, wanting to be amiable and not wanting to be at the same time—the result was no one knew what we were going to do and the servants came at intervals to give us advice, and finally there was a great packing of tents after breakfast and the rest of the morning sitting quite happily on the shore watching to see if the waves would get worse or better, the Failichah maximum being known to come at noon. The Arab notables came and sat in a circle on the sand with a slave pouring out their little coffee cups. There is no motor car on the island, no paper, post, or gramophone: a blessed place. I wish one could buy it and keep it so. If one wants a house, one just goes, chooses a bit of ground, and builds, with no buying of land. We got back racing through green and white waves and a little fleet of boats—jalboots they call them—their white curved sails fully stretched. And in the evening dined with the Oil people!

D. G. is being very nice to me. I think he likes having me here. He tells me that a woman friend wanted to come and he put her off by saying she would find no maid: she said she would bring only shorts! So then he *definitely* put her off! I shall be so sorry to go. I am *so* much better; the doctor here says the dry desert air should be the very best thing for me. It has begun to get warm now and I have gone into a silk frock.

22 *March*, 1937.

My dear Jock,

Such nice things happen here all the time. Yesterday I saw the ancestor of all boats—they were flitting about the hideous little black lighthouse which the unaesthetic British have put up at the end of the bay (completely black) and here were these ancient phantoms with one sail on a curved yard or whatever it is that a sail is attached to. The boats are made of palm fronds, just the back-bones of the palm leaf tied together at prow and stern and a sort of open lattice work between: other bits of palm are laid crosswise on them, and then a second floor just like the bottom one, making a space about a foot deep in which the sea can wash about: they never go quite under, though one sits in water. A nice beduin family from Nejd look after the lighthouse and have built themselves a smart new house on a government grant of £30—and I have got such good photos of them all.

One looks down the coast here, into the lands of Nejd, and just longs to make for those horizons and disappear behind them—a quite awful disease. The missionary ladies are surprised I don't go to tea with them. They say I might find time if I *really wanted*: but why the devil should one really want?

It is awful to read European papers when they come!

24 *March*, 1937.

Dearest B,

Yesterday D. G.'s new black Salugi arrived in the hands of missionaries from Bahrain. I asked Iasin, the handsome butler, what is a good Salugi name, and he without a moment's hesitation said "there is no better name than Salfa"—so Salfa she is. D. G. says he will dump her on us while he goes on leave to England. She is so aristocratic and lovely with brown eyes and a white curl at the end of her tail and four large white paws which she lifts very delicately when she walks— and tucks her tail right under her in moments of excitement. We took her out for a walk in the sort of waste open space which makes the Agency and the various mouldering palaces about it look as if they had been dumped in a wilderness overnight, and there we saw a lot of kestrels sitting dotted about on the ground: they were decoys tied down there, and near them were round discs of traps sticking half out of the sand with a worm or caterpillar tied on the outside by the waist and wriggling like a semaphore slowly round and round. The boys lying in wait came up when they saw us interested and said they get five or six captives a day. Then they tie them on a string and give them to the children to play with—horrid.

D. G. has been a perfect host, so quiet and thoughtful and thinking of nice things: and I find it an effort to tear myself away now— especially as a new reason for staying crops up every day. On Monday we are going to dine with one of the Mutair in his little tent, so I must stay over that. We had a grand rather dreary dinner with one of the Sheikly family the other night—all the British colony and only one Sheikh to go round. But he had a delightful ceiling to his dining-room composed entirely of oleographs of ex-queens and actresses of Europe in gilt frames, placed close to each other so you couldn't poke a pin between.

ABADAN, 31 *March,* 1937.

My dear Jock,

I am now sitting contemplating the beauties of civilization—a forest of tall chimneys, an expanse of iron aluminium-painted tanks, a belching column of smoke which burns year in and out—the Anglo-Persian oil port: the tanks "that launched a thousand ships" and lost us 31,000 dead in Mesopotamia!—I wonder if Oil is worth it?

Looking south, the great river flows quiet and flat between palm groves just as the Sumerians saw it: and looking north, it might be Glasgow except for the sun.

I get to Baghdad in three or four days, going by way of the Garden of Eden and Kut.

Dreary people on board! Men in the East do get the most boring sorts of wives: I think it is because they get them at home irrespective

of any suitability to the East, and they go on living at home in their
hearts ever after, to the infinite detriment of their conversation: and
the wretched men who really like the sort of life out here become
exiles in their own homes for ever after.

BAGHDAD, 9 April, 1937.

Dearest B,

I don't know what I shall have to pay to ransom fate for one
month's perfect happiness in Kuwait. It was *quite* perfect—everything being right in the right surroundings, the lovely place and
people, the comfort of the cool and empty house with nice servants
running round in yellow embroidered gowns, and D. G. who was the
pleasantest host in this world, always thinking out new and amusing
things for us to do, liking the same things, and with a pleasantly
sympathetic mind ready to go from politics to literature or gossip, and
so ready for conversation that I got no work done at all! I think he
enjoyed it too, and sent a telegram after me to wish me bon voyage,
and wrote to thank me for my visit—and altogether it leaves a pleasant
memory of friendly comradeship—and I must say it *is* nice to sit and
talk the same language and, if something funny comes along, to lift
one's eyes and catch a corresponding twinkle. It is unfortunate that
I always like people who are so unsteady in their affections. A lady
in the train with me coming up said: "It is no doubt that safe husbands
are dull"—and that is what it is, no doubt. D. G. would be very
unsafe but not at all dull (not that there is any thought on either side
of such a matter as far as I am concerned). He is the most casual
man I have ever met. He made me take the boat to Basra so as to
see the Shatt el Arab, and forgot that it takes an extra day!

The river is fascinating—the shapes going up and down it in the
way of boats quite incredible. I spent a day with the Dawsons, who
manage a huge date-growing estate: and as we went by car across a
waste bit between them and the town, and flocks and beduin tents
quite near, we saw what looked like a greeny Alsatian—and lo!
it was a wolf—fat as can be, all out on the flat with no cover, no
doubt waiting for night: and we chased it in the car, zigzagging over
its path, while it galloped easily along. D. G. tells me a curious
thing—that gazelle or sheep will always converge on and cross your
trail if you go parallel with them in a car, which seems a silly thing
to do.

It is strange how the things I have seen coming in these lands are now developing, so that I have an almost uncanny Cassandra-like feeling—and what no one would believe six years ago is now becoming commonplace. And perhaps I shall have some hand yet in the history of the future, though no one except myself and one or two unusually discriminating people will guess! Anyway it is good to be here and see the stream flowing.

Yesterday I went to a little female gathering of every sort—Iraq, Turk, Syrian, American and British at the house of a dear little pretty Welshwoman who runs the girls' school. They meet once a week to discuss the universe and they asked me whether I feel myself more cut off from other races than from my own people—and I can truthfully say *no*: it is only a very small section of one's own people with whom one can talk the same language, and one may as well make up one's mind to being essentially alone. I feel very much alone at all these big dinners, and gatherings. But I had a pleasant meeting at the Courtneys (Air Vice-Marshal) with the French Air Officer-in-Chief beside me, a pleasant man who shared my views on civilization and asked to see me in Syria. I am invited also in Damascus to the people there and it will be fun to see the country from a new angle, though I believe the French are a good deal less sympathetic than we are as far as the native is concerned. Their minds are so tidy that they cannot possibly contain the infinite.

Everyone tells me it is almost impossible to call on the little Queen as she sees no one, but I met her brother at the races and told him how much I should like to see her, and he says she will be delighted, so I hope to go one of these days. On Friday I leave and sit for two days amongst the ruins of Ukhaidhr in the desert, an old Sassanian palace (or later) and then go for the week to Nejf to see life in the Holy City. Major Edmonds has been a dear and is arranging this, which is rather difficult as no one has done it before. A delightful Persian in Basra, Mirza Muhammed, keeps—entirely for his own pleasure—a priceless collection of Persian and Arabian MSS. I can't tell you what a lovely morning I spent there. An MS. belonging to Saladin, with his name in it, an MS. of the 8th century A.D. and one stamped by the 4th Sultan of the family of Tamerlane—and such lovely illuminated pages in the later ones—treasures beyond price. The little Mirza with a quick, rather mocking mouth, grey hair, and clever eyes and hands, talked of Lionel Smith whom he has a really *deep* respect for. It is nice to see how those great qualities of his, which he never tries to show, make their own way! I said to the Mirza: "You are getting very civilized here." "Not quite," he said, "we don't make our own poison gas."

13 *April*, 1937.

Elsie Sinderson and I spent this morning visiting royalty—we began at 10 o'clock with the little Queen and her baby son, out in a hideous new suburban castle surrounded with new flower-beds rather haphazard but very gay, and all full of modern furniture, very clean and neat, inside. She came down very simple and gentle, a dear little thing, and said she remembered me. The baby boy, Faisal,[1] was brought down, a gay little two-year-old, with a most ready winning little royal smile that ought to make him popular. Practically no one, except Elsie, is allowed to see the Queen—the ministers discourage it all they can and they live almost in seclusion: I can't help thinking their own choice has something to do with the matter, as the seeing of a lot of speechless British women must have been very dull. We took the little prince for a joy ride round the garden, and then called on the Queen's Egyptian sister-in-law, Princess Malik, a dear little bride, plain by our standards but with a profile exactly like the ancient Egyptians—very much more Europeanized, and easy and friendly. She is going to Alexandria for the summer, and I have offered her a letter to the Bramlys. Her husband[2] is a charming boy (almost), fine, thin and nervous, with a long neck and large eyes, like the young Shelley—and one sees him by himself in a corner of the terrace at the races, watching his horses.

After lunch I called on a Daghistani lady, one of the great families here—originally Caucasian—their grandfather (I think) being the man who fought there against the Russian Conquest. She (Fatima) and I went together to some old friends, Kurds, with a house crumbling to bits on the river wall above the town: it is at its widest and is now swirling down in flood, and gangs of workmen are rushing about with poles to prop the crumbling banks. On the other side one looks out to an unbroken edge of palm trees. My friend Rafi'a's mother was there, an eagle-faced woman with a Kurdish turban,

[1] Now King Faisal of Iraq.

[2] H.R.H. Abdulillah, now Regent of Iraq.

black and gold with tassels, held on by a pearl and gold chain under the chin and a white muslin thrown over: a black and silver kaffieh tied like a cape over her shoulders and a cotton gown under.

SAMARRA, 7 May, 1937.

Samarra has a gold dome and a city wall and with a landscape blurred with dust looked like some celestial vision. Beside it the strange old minaret has a spiral gangway climbing up it on which masses of small grey workmen like lice were working at restoration —it is 800 and more feet high and we went to the top, slightly giddy, and saw the dust-coloured land below, the Tigris in its shifting bed, and the walled town and golden dome and the trenches of the British in the war. The wall of the town is being pulled down: its bricks were taken from the old mosque and are now being restored, a piece of pedantry which troubles the inhabitants who say that a safe government to-day may be anything but safe to-morrow: and of course the look of the town will be spoilt. When Iraq rebelled in 1920 Samarra had a good political officer and remained loyal and they would like the British back again now (like a good many people here and there). This was told us by a young local policeman on the top of the tower, who gets 10/- a month and his food, and all his clothes except a pale green shirt which he bought himself. He seemed rather sad that the workmen get more—2/- to 1/- per day—till I said he had a profession full of honour, which the Arabs are still innocent enough to value.

We took a nice little mild Iraqi director of excavations with us and visited some of the ruins. The whole town was founded and abandoned in less than 60 years (A.D. 835-892) and the 8 Caliphs spent all their time and revenues on building palaces while their dominions went to pot. The town covers a long narrow band of 30 kilometres: we went up to the very end this afternoon, where the second mosque stands like Stonehenge, a series of amputated piers of brick with arches—all brown with a pale brown dust-storm in the air above and two bright blue jays the only bit of colour against a white almost invisible blob of sun. It was full of majesty, so vast and derelict and made of the dust which flew around it: and one reached it along a wide and ancient highway with the rubbish mounds of the city houses in heaps of small dunes on either hand, and infinite hillocks of

L

ruins with the old lines of straight streets through them here and there.

We came back to the house fixed for us by Vyvyan [Holt] belonging to the Rajah of Pirpur: he keeps it here for pilgrims and one goes in through an archway of carved brick and through various rooms to the Harim, opening on to porticoes of carved wooden columns and a paved court all small and quiet where three *cawasses* and a Caucasian servant welcomed us. They are so hospitable. They had four camp beds all arranged and wired an electric light specially for us, and seeing us three women alone, the Sayyid whose special guests we are is sleeping in the outer house to guard us. Sheikh Salih—an Arab with a typical close Mesopotamian face—has given us a delicious dinner of rice and stews and fritters, and talked about the road, and the bridge which they are all sighing for (as there is nothing but ferries between Baghdad and Mosul) and the systems of agriculture and the difficulties of government, and now we are washed and undressed and I must put out the light to go to sleep. He gave us a nice Arab proverb: "the sparrow went bail for the starling, and both have flown away."

We paid a call on the archaeologists—three nice young men rather pathetically and eagerly running their own show. Iraq is doing its own Islamic archaeology and the palaces of Samarra are disgorging most lovely stucco friezes.

We came down the west bank from Tekrit and saw Samarra across the green flat and the winding Tigris, a lovely sight like a Persian miniature with the ancient spiral tower and the golden dome and minarets. And then we crossed the railway line with several bad bumps and climbed across the old trenches to the Lover's Castle, a ruin standing up very fine with a few windows and rounded brick buttresses left standing. There is something extraordinarily poignant in these desert ruins, so solitary and complete in desolation.

It was getting late but we still had one part of our programme to do—and that was to turn aside and visit Sheikh Hamadi in his tents. He was away, but his sister and two wives were there and two sons, and all the tribesmen, and it was fun to sit at coffee. They have a schoolmaster now who comes every day from the village and has a tent and tables and few chairs to teach them: standing on their head in a little black-and-white gym costume seemed to be part of the training

[146]

which the small bedu enjoyed. I bought a blue lapis cylinder seal from one of the women, rather a nice one.

We came back with a pale silvery yellow sunset behind us: refused the offer of a policeman: and got in quite safe after dark.

To-morrow I go to Nejf—I seem much better.

NEJF, 11 May, 1937.

Dearest Venetia,

It is rather nice to have got to the Holy City in spite of obstacles— first the Euphrates rose in flood: then my operation: lastly the tribes to the south began their usual summer rebellion. However the Government acted promptly, intercepted a lorry-load of arms, took away the Parliamentary immunity of three sheikhs and sent them to exile in Kurdistan: and I got away as quick as I could when the railway line was cut, for fear of being stopped by government—however, all seems quiet now. I got into a car with five Iraqis in the back and we ran into a dust-storm, very unpleasant in the open—the lights throw no light at all and the soft dust comes pattering with every gust of wind, giving one an unpleasant feeling of being buried. Incidentally I was worried about my nose as the wound is still open and dust the one thing to avoid. The little driver was very good and crept along an invisible road telling us that "his hand was on his heart" while we said: "May Allah make it easy to you" in chorus. I got tea with missionaries in Hillah, and a bath. We ran out of the dust before that, as suddenly as we got into it, and stopped at a wayside tea-house, and the owner of it brought me a bowl of water to wash my face as I sat in the car. How can one help liking people who think of this on their own?

I got a car all to myself from Hillah and came along in the dusk. One has such a feeling of desolation and the power of time in this empty ancient land—the tower of Babel on the right and the line of humps that once were the walls of Babylon. Ezekiel's tomb, under a crumbling minaret with a stork in his nest at the top—and Jews from Baghdad very blatant in their European clothes, sitting in hundreds along the banks of the canal to celebrate Ezekiel's feast. By the time we crossed the Euphrates to Kufa it was dark: it is such a pretty little town, all strung along the bank with sailing ships moored beside it and all the male inhabitants trying to get cool out of doors on benches, and the domes of its mosque lighted: and from there one goes into darkness and desert again—till the mosque of Nejf appears with the lights outlining it in the night. It is always a very moving place to come to—the end of so many pilgrimages.

I have three days here and then go to Ukhaidr in the desert either with or without a party from Baghdad—and then another week before I go to Syria if the doctor lets me: at present I have to go to him once or twice a week.

11 *May*, 1937.

Darling B,

I nearly left my little life in the Tigris the other day. An enthusiast from Hinaidi (R.A.F.) asked if I would like to try his speed boat: I was of course delighted and he came to fetch me with another R.A.F. man who looked rather frightened I thought at the time. The difficulty was to get through the upper bridge where the water is so high now that one can't get through sitting even in a canoe (there is an opening as a matter of fact but we didn't see it or hear till after). We drifted down rather swiftly—the river going strong, tried to clear the wire cables that go criss-cross all along, got nearly stuck and lifted the engine to get clear: water of course poured in: the other man said "jump out on to the bridge pier" which luckily I didn't attempt. The bridge was packed with a yelling crowd. One man with great presence of mind came out on to the boat-like pier and reached us to give us a twist into the current which was rushing through: and we lay down more or less and got out below the bridge rather ruffled, wet and safe. It was great fun after that, leaping about on the water in circles with no bridge about.

It is unreal still to be in Nejf and settled here as it were, as most people go through in an hour or so. I feel rather slack too about the uphill job of conquering the hearts of the religious here, who look on women as regrettable anyway but specially when travelling alone. But the governor (Qaimaqam) is a most cheerful and friendly man, a middle-aged bachelor who confided that there are many reasons against marrying, as no doubt there are! He took me all round the town and showed me the places where Captain Marshall was murdered in his sleep and where Frank [Balfour] risked his life to get his men away. The town is a romantic place, crowning a long brow that overlooks the desert—a strip of palms with water and green beyond

[148]

and then the desert and the pilgrim road to Mecca, the Tariq Zobaida, lying white upon it—and as we came back we found a herd of camels resting in the suburb, and Shammar beduin from the Nefud, the great sand-dune waste five days away, fine-looking with long pig-tails made reddish by the sun. And the Qaimaqam is so nice because he likes the beduin and the old things—more than any effendi I ever met here. I dined with him in his little house all decorated with Persian gaudy mats diagonally nailed on the wall (one representing a map of Iraq with most regrettable ingenuity). I myself am in a modern little two-roomed house opposite, with running water and every modern convenience. They say the water is good as it is filtered through earthenware and comes in pipes from the Euphrates.

The bazaars have nothing very special in them except rather fascinating gold ornaments, but they are attractive, cool and dark and high, and winding into all sorts of dark labyrinths where abbas are being sewn or quilts being made—and the people are most at-tractively varied, Indian and Persian and Arab. The most useful thing to speak is Persian, as it softens the hearts of the most fanatic part of the people.

Now I have just wandered round in the dusk, outside the town where another town of graves and tombs lies crowded with small blue domes here and there below the round brick bastions of the walls, all lovely under the strengthening crescent of the moon, the old moon a perfect disc in its arms.

I have been this morning to see a very great person, the Refuge of Islam, the religious leader who went out of Nejf with a white flag and settled the peace in 1918. Hamid Khan wrote a letter of intro-duction, but then there was doubt whether, being so religious, he would see me at all: then yesterday one of his disciples came with the Qaimaqam and we talked about the history of Islam, and he was so pleased with me that he must have spoken to the Sayyid and the message came that we were to go in the evening when people would not notice so much: then he changed his mind and said in the morning, and we went through the winding little streets with the houses meeting overhead to a little poor door, up high narrow steps to a poorly furnished little room on the roof—just a rug and two cotton mattresses on the floor, an old servant offering cigarettes and the Sayyid's son Halim and our friend. When we were all seated the Sayyid came looking too fine under a huge white turban, lean face and beard dyed bright red with henna. He told me he is over 60 years and has the most amusing intelligent mouth, very impish and mobile. They have held their position for five generations from father to son. He made a long speech saying that he would give me good advice to take back to England, and told me the feelings of the people here over Palestine. I said that I was glad to be able to say from him what I and many others thought for ourselves. Then he talked about Miss Bell and Cox, and how the people since their time had been lesser people: I find their memory is much more thought of here than in Baghdad. Then we talked of Bekr Sidki and how his government is doing well and how simply he lives, and I said: "Like the early Moslems," which pleased him very much—and I said I would send my book to their new library now building. They were very nice to me. I think in a month's time I would be perfectly at home in this stronghold of religion. The Sheikh who came yesterday is very learned but so poor he makes a tiny living by copying books. Many books here never get printed and are still handed on in this medieval way.

KERBELA, 16 May, 1937.

Kerbela has no European in it that one knows of, but there is a very neat European touch as you approach—a public garden *crammed* with flowers, masses of petunias and coreopsis, and an asphalt street with young eucalyptus trees, all the work of my friend Salih Jabr: and when you come to the end of this highway, you go suddenly into the real East, with overhanging houses and roofed bazaars, high, under ridged roofs of beams and corrugated iron full of holes, and fluttering doves. And a crowd less Arab and more varied than Nejf, many Indians, and women from Sind, like white ghosts with their little embroidered gratings of eye-holes under the skull cap and voluminously gathered gown. And this time my host lived in an old house with two courtyards, and old brickwork solid enough to keep the heat out. He was having a lunch party of Iraqis, three army officers and two Kerbelais and the son of Sayyid Talib of Basra, an engaging but bad old man with many murders on his head who was eventually rather unsportingly seized by Sir Percy as he left Lady Cox's door after a visit there, and sent to exile in Ceylon. His own son is a nice lad who studied in Sandhurst (and his two brothers in Oxford)—but he himself has a queerly shaped head. The shape of people's heads here are so often a disappointment when they take their turbans off.

In the twilight we went to my host's country house in an estate of palms and pomegranate, with a stream and little flower garden and a boat, and the chauffeur boy punted me about in the twilight without knowing in the least how it should be done, and the banks were full of tamarisks in flower, called Tarfa. And at night I slept deliciously on a roof all to myself, and when I woke early saw two storks in a nest about 40 feet from my bed waking up too and making love to each other in the most conjugal way, though it looked very uncomfortable for the lady as her husband bit her head with his beak all the time (to keep her quiet I supposed). However she didn't seem to mind but went on afterwards picking up little bits of straw to tidy the nest, looking as if nothing had happened, in the most refined way. There were storks all around on the golden minarets and beside the red flags on the dome: and the servants say it brings bad luck to chase them away.

I took a car and went to Ukhaidr in the desert—about two hours' drive, beyond a shallow lake which the Euphrates floods have made. Its expanses of tiny gravel the beduin women collect with their hands, or with flimsy little palm-leaf brushes, and load on donkeys and take for roadmaking.

Mustafa Khan (who is a cousin of the Aga Khan by the way) sent a plump and respectable family servant with me, and a little basket with fizzy lemonade and a block of ice, and one policeman. As we went along we saw gazelle bounding away, three of them quite white against the desert, which I had often read of but never seen. They were far off and so white and flat that they looked as if woven in a Persian brocade, most lovely against the warm coloured hill—and we saw nothing more except an old built-up column here and there with remains of blue tiles—made to show the way—till Ukhaidr appeared, an incredible place in the wilderness. It is an enormous size, square, with towers all along the walls and a walk round between two battlement walls to shoot from. In its great court it has an inner wall round the actual castle, also with towers, and vaulted rooms and remains of stucco here and there—and now a horrid smell and droppings of bats in every room. One can still climb up three storeys and look from the battlements over the desert and the depression which

[151]

they say was once the Sea of Nejf, and the ridge they call Jebel Tar (Gibraltar). There is nothing quite like this finding of ruins in the desert, something so august in its nakedness, and so dignified in man's courage and helplessness against the passing of Time. There were kites in the ruins and two little donkeys fanning each other's faces with their tails, and the cloak and sack and short sword of some peasant from the oasis. The policeman was just taking the sword when the owner appeared and instantly vanished behind a crumbled wall: it still shows what these poor people have to fear. But he came out at last and was only a dull peasant.

BAGHDAD, 21 May, 1937.

To-day Jamila came to me in tears. They gave the key of their house to a neighbour to look after and found *all* their things stolen when they got back. This was a month ago and nothing has been discovered. They know now that one member of the neighbour's family is "of a thieves' root" and made by the authorities to sleep in prison. I have got Sinbad [Dr. Sinderson] to write to the police, but I don't expect any result—poor people.

It is extraordinary what a mixture of indiscipline and patience has been produced by centuries of injustice in a country where a basis of physical violence underlies everything from the climate downwards. In the car from Kerbela the other day my driver got furious with a meandering donkey and spat at his driver as we passed: I thought "what a revolting degenerate person this is". Then we broke down and he found his piston broken, and limping along at a crawl told me it would mean nine pounds for a new one: "and one pound yesterday to pay: I have no luck with my car": it meant a fearful loss to him but he had not even an impatient word for that! Of course if he had kept his car oiled and clean he would have avoided the disaster, but that is a separate story. When we finally broke down, all he did was to apologize in the most disarming way for not taking us to a destination. One can't help liking these people. Their manners are always good if given a chance, whatever vexation they themselves labour under: and they are manly and cheerful.

BRUMMANA, LEBANON, SYRIA, May, 1937.

Dearest Venetia,

I had dinner with a cousin of the Aga Khan the other night and two other Shias from Nejf on a terrace on the Tigris. I could just follow the very learned language of the old Shia who is the head of the Shia High Court and a poet as well: and though the other guest begged him to use short words for my sake, it was still very Johnsonian. He was one of these ascetic-looking people in white turban with a beard which looks as if it came just from a few weeks neglected shaving: but when he took his turban off and became animated one could see that he had quite a nice face and quick and intelligent eyes and mouth: it is just the fashion of perpetual solemnity which makes them all look half-dead.

I took Miss X through the bazaars yesterday—and *what* a wasted morning! She saw nothing, took in nothing, and only went to get something to talk about at a cocktail party. But a strange thing happened: an Arab-dressed woman with a baby came begging and I suddenly noticed she was doing it in Russian! I asked her where she came from—the Caucasus: and she had walked to Baghdad. Then she got separated in the crowd and I heard no more. But what a strange history to bring her here begging in Caucasian in the Arab bazaar!

DAMASCUS, 27 May, 1937.

I got here last night by a new native car service that rushes you across the desert at express rate for £4. It leaves at 4 a.m. and is supposed to get in at 6, and as a matter of fact we did get in at 9, with one breakdown, and quite exhausted. I came along in a kind of coma, waking now and then in mirage and glare to see gazelle bounding away, some right across our path. After the dreary bit round Euphrates, the desert grew pale green and *full* of camels, and when we broke down two herdsmen from the 'Sbā ('Anezah) strolled up, one of them spinning camel wool into ropes, and asked for water. The horrid little effendis at the back of the car were for refusing them, but I gave them my water bottle. They go with the camels only once in five days to the wells and tents and live on milk in the intervals and a little bread which they had come to an end of (and one day still to go): and when I gave them what I could of my rye vita biscuits, and a third herdsman came up, they handed him a share, hungry as they

[153]

were. How can one help liking them? I asked them: "Who is your Sheikh?" and they answered "we are all sheikhs"—and, dismissing the matter of their hunger and thirst as of no account, woke up to interest when one of the effendis quoted a line of poetry and gave me the verse of a qasida. They were all in rags, loose and voluminous, and black by the sun, but with small and pleasant features. I happened to notice the insides of one of their hands, with scarce a line on it—the hand like that of some fine animal with no nerves to worry it.

31 *May*, 1937.

Darling B,

The north of Syria seems scarce Arab at all—half the people with fairish hair and blue eyes: said to be descendants of Crusaders, but anyway they might be sturdy peasants in the Alps. It is lovely to drive over that great open country rolling away in emptiness near the hills and then in great red strips of ploughed earth and corn: people riding over it with droves of horses, Arab but a little stockier than the delicate creatures of Iraq—and everywhere you see dotted here and there and rising out of the haze against the mountain ranges old mounds of nameless cities. There is a feeling of incredible age here, an easy country over which armies have marched since the first days of mankind. Usually near the mound some little village lingers—looking, in all the country between Homs and Aleppo, like a camp of tents from the conical fashion of their beehive domed huts, little square mud affairs with a door and a few window holes, very cool they say in summer. They are not beautiful, but look amusing, sticking like teeth against the skyline as they lean up against the more ancient mounds. Homs has a mound, and Aleppo has *the* mound standing high above the town, crowned with walls: till Ibrahim Pasha came and pulled it about, the slope was all smoothly coated with stone and even now one spends hours wandering over it through tier after tier of civilizations—the Hittite lions guard the metal doors studded with Saladin's horse-shoes: the mosque was built by his son, and an old mosque is supposed to mark the site where Abraham milked his ewes and gave the name of Haleb (milk) to the town. I climbed down fifty high steps into an immense Byzantine hall on pillars, and then wandered over the Haram and palace of Egyptian Caliphs and the medieval precautions round the great gate, with secret posterns

[154]

and holes to pour pitch down on the assailants. There is a horrid prison, deep down with no window and a hole in the roof for letting food down—I always dislike going into prisons and offer a little prayer for all the unhappiness that must have been spent inside them.

I went all over this citadel with a Christian of Aleppo, an employee of the French delegation very anxious to tell me how anti-French he was, but as I was their guest and being particularly nicely treated I had to snub him promptly. He took me over the bazaars which are the nicest I know in the East, all narrow vaulted with stone and little square openings in the vault letting down shafts of light. As you look at Aleppo from the citadel, you see a green expanse in its middle, and these are the roofs of the bazaars. The mosque is not particularly beautiful—a long carpeted expanse, only pleasantly peaceful as they all are. But there is a little mosque nearby, adapted from a Byzantine church, with capitals of wind-blown acanthus very pleasant, and a beautiful medieval minbar of carved wood. In the sunset we went through the Arab suburb (half the inhabitants are Christian and have a very European half of the town)—and came to a mosque outside called Paradise—and so it seemed with a little walled garden of pistachio trees before it, and a pergola over the cistern in its court, and an old priest who would have been nice if he could have found it in him to think kindly of a Christian. As it was he showed us over in a severe silence and gave no answer to my salaam so that I had to'say "Salaam is to Allah", which no doubt surprised him.

I am still rather exhausted, as we had such a gay life in Aleppo and did not get to bed till 3 a.m. either night. Everyone was very pleasant and General Nogues a charming old man who travelled in Thibet.

There is the most fascinating antique shop you ever saw in Aleppo belonging to an old Afghan who adapts his prices to his feelings and if he doesn't like you won't sell anything at all. I talked Persian to him and he liked me more and more and lowered his prices every time he thought how nice I was, and I came away with two old mosque lamps of engraved glass and a dozen pieces of Roman glass for £2. 7s. —after hearing all his travels from Herat to Baluchistan and Aden, Somaliland and Abyssinia, and Asia Minor as a prisoner of the Turks. He showed his ankles still swollen with Turkish chains, from which he was rescued by General Townsend. You never saw anything like his house piled from floor to ceiling with every conceivable antique, genuine or faked.   He himself doesn't know what he has and he tells me some well-dressed Europeans come and steal.   "You treat me like a man, but some talk as if I were an animal," he said, and successfully got rid of four ladies whom he disliked by asking preposterous sums for everything they asked for.   An awful thing happened when we got down to the car.   The chauffeur had left it for one moment and my camera was stolen.   So we spent the rest of the morning with the Arab Governor of Aleppo, and talked about philology while the chief of police took steps—and lo and behold the camera has been found, carried off by a bedu to the stony wilds of St. Simeon in the hills—I am so glad.   This is really an unfortunate year.   My fountain pen was pinched in an Aleppo hotel and two cameras would have been too much.

St. Simeon chose an extraordinary site to settle on his column—a wide view over the Amok plain with mountain ranges in sight, but nothing around him but stones, hills of grey boulders with one little flat patch of cornland enclosed in stony slopes below.   A few optimistic attempts at growing fig trees in the tiny patches of red earth are now being made, but really one notices nothing except the stones and the remains of the deserted villages built of the same hillside material.   The colour is light grey where weathered and yellow in the shelter of archways, and the villages are basilicas and pilgrim places of the 5th–6th centuries or thereabouts, built for the worship of the saint and his column.   It is pleasant Byzantine, and the loneliness and aridness and completeness of it all is very suggestive.   A woman in black with lovely eyes came and made us write in the visitors' book, her baby in a sort of pillow-case completely airless slung over her back.   A lot of children came and talked, some quite fair, their wrists stained with circles of mulberry juice "for beauty".   They had the tiniest baby donkey you ever saw, just like a stuffed toy, who came up to have his ears stroked and liked the thought of eating my hat.   Lizards in all the crannies.   People come up, but it is an excessively bad track from the last village, and no arrangements for tourists.   The place was quite perfect in its desolation, only a few blackgowned women harvesting in the tiny island below.

We got back to Damascus late on Sunday and spent yesterday quietly till the evening when we looked at the glass factory with disastrous results as far as I am concerned.   You will see me arrive

[156]

with a huge crate of glass and if you know what I can do with it when I reach Trieste and send me a line on board (22 June) I shall be very grateful—lovely glass it is and very cheap, but fragile.

We went after into a little mosque nearby where there are two lovely Cufic tombs, one wood and one stone, all carved with lettering, said to cover the remains of two of Husain's daughters. Sixteen of the Kerbela Martyrs have their heads in a little place close by and the Shia and Sunni tombs are scattered amicably around, the Shia flat and the Sunni ridged, a difference I had never known before. One of the tombs was a touching sight, for on its flat expanse all sorts of little gifts were ranged, from a shilling or two, to little phials of perfume, rings, and trinkets. The old man was friendly and kept on telling me to go back there whenever I come to Damascus. They are very poor, as it is a Shia place and there are so few Shia's in Damascus. It is extraordinary how some events go echoing and echoing over the world. Here was a little band, 70 killed and their heads and bodies, and the story of them spread about as widely as Islam, and the feeling as strong now as 1,200 years ago. The head of Husain himself is said to be kept in a rather hideous little heap under green velvet in a bare little room across the open space of the great mosque, where another little heap beside it contains the prophet's beard. I feel I am quite well up in the family of Husain by now.

This morning a charming Comte de Chandon de Braille took me over the museums—the new one with a Palmyrean tomb restored— all the family busts in rows of little niches. It would be fun to have such an arrangement if it could last a few centuries and one could see all one's history at a glance, but rather depressing from the point of view of a Palmyrean as they look horridly vulgar, very like some Levantines to-day. There is also a Synagogue reproduced from Dura on the Euphrates with interesting (ugly) frescoes. And then we went and saw the Minister of Antiquities and two unique things found in a tomb—a silver masque worn by some chief on ceremonial occasions and his signet ring—a lovely little figure cut in cornelian. These things were a great joy, and so was the old Azm house, Moslem 17th-18th century, all painted woodwork very rich but made livable by the fact that the very decorated ceiling is separated from the very decorated walls by a band of plain whitewash. *Such* pretty rooms. The ceilings come down into the corners in a charming way to take away any feeling of suddenness.

[157]

BRUMMANA, 4 June, 1937.

Dearest Venetia,

It is strange and nice to be back here—everything so familiar and still with the sort of enchantment over it which my first visit to the East conferred on it ten years ago. Miss Audi is ageing like a lady in *Cranford*, just getting smaller and more refined till one fine day she will vanish altogether. She still trots about her kitchen and her flower pots, and though the begonias are dead that used to climb up over the drawing-room door, a new and vigorous family is growing up. My ear, now used to the decent Arabic of the East, can hardly bear this awful coastal clipping—and Miss Audi begs me to stay a year to study and lose my vulgar pronunciation!

ANTIOCH, 11 June, 1937.

My dear Jock,

I have been seeing so many things and leaping about the ages in such a way that I now long for quite a long time to sit in the garden and sew. Yesterday we came from Palmyra—the Director of Antiquities and his wife and I. She is a Master Mariner and friend of Ella Maillart and stops at intervals to shoot bustards and francolins from the window of the car, and he is a Hellenist with a nice neat French sense of fun. They are both quite charming and took me to stay in Palmyra in a whitewashed house with arcades, in a small court full of round cemented circles in each of which a holly bush or palm is induced with much trouble to grow: they don't like the local water (nor can they be blamed) so it is brought for them from outside. The house leans up against the temple of Baal whose colonnades are cut against the pink and blue sunsets. You can't think what lovely sunsets there are. We had a palm oasis on one side, and a modern ugly village on the other, but otherwise there is nothing but desert and ruins, long lines of columns weathered as gold as sand, and the descending hills embracing them. The hills run together in two long ridges and Palmyra is at the opening, in an excellent position, and the hill above it has an Arab castle with lots of square towers and a ditch. Below it, as you come towards the town, you reach a little neck with tombs on either hand, square towers, mostly ruined, dotted here and there, and the ruined colonnades visible beyond in the dip and opening out of the valley. And in the evening this is full of goats coming home and everything takes on blue and purple and yellow gentle colours.

[158]

ANTIOCH

One knows exactly how the people lived for they sit in full dress on
their tombs—Greek or Asiatic according to fashion or taste—very rich
and rather barbarian. Every year they made a great camel caravan
and sent it to Charax Spasini on the Persian Gulf which is now full of
oil tanks: and they must have been awfully pleased with themselves
till Aurelian came and took their town—and then the whole thing
collapsed like a pack of cards: the desert beduin looted, and the
caravans took the safe road to Aleppo and never went near Palmyra
any more, and some medieval Arab called Abu Na'am built a castle
on the top of a hill architecturally all wrong but just like what a
castle on a hill should look like in the distance. I climbed and wandered into it by a small hole, as the drawbridge has gone, and looked
out over the oasis and the salt lakes beyond and the desert in which
a faint white line shows the pipe-line lost in a dusty horizon, and
thought about the Passage of Time, and came down to a goat-herd
who gave me milk fresh and warm in a tin. The next day we came
straight across the line of hills, which lifts itself in desert steppes all
yellow grass or stones, with trees here and there and traces of old
square patches to show that once there were settled folk: and we had
lunch in the shadow of a temple, the only thing standing of a forgotten city called Sirian: the beduin have made their hearth there of
two old columns and still water at the wells—and through nine hours
of squelching heat we came down to Antioch.

16 July, 1937.

Don't be surprised if Mr. Micanek and Sykora send you a brown
linen dress. It is a very chic divided skirt, so you can pretend it is
yours and you are one of the Dress Reform people.

L'ARMA, 11 August, 1937.

We had a lovely hour or two last night. It was very still, and
some neighbours took us to see the fishing of sardines in a motor
boat, with the sergeant of police on board so as to make all safe.
You can't think how lovely it was, to get out and see all the lights—
Ventimiglia, Bordighera, Menton, Monte Carlo, and the dark smooth
water, and streaks and circles of phosphorus wherever the oar broke
the surface: and then the boats floating slowly with their light at the
prow and a man lying there looking down to see if the sardines were

[159]

gathering below. Every ship with a light has a dark one, like its shadow beside it, and this combination gave a dramatic feeling, like Life and Death, the shadow ship and its unseen rowers creeping silently and now and then cutting across the light. And round the light the water was green and luminous, so that the boat seemed to float on air, and the black oars below to drift in nothingness; and when we got close to the boat we saw thousands of little silver fish turning over in the depths, no end to them. We had almost given up waiting, when we heard that one far boat had what it considered sufficient sardines below its light for the casting of a net: and we rushed off and came to it just as the dark boat, encircling the light, had dropped 30 metres depth of net in a wide circle round it, and having closed it like a bag at the bottom, was now pulling it in at the top: the men pulled it in, six of them in a row in their boat, most beautiful —lit up here and there, with brown arms and chests, by their lamp-lit consort who waited while the circle of the net grew closer round her —till she finally rowed over it and got outside, and helped to lift the far side of the net: the circle got so small that finally the boats touched, and the sardines—60 lbs. or so—were shovelled out flicking their poor little tails, and making a shivering noise all over the boat.

Rather a nice life, to be a fisherman and spend one's nights on the Mediterranean looking down into a strange world.

25 August, 1937.

I am not *really* temperamental—only just appalled at all I have to do before getting into the comparative restfulness of Arabia. I have been learning the Himyaritic alphabet all the morning by heart, and that is very soothing—but if you only saw the four fat Arabic books that are still unopened, you would realize my feelings!

I am beginning to wonder if there is any place in the world where one does not have to lead a Social Life. Do you think we will have tea-parties on the Queen of Sheba's tomb? One seems to have something here every day—and it would be so nice just to sit and do nothing but look at the sea. I do sympathize with the man who fishes: much better and more effective than taking to hashish for instance—I think it must be the one sport that completely eliminates time.

Do you know what we did yesterday? We went to St. Tropez to see my Alsatian friends and pushed on to lunch at Paradou, and

[160]

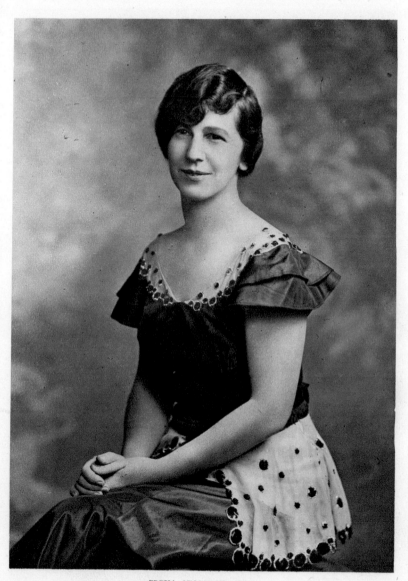

FREYA STARK IN 1934

FROM A SHOP IN TARIM

found A. Besse very cheerful with 7 ladies (including ourselves) around him, therefore fully in his element—and both of them and Meryem as pleasant as could be. I took over your cartoon, which amused us—and spent the afternoon reading accounts from his agents in Abyssinia which made me quite sick almost physically. It made one feel what the man said of Hell: "It can't be true: no constitution could stand it!"

3

The Winter in Huraidha, 1937–38

ON the southern journey to Arabia in 1937 I altered my route and flew for the first time by Italian North Africa to Cairo. I landed in Cyrenaica at Benghazi, and spent a night in the Berenice hotel. In its marble surfaces polished like glass, and bedrooms furnished for comfort with mosquito nets and baths; in the gaiety of the little town, its café tables among oleanders with porticoes behind them; in the clip-clop of fiacres driving in the cool of the afternoon up and down with nothing much to do; and in the sight of the colonial Italians strolling in family phalanxes at leisure after the working hours of their day; in all this one felt as if the clock-hand had moved back some fifteen hundred years—back to the life, easy but threatened, superficial, rigid, rootless, of the last centuries of Rome.

Synesius, a Cyrenaican bishop of the fifth century, describes 'the hour when the Forum is thronged'. I had not read his letters at the time of my visit, but the impression of the thronged forum was there. As they walked, or sat with their coffees or syrups or ices, the people turned to notice the arrival of a stranger —a sign of the smallness of life in spite of its gallant little show. A tall cathedral, with twin domes so alluringly rounded that the 8th Army later nicknamed it Mae West, boasted a double dating from Fascism and Christ: from it I wandered along the sea-front esplanade, by columns that held the she-wolf of Rome; by the square of the Prefecture with public gardens filled with municipal flowers too highly organized to live; by the street, beautifully designed and lavish with marble, where the banks

[162]

and shops were, and the square of the cafés; and here I gradually began to be puzzled. Something was missing, and I noticed that it was the raucous Arab voice of the Levant. The crowds moved in a silence that seemed European to anyone familiar with the East. I began to look round for the Arabs, and there were none to be seen. I walked for quite a long way, sat at a café, and at last discovered a boot-black, who came up and polished my shoes: when he had done, I thanked him in Arabic: he looked at me, startled, and fled without being paid. I began to feel a quagmire beneath this gay little town, a deadening substratum of fear. "There must be some Arabs, somewhere," I thought, and spent what remained of the daylight trying to find them; and did so eventually, in a little ghetto of squalid streets far back from the sea. They watched me passing by in silence, and—accustomed though I was to the nationalisms of Baghdad or Damascus—a throttled horror made me wish never to visit Benghazi again.

A great deal is said and written about the struggle between Asia and Europe, and nowhere can it be seen in sharper relief than along the south Mediterranean shore: but I think the problem has nothing to do with continents or races, but is simply a question whether civilization has or has not the right to exploit: if the voice of Christianity is any voice at all, it stands for the equality of human souls, and the fascist revival of the catchwords of pagan Rome was both futile and impious. The good work of the Italian regime was invisible to me at that time; the saddest point was apparent—the madness of absolute power plunging into unnecessary war. And the heartless anachronism, if it had succeeded, would have been accepted by the world.

When I had flown on to Cairo and reached the Bramlys at Burg al-Arab, I found Whiffey busy with hundreds of refugees from across the Cyrenaican border: he had collected them with lorries beyond the last desert wells where they had been driven and lay dying of thirst among dead animals and men; and a crowd of them, ragged, emaciated and friendly, surged round his car whenever we drove in the direction of their camp, where a few tatters propped on sticks sheltered them from the sun. Whiffey, still smiling, but saying things about 'your Mussolini' that would have put me into an Italian prison straightaway if I had repeated them at home, remarked that in the long run this exodus would be an excellent thing for Egypt, helping to populate her western border; he was already thinking how to organize and settle them. They have now drifted back to their own homes, which are also comfortably depopulated by thirty years of war.

I was driven down to Burg by G. W. Murray, who directed the Egyptian Desert Survey and with Bagnold was studying all those problems of driving through sand which made solitary desert adventures of war possible in a few years' time. He and his wife became good friends of mine, as did a number of people I met in Egypt on these passing visits and came to know better during the approaching years—John Hamilton in Cairo, or Reginald Davies who became my chief in 1940, and was now running the municipality of Alexandria with the help of a philosophic mind. I was laid up for a few days with illness in Alexandria hospital, and he came with a bunch of flowers and discussed poets who have loved the sea. The abstract world is surely one of the essentials for living in the East: it gives an oasis always at hand wherever one may be. I think that my own 'detachment', which never ceased to surprise my mother, was very much a result of a life of illness and travel, for I have often noticed it both in patients and in officials who live much away from their own people and alone.

By the 27th of October I had recovered and was to meet Miss Caton Thompson and Miss Gardiner on the *Narkunda*, to sail for Aden; we were to dig through the winter in Huraidha in the Hadhramaut. It was to be exploring no longer but archaeology, and 71 packages were travelling in the hold. Much of the summer had been spent writing to each other, and eventually meeting, to give the finishing touches to preparations mostly done by the two scientists, who are both admired and esteemed in their work. All I did was to consider our stores in the light of transport, climate and conditions which I knew: there was now a motor road across the jōl where only donkeys could travel two years before, and Harold Ingrams was the first British Adviser in Mukalla, so the problem was not very difficult. The Royal Geographical Society and Mr. Louis Clarke contributed towards our expenses, and Lord Wakefield generously wrote me a cheque for the whole amount I suggested as necessary to the expedition. The world seemed to rock almost physically as I walked up Cheapside with £1500 in my handbag. Stability, after all, like perseverance, or constancy, or even devotion, is one of those qualities whose complexion varies according to what they are attached to: and my ideas of stability were all wedded to poverty. Charles Ker, who had introduced me to Lord Wakefield, met him afterwards and was told the reason for the generosity of this gift: it was not archaeology at all, I regret to say, but the fact that I "looked so little like an explorer".

It is the most difficult thing in writing an autobiography, to determine how much of one's private feelings one must explain. My practice in these books is that of a painter, who can leave out an accidental smudge or temporary sunburn, but must give, however summarily, every feature and even every shadow of a feature, since such structural omission might distort the proportion of the whole. If one has the presumption to think the world interested in a portrait of oneself, it is at least decent to make the portrait as accurate as one can. For this reason I have not left out anything that I can look back upon as having influenced me, for good or bad, though naturally memories that are private in their nature or have affected other people, are not developed to the full proportion of their actual power. There they are, however, in their proper places, and sufficiently indicated for the reader with imagination to follow. I now admit, without any feeling of rancour, a deep divergence with one of my companions. Its intensity surprises me (and indeed it did so even then): it ruffled all the winter horizon of the remote little backwater in Arabia.

[165]

I feel no compunction for this dislike, though realizing how horrid were the feelings it aroused: it is comparatively easy to forgive people defects which are their own concern, but much harder to pardon them for bringing up against you some revolting aspect of yourself: I felt it monstrous that this extraneous presence should turn me into someone so much more objectionable than I really was. And she must have felt the same about me.

The portion we see of human beings is very small: their forms and faces, voices and words, their ages and race perhaps: beyond these, like an immense dark continent of which their obvious self is but a jutting headland, lies all that has made them—generations vanishing into the barbarous night; accidents and impacts not only on themselves but upon their forebears; the cry of the conqueror, the sighing of slaves. Even the chemical variation of substances—airs, foods and waters—are all gathered to that point of light which is the person we know. He himself is unable to communicate, forced to use fluid words as if they were solid, and—if Anglo-Saxon and well brought up—is anyway not expected to wish to communicate at all. And when two human beings meet even in the most simple intercourse, it is not the tiny visible substances, but the immense invisibles that come together. It is these that must determine the liking and disliking over which we have so little control.

My arrival on the *Narkunda* was strenuous enough, for by some mistake I was preparing to board her at Suez and only discovered during the last afternoon that her port of call was Port Said. Either the Delta was flooded or there were no cross-country trains, I cannot remember which: anyway there was nothing for it but to make from Alexandria for Cairo, arrive there at 10 p.m., and hope for a means of reaching Port Said before eight in the morning. The whole thing was complicated by a surging, swaying, shouting, pushing demonstration in honour of Nahas Pasha who was travelling on my train. A young Cairo porter took me under his protection, and having got a taxi, we started for Port Said near midnight, with a driver

full of justified misgivings.   Luckily I had a warm coat.   I lay on
the slippery seat, falling into snatches of dreams and waking to
look at dim vacant streets of the little Delta towns, tucked into
slumber like sleeping birds on the long straight perch of their
road.   The car broke down at intervals, and the driver lost his
way and stuck in a sand dune; at about two in the morning
we routed out a surprised British sentry at Ismailia: but a
series of small miracles always set us off again, and I said
good-bye to my porter and boarded the P. & O. an hour
before she sailed.   The sudden change into that ship's self-
righteous atmosphere of aloofness and games gave me my
first misgivings.

There is no doubt that we English are apt to foster a quality
which other nations object to and which the Americans think of
as smug.   It is, I believe, a transformed humility—a clinging to
outward shapes because of a rooted mistrust of one's own
initiative, and so—by very easy degrees—a rejection of all that
does not conform.   On the Continent it is, or used to be, called
bourgeois and was a sign of social inferiority; but in England the
industrial revolution, or even perhaps an earlier Puritan revolution before it, lifted the bourgeois into power and gave far too
general a licence to this unpleasant characteristic; until its
apotheosis was reached when Dr. Arnold substituted the Team
Spirit for Christianity.   On the P. & O. this rigidity was obviously basic, and—as three of us travelled together—I was not
even visited by the stray little wisps of humanity that usually
approach one when sailing even on the most conventional ship,
alone.   We were immured in the social solitude which belongs
to marriage or accompanied travel—the private compartment
which, when not made for intimacy, becomes the sanctum of
reciprocal boredom.   Intimacy is a different matter; it is carried
on with a glance, a touch, a lift of the eyebrow, alone or in the
middle of a crowd as the case may be; it has nothing to do with
outward shapes and the winds of life blow through it: but here
on the P. & O. it began to be borne in on me that we were
immured not for fun but for exclusion: my companions seemed

not to mind: and this made me feel, dimly but with anxiety, the difference of the continents behind us.

Liveliness and relief were brought on board by Stewart Perowne in Aden. He had been sent to meet some oil magnates and escort them to the Residency, and as he was looking about for them, happened to see my name on some suitcases on deck. As he had just read one of my books, he left the oilmen to their fate and came up to offer the Governor's launch, quoting *Paradise Lost* while he wafted our luggage over the side. He was gay, slim, well-dressed, enthusiastic, with a sparkle that matched the sunlight on the bay. His light-hearted treatment of the duties of an A.D.C. charmed me (though possibly not the oilmen); and, as soon as we were in his launch, amusing things began to happen, for an Arab boat much bigger than ours, listing heavily on one side with most of its crew cheering on the gunwale, charged us amidships and, deviating seconds after a collision had become unavoidable, nearly sent us down among the sharks of the bay. This was the casual world again, and Stewart has told me that it was at this moment that he differentiated me from the P. & O. background. As for me, I was too delighted to be back among the noises and untidiness of Aden to share in anybody else's ruffled feelings.

We spent a week in Aden and then flew to Mukalla, and the story of the following months is told in *A Winter in Arabia*. What has chiefly remained with me from that winter, apart from the beauty of the valley-pictures that lie deep in my mind, is the *intimacy* with a world so strange and remote: it amounts almost to an annihilation of time, for the then scarcely visited smaller valleys of the Hadhramaut seemed to be separated by centuries rather than by space from the life of Europe; I thought constantly of some illuminated manuscript, roughly painted with draped sandalled figures and crowded backgrounds of towns, coming suddenly awake and living and moving beyond its frame; and the history of the Middle or even of the Dark Ages will never again be mere history to me, since I have lived in it and known what it has been. Its difference from our world went far deeper than outward circumstances: it went beyond its permanent insecurity, which is now no longer a stranger in Europe: it was perhaps the *acceptance* of insecurity as the foundation of life. This gave to everything, even to very small things, a significance, a sharper outline as it were, such as you may find in Gothic carving or Elizabethan writing: the whole landscape is illuminated by an eternal light. People have told me that this has happened to them in concentration camps and has given a serenity even to terrible horror. It is, I feel sure, the secret of great art in difficult ages, and the truth of the commonplace that the artist must be unhappy to be great. In the Hadhramaut a permanent threat to human existence was taken for granted: under its hard light the important and the unimportant disentangled themselves, and goodness and courage remained: and any number of figures that might pass unobserved among the milder outlines of what we call civilization, stand there with a strange majesty and grandeur, as clearly remembered as companions in war.

The other impression that has remained is far less agreeable, for it is the feeling of being haunted by sickness, a pervasive, intangible presence in everything one ate, or touched, or did. My companions, who did not share my pleasure in the medieval aspect of life, felt this even more than I did; they succumbed, one after the other, and so did I, and we were hardly ever all well together. With memories of my last expedition vividly before me, I flew to Aden when sickness began and recovered there and flew back, stepping through the centuries as Alice did through the mirror, from one world to another. The winter passed like a Balzac novel, its events unrolling slowly in an atmosphere of dramatic squalor far more intense than their apparent smallness seemed to warrant. Tribal wars surrounded us: archaeology went on its way unearthing inscriptions and pots and a complete temple, the second to be dug in South Arabia.[1] And when the spring had come, on March 4th, 1938, when the

---

[1] Carl Rathjens and Von Wissmann dug up the first in Yemen in 1928.

temperature was already 82 in the morning and 98.6 at noon, I set out for my last solitary exploration in South Arabia.

It always surprises me to notice how short a time is taken by events that have been so slow in coming. In war, in love, in history, in art, and in everybody's life, the long preparation, conscious or unconscious, rushes to its climax and is gone.

> The lyf so short, the craft so long to lerne,
> Th' assay so sharp, so hard the conquerynge,
> The dredful joye alway that slit so yerne,
> Al this mene I be Love . . .

or by any other endeavour on which the heart is set. The cleverness of living is to distribute climaxes—to savour them beforehand and to remember them after in such a way that the labour of their making is lightened and the memory of their passing is without regret; for one might as well take to drink as seek for climaxes all the time. Perhaps one of the advantages of my habitual see-saw between illnesses and activity was the learning of this lesson—the saving up through long periods for some treasured enterprise, which came and went like lightning, but illuminated the past and future as it flashed by. This rarely happens with things that have cost nothing to prepare. Now that I am known to be a traveller I sometimes receive letters from unknown people who seem to think that I would like to take them exploring: they usually give me no reason to suppose that they have prepared themselves in any way, except that sometimes they tell me they can ride. I have never been on an expedition that has required less than one, or often two years of drudgery, in the learning of language, history, and such things; and I now know that this drudgery is a great part of the journey's happiness, and that to labour with anticipation is one of the secrets of enjoyment.

I closed my stay in the Hadhramaut with one of these rare climaxes, a month's camel riding to the coast through the tribal borderlands of the west, by the little sultanate of 'Azzan, down the great Wadi Meifa'a, to Bal Haf and Bir Ali on the sea. This country was as lawless as Luristan, and the beduin of 'Azzan were much more exhausting than the taciturn Lurs; but in these empty lands even diplomacy and peril are washed through with great hours of clear space and silence, and the pattern is one of solitude with all its interlacings of human difficulty. The waterless road, the little fortress groups built with flat desert stones, the chaos of wild ravines uncontrolled by the hand of man and left to the impetuousness of geology; the tribesmen, painted blue, with kilted skirts and Greek filleted heads and dancing steps, so much more like the ballet than ordinary life; the stillness of their sacred walled hill which they surround with danger; the great caravan along an ancient prosperous way desolated by war; and the bales of the Indian merchants on the sand: all this was as a flower on the branch of the years, the studies of Arabic and the learning of maps, transformed and justified by the brief blossom at their end.

Perhaps the secret of a happy life—and mine is hitherto a happy one—is the feeling of an aim in one's journey, so that one may take pleasure in the milestones as they pass. And this of course is the triumph of religion, placing its goal safely beyond the frontier of death. But in a more temporary way, it is also necessary to travel with some object in sight for the end of every day, so that the routine is routine no longer and the dull straight stretch of the stalk ascending can solace itself with the thought of its flower to come. This is a happiness which I have always had, as far as I can remember: when I climbed, I thought of all the mountains in the world before me: and when I embroidered I looked at the collected patterns in books and museums, until life seemed too short; and the dullest exercise on the way of these objectives has been a labour of love. The fact is that every happiness must be paid its price, but it is often forgotten that the paying of the price is the greatest part of the happiness and essential to its enjoyment when it comes.

I reached Aden on the 27th of March, coasting in a dhow for two days westward from Bal Haf. When I landed, I looked at once for a hotel and bath, thinking to make myself more civilized before telephoning to friends. But when, for the first time after months, I saw a long mirror, it reflected me a bright unnatural pink all over: I telephoned the doctor, who took me into hospital to nurse the departing effects of dengue fever, which I had suffered without knowing, attributing a strange fatigue to the long hours on a camel's back. Delighted for once to have got away with an illness so easily, I rested in the familiar hospital, and sailed on the 5th of April for Egypt.

I stayed in Cairo with Mrs. Devonshire, a charming accomplished Frenchwoman, to whom I was devoted. As a young widow, with two daughters, and poor, she had settled in Egypt, and by her work and studies in Islamic history had made enough to live pleasantly and bring up her girls. She took visitors and showed them the old mosques and out-of-the-way corners of the city, and during the war, half crippled with rheumatism, would still do this twice a week for parties of soldiers, driving at the head of a fleet of ramshackle Egyptian gharries. She would step out with gloved hands and an ebony cane, her walk stiff, her hat a little unlike anyone else's, evoking an atmosphere of distinction and femininity, not visible any longer, but real, like a pressed rose. She once told me with simplicity that "if a woman has been beautiful, she acquires the habit of expecting to be attended to"; and now, beautiful no longer but very fine, she carried that subtle essence which would make even a barbarian recognize a lady.

Leaving her, and the kind Davies in Alexandria, I flew, towards the end of April, to Athens. My book had done well, and I was able at last to give my mother a holiday in Greece. The years of peace were running out, and every little set of happy days was now visibly fragile, precious and personal as his treasure to a connoisseur, and astonishing, like a miniature saved from a flood. I flew in sunrise over the Aegean, the colour of metal, dinted, and scattered with Cyclades, with a pet lizard with me, rescued from the beduin of 'Azzan. I had meant to let it go before leaving Aden, but my illness prevented this and it now lived—still uncommunicative but no longer panic-stricken—in a warm little corner under my jacket, whence I pulled it out to look at the world below while the steward made suggestions for its breakfast. I had now had it for over a month and still, as far as I could see, it had not eaten: it contemplated, getting slimmer and slimmer but bright, with an inscrutable look in its little triangular eyes. I called it Himyar, from the tribe where it was found, and spent any odd hour I had sitting with it on my knees to make it friendly; and finally, before reaching Asolo, I induced it to nibble lettuce from my hand; it then gave me a delightful feeling, as of a barrier broken in the exclusive world of man. At present we were still strangers and the sympathetic steward, who obviously preferred animals to other passengers, advised me to hide it from the customs because "they mightn't understand".

In the middle of the morning, in the incomparable Athenian light, I landed again in Europe.

*   *   *

CAIRO, 5 October, 1937.

Dearest B,

It was such a relief to get away from Benghazi, where the atmosphere was quite too oppressive for words. It lies in a God-forsaken desert and we flew for hours over little naked brown hillocks and empty barren stream-beds and over the frontier where a barbed fence and a little obelisk talking about sanctions testify to the love of peace. We flew over completely red lakes, red as wine. When one comes to the irrigated Egyptian lands it seems like the Garden of Eden—a wealthy incredible expanse of green: the thought of how nice it would be to own it must come inevitably to anyone who flies over—and everyone flies over on their way to the Red Sea coasts farther south.

Feeling here very friendly, and the poor beginning to wish us back more definitely.

[173]

MARIUT, near ALEXANDRIA, 10 *October,* 1937.

A charming Mr. Davies of the Sudan Service who sat next me at lunch agreed that Pontius Pilate was a first-rate government official and told me that during his own service various Christs had appeared thirteen times and most often had ended by being hung! Anyone who makes remarks like that at lunch is a treasure.

I am worried about your finances. Will you be able to lay your hands on any in case of need? I could send, but there may be difficulty in getting letters to you and I think you had better arrange this in time and let me know.

12 *October,* 1937.

My dear Jock,

You do neglect me in the most disgraceful way! I saw and seized on a JM envelope, and only found a miserable letter from an idiotic female who wants to come with us because she can ride "any sort of quadruped".

We are in the familiar detective-story atmosphere of the Near East. A little spy wandering about by the gate whenever anyone comes to lunch—and rumours and counter rumours from the barbed wire of the frontier. I have never really doubted for the last few years that Italy means war, and feel more and more convinced. I expect if Mr. S. [Mussolini] has to lose, he will prefer to do so in a good blaze rather than in a quiet way all on his own.

Whiffey is as delightful as ever and full of good stories of Egypt under Kitchener. His mosque has been dedicated but is not finished, but getting on and he is having great fun with it. He has found some old Græco-Roman foot stamped into a stone and it is up at the gate of the mosque in the wall and in process of being turned into a relic—we incline to Moses, but keep an open mind. The mosque is dedicated to the memory of a good old tribal Sheikh here—Whiffey knew and liked him: he used to sit in his diwan and if a very poor man came in asking for help, would look round, pick out a rich Beduin, and say "Give him five pounds". The man would hesitate, but took them out and put them on the floor and the old Sheikh would brush them towards the poor man. Whiffey sometimes protested in private, but the Sheikh always had his answer. "Don't you do it with taxes?" he said. "*I* am the government here, and I do the same." He fell on bad times, and the British, whom he helped

[174]

a good deal, collected £25 for him: as he went out a poor man came up and asked help: he gave £5 straight away. The Englishman said: "You can't do this. You are as poor as anything yourself"—and the old man said: "That is just why I give—because I know what it feels like!" Kitchener picked him up one day as he walked along under his umbrella and drove him to the Government House where he had some business, and the next day saw him on the kerb asking again to be given a lift, and got annoyed: but the old Sheikh said: "Don't be angry. Yesterday when I was seen with you, three people came out as I walked up the stairs and pressed five pound notes in my hand asking for my good word with you—and it seems so easy that you might just as well take me again."

I must stop this—I am sitting in the shade of a little kiosque and there are white pigeons on the roofs around against a blue blue sky—and a noise of wind rushing about in the sunlight.

Do write soon, you *horrid* Jock.

13 *October*, 1937.

Dearest B,

I woke up this morning feeling pleasantly well, and realized that this was the first time I had had that ineffable sensation since my operation last April! I hope it may continue. How easy life is for the really robust. It makes the world into a different place, people are all pleased with one so easily, nothing seems hard. I wish I were one of those to whom it is a surprise to be ill and not the other way around.

The desert is full of little scrubby plants that look purply like heather, but it is only their little red fleshy leaves.

18 *October*, 1937.

Dear Jock,

We are very excited to-day to see at least a sign of life, patrols and lorries along this desert edge. Every prospect of a fine good battle quite close as soon as the fireworks start, and I am awfully sorry to think of missing it. Whiffey is great at strategy and has been showing me exactly where it will be.[1]

The people in Alex, meanwhile, are rather nervous, as they think they may be wiped out while the British lion is getting out of bed—

[1] Alamein eventually was thirty miles away.

[175]

but I can't think we are quite such fools, and we have had *heaps* of warning. In Cairo I met General Cornwall, who is head of the Military Mission here and seemed to me very much on the spot. I think I would stay here if one could in the least tell when it will start, but it may be delayed a good deal. I am convinced it will come: the news from Abyssinia seems to get worse (from the Fascist side) and I feel sure they will prefer to say they lost it in a general war rather than quietly on their own as would happen otherwise. One does feel *revolted* by them out here. Their Cyrenaica colony is simply *depopulated* of natives, because they thought they would settle the land themselves: so those people not exterminated fled over here: now they (the Fascists) find they can't live and work in that desert and are bribing them back, but only to work like serfs on their own land. During the Sanctions trouble, a Captain Kenneth who was Intelligence here was taking photos on our own side when two of the other side whom he knew invited him in to coffee in their little hut: he went unsuspecting (which I must say speaks badly for his knowledge of them) and they asked him for a photo of their room: while his hands were busy, they covered him with their rifles and took him prisoner. He got at our Consul and a message came through from General Balbo to free him.

Last night I got my typhoid injection in Alex, and am rather depressed to-day—also worried because my blood-pressure refuses to go beyond 95—and that is absurd: I can't think what to do about it nor can anyone else. I think of turning Christian Science. One takes to God as a last resort, though it is not the right way round.

A few nights ago, in lovely moonlight with white clouds scattered here and there, we heard high sweet voices in the sky as we sat outside at dinner. Those were the cranes flying south. One could not see them, but just heard those voices calling to each other in the moonlight spaces, flying over the desert. A lovely world.

ALEXANDRIA, 24 *October*, 1937.

My nice little nurse came in here just now and I asked if what we look out on, beyond the houses, is the harbour. "No," she says: "it is the salt lake. It would be nicer if it were the harbour, and so I often pretend it is." What a *sensible* thing to do!

Another nice thing happened last night when the Greek (?)

A SŪQ IN THE HADHRAMAUT

AL KĀF SAYYIDS: TARIM

SONS OF SAYYIDS: HURAIDHA

photographer with the Yankee accent brought my poor little Compass camera to my bedside, already smashed by falling but now mended, and asked me to let him know if he could do anything for me as I must feel very alone in Alexandria. This from a perfect stranger—the world is not so unkind!

25 October, 1937.

Dearest Herbert,

This letter is to send my news to Asolo before leaving. I go on Wednesday morning to Suez and meet my two ladies there. Meanwhile I am spending these five days rather tiresomely in hospital with a *tummy*. One always gets a tummy, so it is as well to have it over and done with: I only hope this will cover the Aden variety as well! In any case I have now found the ideal thing to do when anything goes wrong—go *straight to hospital*: one gets it put right and one is able to keep quiet without any devastating effort of one's own to do so and all the thinking is done by someone else.

Mr. Davies came to-day, with a huge bunch of dahlias and sat talking poetry: he used to spend his long camel riding days learning by heart to fill in the time. What nice things one comes upon in unexpected people! I think one is liked in just the measure in which one can elicit from people their secret loves, the things they rarely speak of. Our discovery of poetry came through Maurice Baring's book of quotations; it has a blank page under each one which one is to fill in oneself, and I am being tantalized by all the half-remembered lines I would like to quote.

P. & O. NARKUNDA, 28 *October*, 1937.

Dearest B,

You can't think how glad and surprised I am to find myself safe on this large boat. *Everything* went wrong with the start. G. and E. had booked from Suez the first time and never mentioned that this time they were getting on at Port Said. The doctor said a day's extra quiet and diet would be all to the good; the distance from Aden to either place is the same, I thought I might just as well get on at Suez a day later: to make *extra* sure I wired the agency to ask if the train was sure to be in time. The answer never came till the last train from Alex to Port Said had left, and then it said the *Narkunda* does not stop at Suez! This was an awful dilemma. The matter was made worse by the hospital sister who told me that there was a night train at 7, so I lost three precious hours before discovering that the young man in the office who looked it up had omitted to see *where the train went to*; he saw that one started, and troubled no further. It was now six, and I had to be in Port Said (about 300 km. away) at 8 next morning. There *was* a train to Cairo, and I took that, hoping that G. and E. had some special arrangement to get on at Suez with the pilot's boat and I might find them in Cairo. So the kind De Cossons gave me dinner, and put me in the train with Nahas Pasha the Prime Minister who was driving through crowds cheering at every station, packed and shouting. Cairo at 10.30 was a seething mass, with banners and all. I and my little porter were seized by an enterprising shifty-looking sort of tough and smuggled out by a back way, through empty trains, by an unwilling little sentry trying to guard offices with a gun whom we just pushed aside like a fly, till we came through a padlocked gate with a chain thoughtfully left wide enough to let us and baggage through one by one. The tough got into a taxi with me and we reached the hotel all wrapped in sleep with a one-eyed porter on his bed in the hall; the two ladies had left for Port Said that afternoon. I was still 230 km. from the destination and it was now 10.45.

The tough said he would find me a brand-new car, he knew the road, he would come too—in half an hour he was back with a Hittite-Armenoid-looking driver and a car which seemed all right except that a bug was running about the seat. I meanwhile had fortified myself by sucking raw eggs provided by the porter; got packed in; and we went. I knew that all sorts of troubles threatened, but it seemed the only thing to do. I settled myself down in my seat: I luckily had my thick coat: and I tried to say to myself that there is no need to find anything tiring if one can lie down and sleep—which I did, waking at intervals to see a flat lemon-slice of moon, palm or tamarisk trees, crops and a lonely bad road in a flat land with canals and bridges. We should have gone the longer way by Suez where the road is asphalt, but nobody knew of this, so the tough asked all the policemen whom we passed, standing with their rifles under trees, or in little wayside huts. We met only a lorry or two and perhaps two cars. We made quite good going till somewhere between Zagazig and Ismailia; the tough gave me chocolate which he had had the thoughtfulness to buy, and sat in front and smoked. A

[178]

beautiful calm descended and I slept, and woke to find that we were stationary with our first breakdown. A rubber tube had given: the machine had worn it out by going round and round, said my tough, and they were replacing it with a bit of rope. Anyway, they said, it was no good getting to Ismailia before six, as no one was allowed on the road by night. "That is all right," said I. "I will make the English officer give permission." This was received with much respect. "The Engliz how they love one another." We had a little group round us—and soon started.

Next time we broke down was where the road was up: this had the advantage of providing a wakeful gang of workmen, and rope and wire to tie up the inside of the engine with: but we were sent by a roundabout way through desert so bumpy that it was impossible to lie down. Also it was 2 a.m. and I knew by many familiar signs that the next breakdown was only a matter of minutes. We got providentially over the desert track, where no help would have come along, and found ourselves at the gates of an R.A.F. camp with an immaculate vision of a young airman at the gate, his trousers just pressed, his face just shaved, absolutely breathing security and peace, but most surprised and concerned with me and my story. He put us on the right road and we went beautifully on asphalt for a while till the devil prompted the driver on to the wrong road and in a moment we were deep in sand: the feeble creature lifted his arms in a despondent way and said that "the machine is finished". This was 3.33 a.m. Providence meanwhile sent a horrid sort of effendi lorry driver sailing along the right road about 300 yards away. He was hailed. He seemed quite disinclined to do anything but offer me cigarettes—but eventually conjured about fifteen wild-looking gowned road-menders whose Sheikh came up and shook hands and they pulled the car out on to a decent road again.

We got into Ismailia where we broke down definitely and the tough went off to find another taxi—I tried to spur my effendi on to some effort and told him my "people" were leaving on that P. & O. and would go off to India without me. "Your little children?" he asked. "Yes," I said: "Three of them, all small, and no one to look after them They will be like orphans. Do look for a car please." His heart was touched, but all he did was to say he wished he could offer me tea! Luckily the tough now reappeared with a taxi. The crushed Armenian accepted half the price without a murmur and was left derelict and we got to Port Said, very cold in the open car, at 5.30, found the other two at the hotel and got safely on board. I was so grateful to the tough that I gave him £2—which he really did deserve. I was almost dead with fatigue and just begin to feel like a normal human being to-day.

ADEN, 31 October, 1937.

We woke up to-day to see the coast of Yemen, the Indian Ocean very blue, and were presently sailing into the bay of Aden. As I went into the saloon for passports, Mr. Longrigg brought up a nice-looking enthusiastic young man who had been reading *Baghdad Sketches* (the old one) and welcomed me *most* cordially. His name is Perowne and he is political here, and keen to dig and ready to give all help and encouragement—so pleasant, and he quoted Milton and Tennyson before we got off the boat into the Residency launch, in which he took us regardless of the Oil party he was supposed to be attending to. The launch was full of dignified old Sayyids in white with coloured turbans, and we were speeding through the wide open waters of the bay when another launch, *much* bigger than ours, came also speeding along at a right-angled course obviously ending in our middle rib. For a second or two we watched fascinated till it dawned on all that, far from deflecting its course, the Arab meant to sail straight through us: shouts went up: the thing came on without an attempt at a swerve. Luckily our man, probably from incapacity to think quick, kept also on: it is funny how detached one is in such moments—I wondered which half of the launch would be the easiest to be in when we were cut in two: we watched the sharp bow hit and slide off—at the 99th second both boats had turned a fraction so that we did not hit at a right angle, and the other went sliding away off our rope buffer carrying nothing but our paint with it. The old Sayyids embraced, but all the Arabs recovered in no time and thought it a lovely joke: I said "haste is of the devil" which was greeted as a *bon mot*: only Mr. Perowne looked worried. It would have been rather sad to drown the Wakefield expedition in Aden harbour at the start.

This place is now a large military station with the result that the hotel is full and we had a long time to wait in uncertainty as to rooms. But we sat and had lots of talk and Mr. Ingrams, who is here for some days, stayed to lunch. He has not got Shabwa under him and we shall have to tackle Colonel Lake for that, but he was quite welcoming for his own district of which he is absolute king. It sounds *dreadfully* civilized: and you can address letters from now to P.O. Shibam, via Mukalla, Aden, and they will go from here by A. B.'s [M. Besse] plane: he has a weekly service and all the Hadhramis fly over for week-ends. How glad I am to have seen the country still untouched, two years ago.

This afternoon I went to see Colonel Lake, but he was out—so looked in at the hospital on Captain Hamilton[1] who has just shot himself in his own foot by mistake. He had been out running a small tribal war and had himself carried back to the assembled enemy whom he approached waving his leg and saying: "You needn't bother to shoot: I've done it myself for you"—and they gave him a marvellous reception and killed a sheep instantly. Mr. Perowne has a lovely ruin also waiting for us in a place where they received him with a brass band of eight trumpets which marched before him, only pausing to drink by filling the trumpets at a stream, and then *blowing* to clear them when finished.

GOVERNMENT HOUSE, ADEN, 2 *November,* 1937.

You are a dear Jock to send that lovely long letter to greet me here—also the telegram and the Book: it was very exciting and I must tell you I think the pictures really look *lovely*. On the other hand I thought the writing seemed silly, but I always feel that: one's book is, I take it, like a husband—one just has to get accustomed to it! I was so surprised that you like the poems—I don't think they are good really: one cannot make words do one's will. Like the colours I see here overlooking the bay. They are things ineffable, intranslatable even into thought.

I am being taken as the Head of this Expedition, which is really absurd—and you can't think how unsuitable I am for the job. We haven't got a cook yet! And we have 71 pieces of luggage. And one parcel with all the instruments has gone to Bombay by mistake. And our food has been opened and subtracted on its way from Cairo.

[1] Now Lord Belhaven.

4 November, 1937.

Darling B,

I find I get through much more with far less exertion than my party. The Arab has the charming attitude that anything he does is done as a kindness, so it is no good chivvying him about for it. It is the same with the English. Everyone is *so* kind and laying themselves out to do all they can, but I think it is because I look less efficient than most female travellers; I do notice quite a difference. It is a great mistake to look as if you can do everything yourself if you *want* people to put themselves out for you. For instance G. wanted a cut-and-dried arrangement about the division of antiquities; but I have spoken to Colonel Lake and asked him what he would like, and he says he would like a few things for the museum here, but will leave the deciding and choosing entirely to us. He is such a nice man, very quiet, but with a pleasant sense of fun: his description of his time leading Arab potentates about the Coronation is very funny.

MUKALLA, 8 November, 1937.

It seems more like a dream than real life to be here again. I had forgotten how almost incredible is the beauty of this little town. We drove last evening to the Custom House, the sunset lying on the green sea, the mountains running out in purple ranges, to Ras Burum in the west, the lovely houses white and grey like pearls, and everyone busy with their suppers, buying radishes and fish to carry to the camp outside the walls, or settling round eating booths, when the gun went off for the end of the day's fast. Old Yusuf Sherif came waddling down, very prosperous in the same blue serge you would swear he had on three years ago. Nothing could be done. Ramadhan is spreading a canopy of procrastination over everything.

9 November, 1937.

I have no leisure at all for writing or anything else. The temperature is 87 in the bedrooms, so that one can't help sleeping till tea time, and all the odd times are taken up in being diplomatic with Harold [Ingrams] who shows every sign of becoming fussy. G. says, "Why not do as we like in spite of them all," but that would just dish us for anywhere this year, and also I can't help feeling that it *is* unfair to

[182]

go right against authority when it is reasonably kind to you. But there is no denying that we are a Nuisance only slightly inferior to Oil! Harold looks at us in a pained way: he has a sort of angelic look, like an angel whose temper has been tried rather often—a mop of very light hair and *very* blue eyes. He and Doreen have the whole show here on their hands and all to make out of nothing, and he has succeeded in getting a tribal truce over the whole district for three years. You would think this would make it lovely for travellers, but the truce is such a fragile delicate creation that they are far more afraid to see it damaged in any way than they were before, when it only meant one more little war on their hands.

The motor road, too, only means that one has to pay 200 rupees for one car along it rather than 50 rupees for four donkeys before. Such are the pleasures of civilization! I have refused to pay that, and so now Time is being left to act on the morals of the chauffeurs. It looks as if it would be cheapest to *fly*!

Two rock pigeons with lovely blue necks that catch the light are standing on the ledge opposite my window. They croon and fly in wheeling flights in the morning sun.

Apparently you only find palæolithic flints in gravel. It seems peculiar, as one can think of nothing more dreary for primitive man to choose as a habitation, but there it is: a wide expanse of horrid hard stones, mostly rust coloured or crinkly limestone or black.

We are staying an extra day as E. wants to find a missing beach: she has got two, but as there are three gravel layers, she has just got to produce one more somehow and only to-morrow to do it in, as we *must* get up to Tarim if we want to see anything at all of the main wadi. We have chartered a lorry for 200 rupees to take us and our food and all our belongings to Tarim and Shibam and sleep on the road as often as necessary. It is all very expensive and quite extraordinary how much cheaper it is to be unassisted and alone: and we have to allow for lots of blackmail to beduin tribes later on! However that is quite a minor affair.

Road on the JŌL, 14 *November*, 1937.

This road would not be considered worth paying one rupee for in any country except Arabia, but here it is unique and goes up by long clever turns into the broken country that leads to the jōl. It is a much softer approach than Wadi Himem and one can't judge of it as the locomotion was so different. Trails of camels were coming down carrying mostly rushes: they looked lovely in the afternoon light against the skyline. They are so perfectly adapted, the camel and his beduin, to the arid life of the jōl—it is a pity to spoil it by bringing a life which can never really belong—and when one thinks that the beduin has evolved a life that makes him dignified and happy out of *such* conditions, one must have a respect for him.

We have only met one lorry and car travelling together on the road, and they stopped to tell us the news and that someone in Shibam has dug a trench across the road so that cars can't pass.

Now our chauffeur has found us a lovely place in the shadow of qaradh and samr trees and I hope we shall be left for a little rest. Only seen one lizard, a bird or two and a swallow-tail butterfly today, and eight gazelle.

15 *November*, 1937.

It was a very tiring day, from 7.30 to 5.30, with 2½ hours off, one of which was taken by G. who wandered and came back to a frantic lorry with two palæolithic flints and some lichen in her hand. Bakhbukh, the negro, came to me at intervals to beg me to remonstrate with her: but no one was cross when she actually came—just one of the Inevitable Delays of which another is taking place now, with our lorry stuck in the sand in the Tarim plain.

18 *November*, 1937.

Yesterday we went to the ruins where my inscriptions came from last time. It took us three hours to get there, a car and three donkeys, one chauffeur, Qasim, two headmen and three slaves. With all this assistance arranged for us beforehand, all went well and we found the square heaps of untidy and rather unattractive ruins by a little side wadi of their own, with a few nebk trees about which the main water drains down an eroded sandstone bed where E. found tiny and uninteresting-looking shells that the British Museum is panting for. It appears that the ages of the world are chiefly dated by molluscs. She also found two flints embedded, but is not quite sure whether worked by man or nature—and everything depends on that! I am rather worried by this passion for flints as I am sure Lord Wakefield cares nothing for anything so unemotional and what

[184]

he wants is the incense road. I believe however that I could find him the site of the old harbour of Cana if all else fails!

TARIM, 20 *November, 1937.*

We went over the market this morning and collected the familiar train of small boys about us. It was quite a tiny crowd compared to some, but rather a pain to E. and G. and by the time we got through the market all photography was impossible, we moved about with a small shouting screen hemming us in on every side. I got photos of the pottery all laid out in the street: it is fascinating, done in red or whitish *very* rough clay and with brown or cream geometric patterns like bad prehistoric work. I am sure anyone digging it up in a hundred years or so would date it 3000 B.C. We found popcorn in the market; dried shark, millet, biscuits, a few celluloid toys, a glass revolver filled with sweets, most dangerous-looking coloured sweets, various sorts of grains and salt from Shibam—all in open baskets with little round wooden measures to measure out the grains—and a bit of sacking above for shade. In another street was the meat set out in little shreds and pieces on wicker-work trays and the owner fanning off the flies: E. tells me she is not going to eat local meat any longer. Little patches of white goats for sale: little bunches of grass all ready done up to stuff into the mouth of your camel. They are nice to their beasts. When the ox or donkey has reached the end of his walk, either drawing water or ploughing, and is about to turn to begin all over again, he is given a stalk of grass or millet to comfort him. The millet is all out and green in the fields now and looks like Indian corn except for its heavy grey heads, very pretty.

SEIYUN, 22 *November, 1937.*

We left Tarim yesterday morning. The old Sayyid Abd ar-Rahman never came to see us, ostensibly because of Ramadhan but really because I alone was almost more than he could bear and three of us is above the maximum. But as I took a little bag to his wife, he sent along at the last moment a square blue box wrapped in a towel and inside it a brush and comb with imitation gold flowers on an imitation silver ground and with it two little boxes for razor blades and two rings inside them. We tried to pack them up with the

[185]

palæolithic flints and send them to Mukalla, but there was no room, so we have to take them travelling with us—and he will be sent a present in return.

It was awful starting off anyway and makes me feel like a Cook's agent because of the enormous amount of things E. and G. need to have with them. They simply wouldn't go into one car, but a camel man happened providentially to stroll by so I pressed three suitcases and various bundles on him and he arrived here almost as soon as we, all for 3 /-.

We strolled along and took our lunch in the shadow of a big rock rolled down from the jōl wall. On the other side it had tilted up and the shepherds had made a cave by piling stones for their goats to creep under from the sun. There are lots of these little holes about and people appear from them unexpectedly in what looks like an empty landscape.

We stopped at another ruined tower and a mound with palæolithic flints on it but nothing otherwise, and then at a ruined town called Mariama, a dreary place in spite of its pretty name. The mud buildings make dingy ruins, just a *mass* falling down and there was nothing left worth looking at except a few columns in the mosque, filled with hornets that came buzzing out trailing their legs in the air in an aggressive way. I sat by a well in the wadi below and talked to some women and admired the tooth of a rat or some such animal hung round the neck of a small boy to keep away the jinn—it was all he had on except his top-knot, right at the back of his head. Some of them wear two, one in front and one behind, but I can't make out if this is just fancy or with some reason.

My dear Jock,

We took the journey gently and slept two nights on the jōl, and it was still marvellous to lie out and look at these Arabian stars though nothing like doing it with your own beduin in reasonable slowness, and I feel a little like a Cook's Courier trying to please the rest of the expedition which is much more fussy than I am about physical things. They are as nice as can be, but share the British extraordinary idea that you can go about expecting perfect strangers to put themselves out for you and then leave you in complete solitude, and think it rather an idiosyncrasy of mine that one should spend some time sitting about and being pleasant to the people who are taking ever so

[186]

much trouble over us to make things easy in their country. They have been sending us to see ruined sites. I wish you could see what a Hadhrami driver considers to be a way for motors! We did one on two sides of a dry channel with the path down below us between the wheels. The motor road down the Tarim aqaba was great fun: when the little row of boulders that separates the edge of the road from the precipice got in the way, the boulders were just shoved over—so as to let our wheels get round on the very lip of the edge. Four men tugged the wheel round. They were all a little hurt because everyone got out and walked and seemed to think it showed a want of confidence. I did sit in it, merely because I had never been down such a slope in a car before.

I wish you had been with us this morning gathering flints. We came suddenly in the chaos of the rocky valley to three deep pools each a little way above the other, the last just a dark cleft of water between crumpled limestone ledges, and the signs of the camp-fires all about: and went on up still finding flints strewn about in hundreds till one stood near the top of the last shelf under the straight-up cliff of jōl. I didn't go so far but lay in the sun with the cold stone under me to make a reasonable average temperature and thought of all the ages in the valley, just more or less as it is now, as one could see by the weathering of some of the flints that they had hardly changed place in all those thousands of years. There was nothing but a great silence of rocks all round. I went down to the middle pool, and there were reeds at the edge and a fluffy-headed tall grass in bushes, and scrubs of wild palms: and I sat on a rock with my feet in the water quite still so that all the frogs came floating slowly to look at me, with just a languid movement of their horrid long back hands now and then and little wide-awake slits in their gold eyes: and the most strange-looking newts were nibbling the weeds with figures just the shape of an egg and a long tail and two legs at the base of the tummy: they were so lazy that even stones didn't matter to them when one splashed them. It was lovely—there was a little wind rustling very dry in the reeds and the water as green as the shadow of palm trees with ripples and the reed-shadows zigzagging in it like lightning—and suddenly on the path above a little wild bedu appeared, just like palæolithic man in person, with a tousle of hair and a black shawl thrown back over his naked shoulder and a wand in his hand, walking up the stones bare-foot with that lovely spring that people have who can walk uphill or

[187]

down with equal ease. I called 'Salaam', and he was like a startled wild creature, stood stock-still and looked at me and began then to move slowly on, keeping his eye on me: then before he vanished he lifted his right hand and arm to salute—and I did mine—and the palæolith vanished. But he had made the whole valley come to life.

25 *November, 1937.*

Darling B,

Yesterday all the Abu Bakr ladies came and sat with us in the evening and I put on my taffeta dress to please them and did my nails and toenails a lovely pink. They were very pleasant and friendly. I suspect H. of being rather a villain.[1] I think he is terrified of my coming to conclusions of my own and announcing them. His clerk comes along and asks us to say exactly everywhere where we are going and yesterday I got rather bored and told him we were not used to having to say everything we meant to do or didn't and who had told him to bother us anyway. Whereupon he collapsed and said it was Sayyid Abu Bakr—anxious to smooth our way: so I said it was very kind and I would be sure to write to the Sayyid if ever we were in need of help. But I think it is H. who has told the poor old Sayyid to keep his eye on us. I then asked why the Sultan had not called. Oh, it is Ramadhan. So I gave a message to say that I hoped he would call next time I came when Ramadhan is over. It seems impossible for us to administer anything without bringing this tiresome atmosphere in. Doreen when she comes up does not mix with the men at all as she has a husband to do that for her: but it is a very tiresome precedent for us, who have to do all the doing there is on our own. After this little tussle I restored harmony with the young clerk by getting him to dictate me an arabic letter to Sheikha Alawiya to whom I sent a prehistoric flint as a present with a short summary of archaeology which she will pass on no doubt to her flock.

SHIBAM, 26 *November, 1937.*

Such a time arriving here yesterday. E. has a bad throat, and looked very unhappy. I was rather exhausted, and also worried by

[1] Harold Ingrams was kindly anxious for our safety as we travelled towards the West, but official solicitude was of course the one thing I was most concerned to discourage.

the signs of disapproval which three women do rather arouse: I got eggs, saw to the water supply, saw to nails to hang up the mosquito net for poor E. who lay with a suffering look on her camp bed which looks as if it means to collapse under her.

This morning we left E. to rest and find a lovely little new shell, steel grey, in the household wall—while G. and I went round the town. It is so lovely. Even the atmosphere of a British Conducted Tour cannot spoil it. I went for the first time into the narrow little by-streets where the houses lean away from each other into a lovely mellow sunlight. I looked last night at the rocks in the moonlight: the cliffs hang over our very head and look as if at any moment they must come crushing down.

ADEN—as from SHIBAM, 18 December, 1937.

My dear Jock,

At last you have sent a nice long letter instead of your horrid little typewritten snippets: I was so glad to get it and hope you will have lots more fog, then London may be so disagreeable that you will be forced to remember your distant friends! Your letter got me in Aden because we have all been down with fevers—I was the last to go (thank goodness) and as G. was still laid up for four days at least I thought I would fly down here for a week and be looked after. And now see the workings of providence (?): the doctor simply refused to let me return on Thursday and has kept me for an extra week, and the aeroplane took the opportunity and went and smashed part of itself while landing. It is up at Tarim, and I have no news of my party, and only hope all may be ready again to take me back on Thursday. The fever has gone by the way.

You needn't believe the Italian newspaper when it says that the Hadhramaut is "wading in blood". It is what is happening their side of the water and they like to pretend. But there has been a little trouble, looting of camels and a consequent thought of bombs: not yet decided whether they will be necessary, and I hope not as it has a flustering effect all round. I looked down on the little tiny village plots as I flew over and wondered how they can ever distinguish what to bomb—such *tiny* little places. It was very exciting to fly from Seiyun to Mukalla and see the jōl below—really an *incredible* sight, so tortuous and eaten into in winding filaments of gullies—and all a dusty rusty colour which somehow *feels* like a colour of death—and, looking north beyond the wadi, the jōl goes on and on till one guesses the sands of the Empty Quarter there beyond the north horizon. I was feeling rather ill, as it was in the middle of the fever, and glad to get here into bed and pleased to be commended for prudence once in a while: but now long to be back again, especially as this is just the week we are supposed to be settling in to Huraidha. We have the house fixed, and my nice bedawi Sayyid is there to help, so there should be no difficulty—but one can't help feeling oneself quite unnecessarily indispensable in this world.

Meanwhile I have been enjoying myself reading Anatole France and the philosophy of M. Jerôme Coignard. What a charming creation. "Il méprise les hommes avec tendresse." It is all full of wisdom and human kindness—and does one good to read. What I like about Anatole France is that with all his biting wit he always recognizes and loves real goodness when he sees it and I don't think anyone has more endearing simple good people. I must not wander into philosophy as this letter is to be finished some time.

It seems strange to think of Christmas next week—the sun is dazzling, the sea a gay sort of blue, the hills of Yemen showing like some dream almost melted into daylight beyond the bay of Aden and its sands. All sorts of little boats and launches, tugs and sailing dhows are running about the harbour—I wish I could send you a little parcel of all this life and gaiety to empty out in Albemarle Street for Christmas morning.

HURAIDHA, 5 January, 1938.

Dearest B,

The temple is nearly dug out: another two days should see it through and then G. will search for the next object and hope it may be something more ancient and less gimcrack. So far it is rather disappointing—only one small hideous idol and no little knick-knacks, and the inscriptions all taken from somewhere else haphazard.

I sat out on my roof and went on with my manuscripts, distracted by bevies of women wanting medicines for what they call 'wind', i.e. pains from sitting in their perpetual draughts with no clothes under their gowns. The manuscripts are pleasant to read here: all the raids and battles, talk of the places I know, and the turbulent medieval life rises vivid before one.

[190]

E. and I had a pleasant lunch chatting of gardens in England. She is a dear, always doing the dull things, always to be trusted and ready to enjoy things apart from their relation to herself.

7 January, 1938.

The night before last we had the Mansab[1] and his brother to dinner, very like two portraits out of a Vandyke and very pleasant. I still go to bed at sunset, as it gets chilly, so we spread G.'s fur rug and a table-cloth on the floor beside my bed. G. was laid up with fever, so there were just us four and Qasim and Sayyid Ali squatting on the doorstep to join in at intervals. We had tomato soup, Arab rice and chicken and the poor little white kid, and tinned fruit, and it was all very agreeable though difficult to eat fruit salad with one's fingers. I think E. enjoyed it, and they like her, it is extraordinary how quick they are to catch people's real feelings under their various manners. The Mansab says he wishes no one to touch the temple when we leave—it is to remain as a monument and no European except us is ever to come to dig here. As a matter of fact the temple stone is so rotten, it will melt away almost without being trodden on.

Yesterday E. went alone and found part of the older building in the north wall. So now there are three periods, none yet dated but all probably late-ish.

I am getting hold of a copyist as there are various exciting manu-scripts here and I can't deal with all myself. I have nearly finished one and it is full of useful information—for instance it gives the date when the old Himyaritic ruin we went to see east of Tarim was renovated by the Arabs and finally ruined. The oil people down there have found inscriptions too and kindly sent us word. I think it will be a useful winter's work though not as sensational as if we could have done Behan.

8 January, 1938.

The days pass here and we seem completely cut off from the world: no news even of Seiyun has reached us this long while—whether Harold and the R.A.F. are there, what the oil people are doing—nothing, whether Hallett and his little plane are dead or alive!

---

[1] The religious head in a district.

[191]

9 *January,* 1938.

Dear Jock,

I am a poor thing and I have been lying in bed and thinking that I must give up exploring and Settle Down for ever and ever: I don't think I really mind—it really is *how* and not *what* one sees that matters: but I would just have liked to have done one more journey without fifty thousand microbes struggling inside me.

The dig is going very well and there is enough here to provide for a whole season and more. The temple turns out to have three separate periods, all late unfortunately, and singularly unprovided with pots and pans or idols. But there is lots more all scattered round.

Yesterday I was telling Ali Bedawi how Mr. Eden went to visit Mussolini. "Did he eat in his house?" he asked, very surprised, and when I said yes: "And wasn't he afraid of being poisoned?"

I have found what I hope is an unknown and useful manuscript of local history and am copying it out. It has a nice miracle recorded. Someone made fun of a holy man at his prayers: the holy man, without turning round or interrupting his devotions for one instant, turned the scoffer's face into the face of a pig.

10 *January,* 1938.

Darling B,

Our peaceful valley is to go up in smoke. I told you that my woolly old Bedu gave me an inkling by dictating in his letter that the Government was going to go. Well, it's gone! The Qu'aiti governor, who has no pay and no soldiers to help him out, fled here for refuge from the inner recesses of Wadi Amd and the Bedu are busy pouring paraffin over the roots of each other's palm trees—all because of a man who was killed in his sleep the other day, and possibly a bit of stirring from outside.

The Mansab is going to Seiyun to-morrow and I have given him a letter to Harold and advised him on things in general. I hope Harold too will take my advice or hit upon it on his own, because it is good. I hope too that the conflagration may be limited to the palm tree roots as it would be most inconvenient to have it spreading here.

The Mansab came back and sat with me telling me his troubles. He *is* so handsome: his nose quite straight and small and his eyes heavily kohled: a mass of curly longish locks round a completely bald forehead, which is covered however by his little cap, so that he

[192]

LOOKING TOWARDS OUR HOUSE: HURAIDHA

THE ROAD TO THE DIG: HURAIDHA

A SIDE STREET IN THE HADHRAMAUT

CHILDREN PREPARING TO DANCE: HURAIDHA

WORKER ON THE DIG: HURAIDHA   WOMAN OF THE BEDU: HURAIDHA
THE TRIBESMAN'S SON   THE POSTMAN

looks just like a portrait by Raphael, with that rather girlish delicate expression of the Renaissance youth—and those *lovely* hands.

11 *January*, 1938.

A little girl in a magenta gown appeared and drew out of her bosom two dolls for me this morning. They are little marvels of horror, their faces painted "for a festa" with the fashionable green marks and red eyelids and their hair represented by long black rags: they have *tiny* bodies under the big head and look malignantly alive and strangely obscene—I am keeping one.

15 *January*, 1938.

Yesterday I sent off a fat letter to you. I have been spending my morning photographing inscriptions and copying them—they are all very dull dedications to the Moon God.

G. and E, are off to begin a new site and I began the day with one long struggle with Sayyid Ali over the men's food. He has been cutting down their food and I thought we could make an easy change by installing our nice big black bearded Slave Abd al Izzaq while the other one was away. However the Mansab carried off Abd al Izzaq in spite of a wail of protest: he said he would leave him, but he didn't. He is such a nice slave, always ready to do the heavy and disagreeable work and always amiable and he fetched us our water in petrol tins in the morning. Now I have had to give Sayyid Ali back the food contract, with a serious talking to, as there is no one else suitable to take it on. He tells me he will work only for his good name (an object which would be all the better for a little attention)—and money may go.

I have come to the conclusion that it is more flattering to be a 'man's woman' than a 'woman's woman': a man's woman has to be unselfish and agreeable at any rate in conversation—with a mind broader than her shop, as men have the supreme merit of not always wanting to talk shop. I think I should like women just as much if they made the same effort to be agreeable that men do: in fact I know it, because I *do* like the worldly sort of women who are agreeable to their own sex: it is this idea that if you are busy you need not be polite which seems to me so depressing.

The people are peculiar here. The Mansab is really fond of us

o   [193]

and ready to do anything, but has not hesitated to take away our slave and leave no one to feed us with water except the wife, who pinches her tummy and says "all the meat is melting from her" with the strain.

A rather nice remark about the Wadi Amd when it was in turmoil last week—"it is enjoying European peace," they said.

17 January, 1938.

There are numbers of caves, one above the other on the slope under a flap as it were of sloping limestone: and others to East and West—and to-morrow the tent is to be moved there and a new site begun on the edge of the scree. All that side of the wadi, in the flat ground, must have been gardens: the bedu find old palm roots still, buried in the sand, and an old watercourse runs E. and W., marked only by the sandy ribbon between two lines of stones.

Sayyid Ali seized the chance of my being about with a camera to appear in a gold 'ighal and flowing white keffiah and mounted himself on a Ja'da camel and was very pleased when I told him he looked like Lawrence.

To-day I was asked for a charm for a bullet to shoot ibex with!

That wretched girl who killed her father has been tortured with hot irons on her sides and through her nose and is now on her way to Seiyun. They did not bring her into the town here but kept her in private with relations. The Ja'da are all very self-conscious about it; they came in numbers to the old dig as I sat there and I explained archaeology to them in a highly unscientific manner and discussed the Himyar descent from Qahtan, and showed them the Himyar alphabet. It is very lucky that old Mubarak in whose land the new digs are, is a feudal dependant of our little Ja'far and his family, who struts about among them with a Lord of the Manor air very amusing to see, and told me when first we came that *his* people would be all right!

P.S. The day's finds have been brought in, all the diggers so excited they rushed in with them to show me on my roof. There was a sort of communal grave with about six skulls and the pottery *very* rough, very like what they make to-day—a pathetic little pot with the word MĀT—"he died" in Himyaritic letters. I suggested a sheep for the people to-morrow—*two* sheep: it *is* to-morrow and they have been given 10 dollars to buy them.

[194]

18 January, 1938.

I had a pleasant morning to-day escorted by five or six children collecting plants. They were very useful picking and telling me names, and we went across the little plain which stretches south of us, across to the palm gardens, where I hoped to find flowers. There wasn't one, but quite a number among the outside stones and sand, thorny little scrubs that put out poor delicate blossoms that wither away like love on a cold heart. It is very difficult to press them, the thorns being so strong and thick and the flowers so frail and thin. We chatted to the women who take their goats about there to pasture, and I got a cinema I hope and some lovely groups of women with their *misericordia* headdresses and the pointed hat above, sitting on the mud dykes in the shadow of palms. It was very pleasant there, quiet and not dusty and a few birds about, until we suddenly heard the sound of the bombs from the Se'ar country "drifting slow with sullen roar" and very impressive in that clear sky over the cliffs of the empty jōl in the sunlight.

The women told me that it is no use for them to fast when their menstruation comes in Ramadhan, so they have to take the same number of days and fast afterwards. The Beduin wife yesterday could not stay to lunch because she was doing her fast.

I have just found that Wadi Kasr is mentioned in the Himyaritic glossary by the same name, and also the (waterless) pond which gives its name to our dig—I mean only the generic name of "pond".

The result of yesterday's finds has been a fluttering like vultures over the battlefield of beduin of that district thinking of bakshish, and I have spent much energy putting their frame of mind right again. I have promised a present when we leave, but refuse to pay for finds as it would mean endless trouble once this idea of money has shown itself in tangible form.

I was amused at pay-time to-day at one man who was told there was no work for him next week (merely because the site is smaller): all he said was "So much the better"—such a nice philosophical way of taking it.

21 January, 1938.

It is delicious here now, neither hot nor cold—about 70-86° F. and a feeling of spring. We leave about February 15th and get to Aden a month after, so write to Aden now and tell me plans.

[195]

I have little news these days as I have not been seeing many people because of my voice: there was only one urgent affair, a meeting of the Ja'da tribesmen one evening to decide on blackmailing us for digging on their land. The dear man, the Mansab's brother, went out and dealt with them and kept it hidden from me, as he didn't want me to be worried. I can't tell you how really nice he is. The tribes have been beautifully quiet so far, partly owing to the little we have found, but also to the care with which I have doctored and talked to so many. It is a work of art to talk so as to convince: I can *see* the image I wish to create growing in the mind of the patient; I build it up with all the images he knows and make *him* reach the conclusion I wish. I think this is Science, just as much as anything else—the result of infinite experience and observation: the only difference is that the data are intangible, but they are none the less real—and that *is* the difference between Science and Art—the data of the latter being intangible I mean.

The grave being dug out now continues to produce. Yesterday an inscribed pot—and we hope that something very important may lie in its inner depths. Certainly no intact grave has yet been dug out in South Arabia. E. kindly comes and tells me all the progress in the evening.

27 January, 1938.

A plane has just flown over, low down, twinkling like a silver fish above the palm tops and gone off to land on the landing ground, so I am *rushing* this to get it ready to send.

Seeing my cold hanging on, and as there is a possibility now with the R.A.F. in Seiyun, I asked Harold to get the doctor over from Aden for a day: I know he wanted to come and it will not be very expensive. Poor Harold came rushing over from his bombing expeditions to see for himself, landed here for half an hour and bursting in with all the local notables behind him, kissed me—which must be making them wonder whether I am his second wife or a colleague in the Government. But it was so nice to be kissed by anyone after the repressive female atmosphere. I hope you will kiss me a lot when I get back.

Well, I am really much better, temperature and heart normal, and need nothing but quiet to recover, but I still thought it better to have the doctor while there is the chance, and also the Mansab's mother has a dreadful foot so it would be a double good, and so I let him carry on the arrangement and probably the doctor is on his way now on a donkey from the landing ground.

I meanwhile have been doing nothing except read Jane Austen. I have stopped seeing people for a week, as it hurts the voice to talk much, but had one visit from the Ba Surra of Do'an, very affectionate and inviting me for ten days or a fortnight. They are all so really fond of me now I think. The dig goes on as well as it possibly can. E. has nearly done her map, and pots and skulls continue to pour out of the grave which is scooped away in the mountain-side.

It does make an incredible difference to have the R.A.F. near and be able to get into touch with the comforts of civilization! I only hope they will bring some letters—I have had none since yours at Christmas. No time for more, but will add a line when they have been. Don't worry over me, as I am just as well as if I were at home: only vexed that this bad cold should prevent my going about. But I shall take things as easily as even you could desire.

The watch mended by the old man from Mecca actually goes!

31 January, 1938.

The Mansab has just been. He came in looking so handsome in a sort of brown checked greatcoat of the time of Lord Byron with a yellow cashmere shawl and red border thrown over one shoulder, his amber beads with red tassel in his hand, and a white turban, and he came up to me in my bed and—kissed me on the forehead! I think he is very grateful for all the good advice I gave him which has had the happiest results—and he will do anything for us now. He quoted a verse of Mutanabbi to me to the effect that my "heart and brain are stronger than the body" which is true enough even if they are not very strong. We then had one of our 27 skulls down which G. has varnished with shellac, and I explained the mysteries of anthropology. I was *so* pleased to see the Mansab again. And his mother's foot is improving with my doctoring, which is a comfort as it was a horrid mess and I didn't feel very confident. Did I tell you that an old Sherifa asked the Mansab if it would be allowable to pray for us—as thanks to us she had been able to eat meat for the first time for a year?

Doreen is ill in Mukalla. I *never* knew a country like this for

[197]

illness. And the Hopkins hope to be up here for the feast—in a week or so. That will be very nice and I hope to be out by then even if only for tiny distances.

I have read the whole of Jane Austen and think of beginning over again. What a perfect woman—not only a writer—and what a *sham* she makes all this female emancipation seem! Nothing that is not genuine can stand this primitive severity. But Jane would have been quite at home and talked tea-table gossip with the ladies of Huraidha.

2 February, 1938.

Sayyid Ali is rather depressed. I think they snub him no end out at the dig. He tells me he spends about half his weekly wage in presents here and there "but it is good for his name"; I think it may be true too: he never has a penny in hand. Qasim too is hard up and wants his present now for the feast rather than later in Aden. I talked to him like a mother about wasting money on women, and he got very blushing and apologetic but I do not flatter myself to be more listened to than any other middle-aged spinster advising the young.

Two women came this morning for medicine and told me that one of my patients has died since taking my prescription—I rather wonder it doesn't happen more often! The women are *ever* so much more tiring than the men: they go over and over again and keep wandering off the point. E. says it is inherited: but after all one doesn't inherit only from one's mother.

E. has just brought me her map to look at. It really is a great work—about ten square miles and all the Himyaritic irrigation works gradually emerging: I think it will be really a useful work. It is beautifully done and I would have given much to have been well enough to go about with her and learn a lot. She is always such a dear in explaining things and takes trouble to make one have a share in them.

5 February, 1938.

A youth came yesterday to complain that he was given a boy's wage and he was a man. I explained that only a boy was wanted, so that if he couldn't oblige "and be a bud again" he must go away altogether: so he said "it is all one" in perfect happiness and goes on

[198]

being a boy. I do like these people for being always good-tempered about everything: it is an *inestimable* virtue, and makes all the difference to the pleasantness of life.

6 February, 1938.

Qasim was made happy yesterday by the present of a blue and green checked futah skirt and a white and yellow shawl. He came in trying the skirt at ankle-length and turning himself round in it like a débutante, and then folded it on the table, stroking it at intervals and saying "Al-hamdu lillah" as he had been in great fear that Huraidha might not produce what was wanted. It would be dreadful not to have a new dress for the feast.

While he was there two Ja'da bedu came for medicine for earache. They had been in Java and looked very Mongolian with high cheek-bones and their little tufts of beards, and yellowish under the brown. The patient very often has a friend who does the explaining for him, or else annotates it like a Greek chorus. This one volunteered that the illness came from some woman in Java who had written the charm on a bit of paper for drinking: I forgot to ask whether the Sorceress or the victim has to drink it. "Perhaps," I said, "he treated a woman badly there?" "By Allah, no!" The friend was delighted with the imputation, but the victim very righteous about it. I asked if the local saint could do nothing and was told he was no good—but the Frangi medicines were very useful against that sort of thing.

I have been out again, just down the town so to say. All the houses round us are falling to bits, crumbling into shapeless heaps of mud. I think like all these towns Huraidha is creeping downhill into the Wadi with the coming of greater security. Little Salim met me. He hasn't been near me: he is a proud, sensitive little creature and probably Qasim spoke roughly to him. One need only give him the slightest hint, and he is off, unlike the others. I gave them all little presents for the feast and there is great rejoicing, but it is rather like attracting locusts to give to a few!

I am sending those lovely gold and leather slippers to the Mansab and his brother—I think they will like them. To Sayyid Alawi I gave a little travelling-case for shaving and he was *very* pleased. He is going back by Du'an after the feast, as the motor road seems to be very unreliable: I hope it will settle by the time we go. He went on pilgrimage to an ancient tomb near here (about two hours off) where an unknown saint is buried, he and his sword and his servant. No one knows where they came from. But he died, and the earth opened, and "he buried himself". It might be an old place, and worth looking at.

The Mansab's son of Meshed came yesterday and brought a sack of depressing Himyaritic fragments which we refused to buy so as not to encourage the ruining of the site. But among them was some Himyaritic incense! We put it on the little incense burner and it smelt just as good as new—after about 1,800 years at least!

7 *February*, 1938.

The feast begins to-morrow—there is a pleasant sort of little fever about Huraidha and nothing else is talked of. Everyone one knows comes either to ask for bakshish or to try and sell some possession so as to have a little in hand for the celebrations. We are going to join in the gaiety by having fireworks on my terrace and the children are coming to-morrow to light them.

They have told me the little song they sing to-morrow morning to celebrate the feast, and began to tell me about the stone which is hung between heaven and earth and will open at the last day to let out fire to burn the wicked in Hell.

Sayyid Alawi came again this evening and we talked of books and it came out that a 10th century inscription was found in the old mosque here when they pulled it down last year. I have sent Ali to get hold of it by hook or by crook. Alawi and he say they were responsible for the new mosque: 10,000 dollars had been left to build it by a pious merchant, but the money was being 'eaten' and no mosque built: till Alawi propaganded among the members of the Young Men's Club, and, to persuade them of the dangers of the old mosque, used to go at night with Sayyid Ali and dig picks into the soft mud walls so as to make it more obviously ruinous: and so at last it was pulled down and the Cufic inscription found. The habit of having their mosques completely filled with pillars is not unusual here: I went into another one, and it has four rows of four huge pillars filling it at regular intervals all through.

The Mansab's sister says she is going to make you a dress to send you as a present!

THE QADHI (CENTRE) AND SAYYIDS OF HURAIDHA

SHEPHERDESSES: HURAIDHA

WOMEN AT THE WELL: HURAIDHA

RIDING FROM HURAIDHA

CULTIVATION IN 'AMD

It is so lovely to have been out again. I was away for an hour and not a bit too tired. I hope it was not too unsanitary—a horrid smell of corpses in the tombs—but E. thinks the dead are probably much less risky than the living.

G. is down with a cough now—I am keeping away from her. I have actually taught the little village boys not to come and cough in my face.

11 *February*, 1938.

My dear Jock,

Some day some learned man will ransack the garrets of the Hadhramaut for valuable manuscripts and will find a number of letters from 50 Albemarle Street—but that will be no consolation to me. I got your Christmas one and it was so pleasant, and felt so nice and cold too—now I must hasten all I can into ten minutes as a runner is being sent off to the coast by Mr. Wofford who is here looking for oil, and so I am trying to take this last chance for getting letters out of the country. We shall be descending ourselves in three weeks in all likelihood. Miss G. C. T. is ill now: she says it is horrid to suffocate and not breathe at night, and I can feel for her as I had been doing that for many nights on end: all I feel now however in the way of uncharitableness is that I had rather one of the others were ill than me. I think they are both getting a complex about the climate of Arabia—and who can wonder? There is a special germ here which will make the reputation of anyone who finds exactly what it is.

Such *lovely* sights I have been seeing. The feast is in full swing and yesterday we went to photograph the procession, the tridents of the banners in a blue blue sky, the crumbling walls of the houses scattered up the cliff side that rises like a prow above them; the procession with the Mansab in green cloak and gold buttons, green turban, amber beads and hennaed feet, and the Elders around him and the incense burner in front, and his banners and people behind him and the women shrilling their tongues from the housetops. At intervals they stop and hold out their palms and pray.

All the children of Huraidha are ready to do anything for us except keep away, so we had helpers to carry our stools and cameras and find places, and I hope I have the most remarkable collection of pictures you have ever seen, and anyway being a tactful person you will say so. The procession went to the old mosque on the hill and

[201]

then down to the cemetery where they visited the great grandfather Sayyid who is a Saint, and then all wandered on private visits to their own family graves—and came back and scattered at the Mansab's door. But who can give that light and gaiety and *genuineness* not of a pageant but something born and grown with them—and all mixed in with the shabbiness of their poverty and the barrenness of their surrounding land, so that it is not a *Show*, but just Life.

I am better and able to get about a very little and hardly dare to hope to be well enough to go back by Wadi Amd to the sea—but if I can I will. I should be so glad too to have a last little bit of Arabia to myself, away from complaints about laundry and such irrelevancies.

12 *February,* 1938.

Darling B,

Yesterday was still a feast day, devoted to visiting. The Zina day is for Sayyid ladies to visit each other, yesterday was for the servants, and to-day for beduin. I spent the morning across the way with Nur and Sheikha who had the Mansab to lunch with them. He and I sat in a window chatting over glasses of tea and trying the pink nail polish, and he says he wants a photo of him and me together to send to a magazine in Egypt. He then told me something which touched me very much indeed, for he said he was going to have his precious manuscript copied to give me the original. I don't know if this will materialize, but anyway I was quite overcome even by the thought of it, as he has never even *lent* the manuscript to anyone. It seems he gave the poor archaeologist from Egypt the disappointment of his life: he met him in Aden and told him he had the Iklil of Hamdani here in his library, a book anyone would give almost anything to possess—and the poor man came here on purpose just to look at it, and it is not here at all nor is any copy thought to exist here (or anywhere else).

13 *February,* 1938.

My photographic apparatus looks very gay now that I have put the developer into the empty champagne bottle. It will be a judgment if any alcoholic person tries to drink.

I have promised to leave little Salim a bottle of cod liver oil. He is so tiny and feels it so much: perhaps it will make him grow. I shall be sorry to leave all these children.

[202]

It will be so lovely to get letters. Another ten days and the runner from Mukalla will be back.

14 February, 1938.

This has been a most harrowing day, for every poor bedu shepherdess I know and many I don't have come weeping because all their goats are impounded by the Mansab and not to be released except for one dollar per head! This is an ingenious way of getting taxes out of people and combines two objects as the goats have been eating everybody's young palm plantations. Sayyid Ali had his best little baby plants nipped off and perhaps this precipitated drastic action. Anyway he says the people were often warned and nothing happened, and so to-day they seized on all, goats, donkeys, camels, and had collected 120 dollars by the time of the afternoon prayer and about 125 animals whom their owners unable to pay abandoned on a compromise: the proceeds are to be spent on the prosecution of public works such as evening up the streets (which could do with a little evenness here and there). My poor little bedu bride came weeping and said that, as I drank the milk, would I pay for her goats or write to the Mansab: she had nine taken, and I am sure I don't drink off more than two—so I gave her four dollars on condition I could take her photo with the coral tassels which hang from her veil. Then of course all the other beduin came along, begging me to buy their poor little necklaces and bracelets. Altogether a very harrowing affair.

I am amused because Sayyid Ali, our little villain, appeared all pomposo to-day after his festa and brought presents—a water-skin with tassels for me, and for E. a leather girdle used by pregnant women, and for G. a little leather fringe tied round female infants to hide their private parts! It is done in innocence I know but amuses me all the same and E. too, though G. did not share the joke and perhaps thinks it a reflection on her trousers. She is a little better, but I don't believe she will be fit for very much very soon. E. had a great day to-day, for she found palæolithic flints in the gravel of the wadi, which means that one can date a bit of the geography: there were bits of tufa with the flints, so that the tufa and her fossil plants are dated too.

15 February, 1938.

In the afternoon I went to see the Sayyid's *library*: all in two cupboards with carved doors in a big room with carved pillars. We sat on the floor and looked and I picked out five manuscripts, a history of Shihr about A.D. 1600, a history of Yemen about the same, a history of Aden copied from an 11th century author called Ba Makhrama, a religious book about 1500 and another on what looks like fine parchment in *lovely* script about A.D. 1300. I asked to be allowed to read the Shihr history, by Sayyid Ali. Mansab said he couldn't let me do that as it belonged to his orphan nephews and religion forbids one to lend the property of orphans. That is as may be, anyway I saw it would not do to press for the manuscript: but I am going to photograph them to-morrow and am having the titles, dates, and a few specimen pages copied to show to the British Museum. One *might* find a treasure!

I went upstairs in the same house to see the Mansab's mother and found her poor foot just as black and swollen but bleeding red blood and much less yellow pus in it. I do hope she will get over it as, if she dies, as she ought by rights, it will be now attributed to me. She was very cheerful and friendly.

I am become a Patroness of Verse—and it is rather expensive and very strenuous, as one has to listen to so many odes. Sayyid Ali brought me a very nice one all about my virtues and last night the old watchmender Abdulla appeared just as I was going to bed and settled down with his wife and daughter to sing me an ode in my honour. He had written two lines in blue pencil on a little bit of grubby paper the day before and here were four more lines: they said:

"Faraya outstrips in excellence the most intelligent of women:
By her learning and her breeding she is uplifted beyond Ranees.
She comes to all with gladness, and may the clearness of her face never be saddened:
With beauty of thought and manners she conquers men and women——"

So now you know!

All the people who took part in the dancing and poetry of the 'Id come at intervals to pay a visit—which requires a dollar or two from anyone with nice feelings: it is like the Christmas box in England.

AL-BAHR, a rock pool S.E. of HURAIDHA, 17 February, 1938.

We have come up here to look for tufa fossils, Mr. Wofford, back from Wadi Amd and having a day off, and E. We set off on donkeys, and spent an hour in the wadi bed, looking at its dams and sluices, and *samr* and *nebk* and *misht* trees against a gentle background of cliffs in a spring atmosphere, a watch tower here and there among the date gardens—and then we turned up into one of these ravines with the cliff growing higher and higher and the track so blocked with smooth limestone boulders that at last my poor little donkey gave way and folded its knees under it and sat down while I got off in spite of the impediments of many helpers and walked up the rest of the way.

It is so nice to see Wofford again, so strong and easy and enjoying life, and glad to rest with us from the strain of perpetual Arab sociability. I was pleased that he should talk of it, as I am tired of being considered to be merely self-indulgent when I exhaust myself by seeing thirty different people a day: that is not considered Work! But he knows all about it, and tells me that his five years in these lands have counted as ten with him because of this perpetual strain.

The little beduin girl has just offered us dates: she took her hat off and showed the high crown, *stuffed* with them.

A frog has just appeared in the pond. It is *icy* water. The bedu come out shivering. They use their head-clothes as bathing dresses, a very convenient arrangement.

G. is still ill with a small but persistent temperature and is now anxious to get out of this country as soon as she can. At present the road is closed, so we can't!

HURAIDHA, 19 February, 1938.

Yesterday a mail came from Seiyun and *nothing* in it but one letter from Mr. Guest (saying that I *had* got the right date, about A.D. 1300, for my medieval inscription) and a worried little note from Harold—Humumi rebellion still going on, road still cut, troubles spreading—and I expect he wishes us all out of the country, though as a matter of fact we are having a remarkably steadying influence in this western corner.

We were *all* more or less ill yesterday. I got up with a funny heart, so did not go out, but was able to get up and poultice E. at intervals, who had no voice. G. has malaria and now that at last she has taken quinine, the fever has gone. We may have to go by Du'an if this trouble continues. I expect you have been hearing awful things in the Italian papers. I only hope they let my letters go through!

[205]

Great amusement here over Philby's quotation of the Sultan Ali of Seiyun as hostage at Mukalla!

I can't remember whether I told you about my manuscript. I have *bought* it for £7. 10s., whether it is worth anything at all remains a perfect gamble. Sayyid Ali Mansab came along with it tied in a cover made of mattress ticking and begged me not to show it to anyone: in the secrecy of his green cashmere shawl he had four more books, one of them 14th, one 15th century and a History of the Himyarites written over 200 years ago: he has offered to sell but I dare not buy any more, and they won't let me have them to look at first: so all I can do is to have their names and offer them to the Museum by hearsay. He is such a dear, and so affectionate and genuine. He kept me an hour from my lunch to-day asking about politics and the administration of the R.A.F. and who is to pay for this war: and was much amused when I told him that the R.A.F. would treat it as exercise for the next big one. Then I had to explain the rites of Christianity, translate the Lord's Prayer and the Ten Commandments, and all before lunch.

We went to a place called the House of Brass to look at a cave where they now store millet stalks for fodder, but they said that once a metal trap-door was in the middle of the floor, and a bracelet found —so I went to look around and found the Ja'da beduin there very friendly and mostly already known as patients. They were not awfully anxious to show the cave however, but did take us up to a small door in the stony scree, just like the Arabian Nights. One looked north from there and saw the wadi and its little fringe of palms round the small village, and 'ilb trees around, and the thin line of samr and 'ilb trees along the channel of the seil: and, beyond, the old Himyaritic oasis stretching across the wadi from side to side in small waves of sand dotted with stones like foam flakes, like a sea in which the old histories are drowned: a train of four camels was ploughing its way slowly in the middle of that sandy floor, and there was a feeling of great peace in the motionless landscape and that slow immemorial movement:

> "E se ne porta il tempo
> Ogni uman accidente;"

and the life so unconscious of past or future of the present people of the land.

The cave was Himyaritic: it had a niche for burial on its right-hand side, half buried in millet and down below they dug, half out of the ground, a jar for water like those found by G. in her cave—and told me that many incense burners had been found and given to the children to be played with and broken.

20 February, 1938.

We stopped to drink coffee with old Sa'd whose grandson had been disagreeable. He didn't appear and there was an apologetic feeling about, but the old man was very friendly and presently said there was a cave with Himyaritic writing on the hillside above: I felt I must go, and left Mansab sitting in the family cave where they live under their own house—a big place with tomb niches in a double row. I climbed up with Sa'd's son and various children—between 1 and 2 p.m., very hot, up steep scree, till we got to where the sheer cliff and the scree meet: and there sure enough was a wall of sand-stone all scribbled over in Himyarite, and a cave on either hand: one has built-up walls of boulders, the other goes deep into the hill: both are nearly filled in and seem not to have been touched for there are no fragments of pottery strewn about below. I found a palæolithic flint, took photos, and came away.

The Mansab says he is going to write to the editor of a Cairo paper to deny Philby's ridiculous assertions. They can do much harm.

21 February, 1938.

News has come through to-day that the Humumi have all sur-rendered, handed in the criminals, agreed to pay the fine, and the road from Tarim is open, so we are once more in contact with the world, and have arranged to leave here on Saturday, March 5th, if a car and lorry will come for us. I have sent in to Seiyun to see about it.

Everyone was feverless this morning and we spent it taking photo-graphs of all the season's finds. I offered to pack for G, but she thinks me incapable of putting cotton wool and cambric round pots and I was quite glad not to wrap up pots really, and tidied our flower collection instead; we have 41 different kinds: I have been collecting on every walk and so has E., but there is hardly anything till the seil comes. Some of the leaves are exactly like the fossil tufa ones: she thinks if she can find some fossil fruit the trees may be identified.

[207]

I have bought another manuscript, a history of the Himyarites written in the late 17th century: I gave Ali £2. 5s.—and if it is worth more I will let the Mansâb know and pay the difference. His brother brought it with another manuscript: he saw me hesitating and told me that he thought the second manuscript had been printed: as he was going away, he begged me not to tell the Mansab that he had warned me of the printing which of course took away my reason for buying it!

A hot south wind to-day and the thermometer 90 in shade at 5 p.m.: the mornings are quite perfect and delightful.

22 February, 1938.

I have had a nice day but am very tired, and disappointed because we were all talking and all forgot my photographs, taken for E., and all *black*: and it means such a weary tramp to take them all again. We were doing the irrigation channels of the sandy flat, now all desert, and zigzagged about, and it was interesting because the old life of those gardens came so vividly with all their sluices and canals and built-up banks, the great waterway that fed them running with just a line of stones lying on the sand to show its course. Mubarak the Bedu was looking after his fields—he had hired a plough and two oxen for 1½ dollars for a day, and the poor little patches of turned-up earth looked very small: his son was going over them with a wooden instrument with which they carry off the surplus that has washed down and pile it on the banks: every bit of cultivation has to be done inside banked enclosures to keep the water in.

We found a number of white flints stuck hard as iron in the cement of the gravel: and soon had the children all round us and a tiresome man who shouted in my ear. It was *blazing* hot and what it will be like in 15 days I can't think if it goes on so quick. I came trotting back: if one swings one's legs alternately against the donkey's tummy he knows he is meant to trot and jogs along.

I believe I saw the Phoenix to-day. Mubarak the slave said it was the Green Bird that comes with the seil, E. said it looks like a shrike. There was a hoopoe yesterday.

E. and G. have decided to leave here on the 5th, Saturday week. I have no plan yet but may either go with them or ride up Wadi Amd and be picked up at Bir Ali.

[208]

23 February, 1938.

The days are going by and in a month I hope to be in Aden—not sorry to think of a good long spell of civilization and comfort before me, and to get back to Asolo with the roses!

I went up the wadi and got pictures of the banks as they are now, all ready for the flood water, with a parapet of brushwood to keep them firm: at one point in the field a bit is walled and made lower on the same principle as the lip of a jug, so that the water may find the lower level and pour in or out without damaging the banks. It was useful going with Sayyid Alawi, who knows all about the modern irrigation and explained the narrow piece in the main canal which had been puzzling E.: It is a measuring point for the water. It was anyway a very complicated system and it is fascinating to ride over that waste ground and see the traces of its former prosperity and to see the modern handed down exactly so through all these generations.

We came to charming Arcadian sort of country, plantations of 'ilb trees in sunk fields, quite dry and grey but ready to burst out with the seil. We had spent an hour pottering with the photos, then for an hour hurried almost incessantly at a short half canter: and I realized what a real Arab pony can do: my little beast was scarcely hot and showed no trace of fatigue: I believe it could keep on at that pace all day. It is a dear little brown thing and loves to be talked to: and when I got off to photograph, all I did was to throw the rein on its neck and leave it: on the way back however Sayyid Alawi tried to catch up with it and it began quietly to walk home: I shouted to Alawi to keep still and then, walking quite a way, found Nasib (that is its name) standing waiting, turning its head round at the sound of my voice.

24 February, 1938.

Such a disappointment—the runner from Mukalla has come and brought *nothing* for us: what the devil has happened to our month's letters goodness knows, and the news has also come that the road is still shut and *damaged* so that here we are marooned: and a runner was taken on the Du'an route by the Humumi and the letters all burnt and this poor old man spent three hours in a hole of the jōl so as not to be caught too. So that it looks as if here we should be imprisoned still for some little time and I feel it is almost as bad as being married to G.: I haven't yet told her the worst and she already began to say: "But you said," as if it were my doing.

P [209]

I am so sleepy again, having been up since six, first doing E.'s photos which thank God are all right this time: then medicine for the Mansab's mother: then off at last to Bahr, that nice place where the pool is in the rocks, and took a hefty dark-skinned Meskin with a big hammer and crowbar to break up E.'s boulder of tufas for her. I turned aside first to look at the house of the bees: it is a square old mud place all brown with loopholes for defence (mishwaz—lookouts they call them) and up dark little low stairs you climb to the roof in the sun, and there the bees fly in and out their small mud houses and drink from shallow trays of water fitted out for them with little island clumps of iron sticking out: and the old beekeeper and his wife with naked grandchildren running about among them all as happy as can be—and the bees could flutter over the parapet and see all their pasture lands, the palm and the samr and the ilb, spread over the wadi below them. They take their honey twice a year, but the 'ilb honey is the best.

I then went on up the ravine, and found our boulders and was joined by four bedus from the time before who all spent a good hour with Sa'id the navvy trying to move the boulder and talking over it. At last he began to break bits off, and every chunk less made it easier to deal with, but it was agonizing to see the precious fossil leaves embedded inside being split into pieces and I knowing so little how to avoid it. I was lucky enough to spot a berry, showing itself by the delicate little veins that still survive, stamped in the stone, and that is the only one so far, but I hope there may be more. I had a time getting those five rough men to be delicate enough with their huge tool. The crowbar was pointed at both ends, so not of much use to hammer on!

The fossil bud was far too precious to leave, so I decided to get a camel and while this was being found in the plain below sat and chipped out fossil leaves from their bedding (a delightful occupation) and talked to the bedu. I wish they would not disfigure themselves with a wad of tobacco between their teeth and lips: the nicest-looking face is spoilt by it!

The camel came looking deliberate and superior and we packed the stones in a basket-woven flat sort of saddle bag, very convenient, and came home with all sorts of meetings on the way.

It seems impossible to get any reliable information as to how long it will take me to get to Bir Ali from here: the accounts vary between five and fifteen days! Time is really nothing. The same Feast began at Tarim on Tuesday, at Seiyun on Wednesday and here on Thursday.

26 February, 1938.

E. and I had a pleasant dinner with the Mansab who was beautifully scented but had dressed himself in Italian colonial khaki with a blouse effect at the back. He was very cordial and took me by the hand up the stairs and we sat in a pleasant white room with carpets everywhere, awfully luxurious after my draughty bareness here: and tea in clean glasses out of a samovar—and heard all the letters with news that come pouring in and then sat and discussed it, with the Mansab of Meshed in a nice clean shirt without his order on, and various Sayyids and a Nahdi beduin from Henin who knew all about me three years ago: and my book was brought out for everyone to admire their own portraits, and the Mansab said that Huraidha had been left on one side till we came. I think it showed what had been wrong with all this bit of country—just the feeling that they were being left in the cold.

27 February, 1938.

E. thinks she has found a new kind of fossil leaf, and four fruits to identify the tree by. Very imposing palm fronds. It is very exciting when the rock splits open and discloses these things. We had three camels to carry all back. They spent the day grazing about the ravine, looking exactly like a primitive rock-drawing as they stretched their necks against the rocky background. It is extraordinary how they eat the samr boughs, thorns and all—thorns one inch long. I got a close-up cinema of one, trying to look like a giraffe, and a picture of the handsome bedu leading them down the ledge towards us: a little camel followed, an orphan who follows another camel about trying to believe it is its mother. This camel had a Himyaritic B marked on its neck as a mark!

2 March, 1938.

I was interrupted last night by Ali's arrival with an *immense* bag of mail, three letters from you and two from H.—*such* a joy to get. I am sorry you have been worried about slowness of posts, but what else can you expect from here? It always seems a miracle that letters should come at all! I suppose these will be the last I get in Hadhramaut.

I must go back to where I left off or I shall never find my place

[211]

again! Sayyid Ali took me up into his mother's house to take a photo of a chimney: they are invisible and are built into parapets and other ornaments, quite unobtrusively: we then went through a pleasant empty room of columns to a little terrace where the local saint, the Habib Ahmed, grandfather of these people, died suddenly one morning as he was praying. There was a charming little column to put a book on and a niche for a light with glass front, so that the wind cannot blow it about, and beyond the mud pinnacles of the parapet one looked across the wadi.

We then went down and saw the old lady's foot, which is improving day by day and would be well now if a month's delay had not been caused by a friend telling her that Christian medicines would break her leg. And after that we went into the Mansab's house across the way, saw the big kitchen, the slaughtering place, the shed for animals, the ovens, and finally found E. and the Mansab very hungry for lunch, waiting for us.

After lunch I went to the Harim, and Raguan the Mansab's sister suddenly burst into tears when she heard of our departure—and it was so hard to say anything, for I don't suppose I shall ever see her again. All the kohl came streaming down her cheeks.

When I got back the Somali chauffeur had turned up from Seiyun with news of the outer world. Sir Bernard Reilly had been and gone with Lord Dufferin, the Humumi had surrendered to the last man, and the road is to open to-day. So there is no reason not to start on Saturday and I shall get off a day before as I have the longer way to go. There was a lot to do, packing, and then I had to go and see Raguan in her house and be taken to the roof to photograph and then I got back to write and the mail came.

This is my last day out, as to-morrow will be all house jobs—and E. and I are up at Samu'a again. E. has got up to the top pool and how she will ever get down again is still an unknown problem. But she is just as thrilled with the place as I was, and says it must have been a lake all on the upper level and come away by the breaking of the lower edge. I promised the bedu a kid, so when I got to the village one rushed off and came with a bleating white kid with eyes the colour of water and a confiding little bleat that made one feel quite dreadful. He went with it like a fur round his neck—I wonder why it is such a pleasure to see sheer strength: all the movements of these people are lovely to look at.

[212]

I had gone ahead to start work with Sa'id who however had completely vanished this morning: so I rode by myself while Hasan went chasing after him in the places where he was rumoured to be— or at least I was helped along by anyone who happened to be near and gave an obliging whack to the donkey as they passed.

We have had a pleasant time and I have photographed the process of food from beginning to end (all except cutting the goat's throat). They skinned and put it back into its skin and came up with the poor little bundle and set to to make a hearth on the rock where we ate the lizard: first they made a circle of round boulders, then put a little kindling and lit it, and covered it over with wood chopped from the *misht* tree we were sitting under: then they covered this with flat stones and we watched it smoke away and the stones get black, till the wood consumed and the stones fell in flat. Meanwhile on one boulder a bedu pounded the salt, and on another, using the limestone hollows as a pasty board, another one made bread: the pieces of meat were stitched into suitable morsels with slivers of palm—and soon a selection of the best came to us on a biscuit tin. The rest, when all was ready, were carefully divided into portions: then everyone handed his dagger to Sa'id with a nice smile: he held the bunch of them over his head where he could not see them and took one after another and put them on the little heaps, so that each had the meat under his dagger. On a feast day, they told me, they make their hearths on their housetops, "and the smoke goes straight up"—a very Biblical touch. It was all just as it must have been when they had nothing but a flint knife to cut with and a flint to make the fire.

From where we are sitting I can see the middle pool green as paint and the buttresses like organ pipes beyond. It is most perfect peace, undisturbed even by the noise of fossils being hammered out: it is just the feeling one had as a child, if one got into a secret place in a tree—so shut out from the knowledge of the rest of the world.

What is extraordinary among these bedu is the variety of type: every one of them quite different, and they are all from the same village. The one with the smile might be an English boy.

4 *March*, 1938.

My last letter from Huraidha. Everything is packed and three camels ready waiting, and as soon as the saddle bags are settled on them I hope to start. The old Meshed Mansab is lending me his horse for the first stage. I hope to get down to the sea in a fortnight and to send you a telegram from Aden in three or four weeks. We were to meet at Bir Ali, but G. changed her mind *last night at 8 p.m.* I might not have started at all if I had not expected to find some sort of assistance at the other end. However, it is nice to be free again— and all is for the best. They both leave to-morrow by car.

WADI 'AMD, 11.20 a.m.

I have got half-way to our resting place after a fearful hullabaloo to get off. At 10 o'clock E. and I descended, leaving my poor little bare room looking very forlorn with only five boxes for Aden and two stools left in it, beside the boxes of skulls which support the dining table: as we got down my caravan appeared, a very proper-looking caravan of three camels with the paraffin lamps brightening up the luggage and the Mansab's orange quilt spread for me to sit on. The Mansab however had offered me the little brown horse, and I had just sent for it when the lorry and the motor for to-morrow appeared and distracted Huraidha altogether. Your letter was inside, and a mass of prints of Shibam sent by Jock, and E. and I looked at these in the middle of a thick crowd all wanting to see.

The Mansab's son saw me off: E. was *very* nice, and offered to delay her journey to Palestine if I fell ill and needed her, which was really Christian—and now I am off. We have driven by all the Himyaritic irrigation ruins of the plain, and are now almost opposite where we rode the other day, under a tree, waiting for the camels. There is a horrid fat man, agent of the lorry, and I have had to snub him in bargaining for his price to Mukalla: now however all is peace: a bedu has come up who knows me from the other day. He has just asked if Harold belongs to my "tribe". Our camels have appeared over the sand against the background of scrub: a little mud saqaya with goats is in the foreground: it is all very pleasant: the cliffs stand out into the wadi, one beyond the other: and the samr tree, in its barrage of thorns, is putting out tiny green leaves.

It was really heart-rending to leave Huraidha, so many affectionate little farewells: a small girl came to ask for medicine, and suddenly embraced my arm and said: "Oh Freya, we love you, we love you so much." The Mansab had tears in his eyes, everyone was so sorry

[214]

at the parting. It is something to feel one has left a place like that however soon it may be forgotten.

p.m.

At 2.30 we turned the big corner of this Wadi to the South—all very sandy. The camels had come up, and I rode along under my sunshade; it must be very good for the liver, but *very* tiring to begin with. Qasim is so overcome at parting with Salima that he just sits in tears, with blood all down his shirt from the burst boil, a quite revolting sight. People ought to be in love in private. I am not on a saddle but recline on baggage and the Mansab's orange quilt on top. The shoulders of the camel, lurching along below, are quite extraordinarily shapeless: he *is* ugly: his silly little ears and fluff of curls on his mane give him a look of elderly and dowdy coquetry.

One has a feeling of not moving at all on the camel: the landscape remains exactly the same for ages, till one suddenly sees quite a lot of ground left behind.

ZAHIR, 5 March, 1938.

I was so sick with tiredness last night I could not write. I hope I shall get more fit for trekking in a day or two—it does take it out of one more than anything I know. It is the sociability after the long day which does one in.

Last evening was very pleasant. We got to our little town, called Zahir, in the dusk and saw it growing towards us, a toothed ridge of houses against the sky and the cliffs in straight lines behind, one after the other like a stair.

All the male inhabitants were gathered in a little group to watch our arrival, and took us to a very dark house on the hill top. We settled down, about 40 of us, cross-legged round the walls for conversation. They are a rougher-looking lot than Huraidha, and also very different in type—lots of little English-looking straight noses, and others with a sort of Etruscan curve. I was dead tired, but had to sit an hour, and then my bed was made and I went up to a tiny little clean room with a roof of its own to walk out on, and after the horrid shock of a huge green insect walking up me inside the net, and a short expression of mutual dislike before I got it outside, I went to sleep till a round mat was brought with rice and a kid from the Mansab (a nice long-faced peasant type), for Ali, Qasim and myself. I went downstairs again for another hour, and sat by the old schoolmaster, and everyone got more and more cordial and Ali gave us an improvisation of the Se'ar and Sayyids at Meshed, most of which I missed, but I looked round and saw everyone with shining eyes and delighted smiles: Ali comes into his own in this country where he is friends with all the tribes.

5 March, 1938.

This morning I have been $3\frac{1}{2}$ hours on a camel and it is as much as I can bear. Now we have settled down under a big 'ilb tree in the wadi bed and four bedu have joined us, one smoking his hubble-bubble with a friendly bubble sound. All the wadi is pleasant, about a mile or more wide, big 'ilb trees, and goats nibbling and palms: the towns at the foot of the cliffs or on little hills have a feudal look, partly from the defensive position and partly because they are all brown and no whitewash. I told Ali I meant to lunch out, away from houses and he was to think of food, but of course he didn't, and we have had a short but amiable struggle, and I am under my tree: Ali has procured dates from the little town near, of course with a dozen inhabitants as well.

I am only the second woman here from Europe (Doreen [Ingrams] came as far as 'Amd last year) and only three men I think. It all feels much more primitive than Huraidha, and the men walk about with curly heads and a cloth tied like a garland, sometimes with tassels and sometimes just like a dishcloth.

NU'AIR, 6 *March,* 1938.

I fear my trip is over almost before it has begun. We got here yesterday at 5.30, after $5\frac{1}{2}$ hours' camel riding in the day, and again I felt so tired that I could have lain down and died. But there is no way out of it, one *has* to see people: the whole town was out to meet us.

By the time I finally got up I felt so ill I thought I had better take my temperature and found it 100. I thought I would cure it as Dr. Buchanan suggested with 20 grains of quinine. Well, it was disastrous. My heart simply fluttered about for the rest of the night, and the electric torch chose this time to conk out. I lay in great misery. To-day I am quite flat and still and the heart is recovering—but it seems hopeless to go down into the most malarial part of Arabia if one's heart can't stand quinine! And I would not have arranged to

THE STONY WAY TO DEYYIN

HIMYAR TRIBESMAN
MY CAMEL OWNER

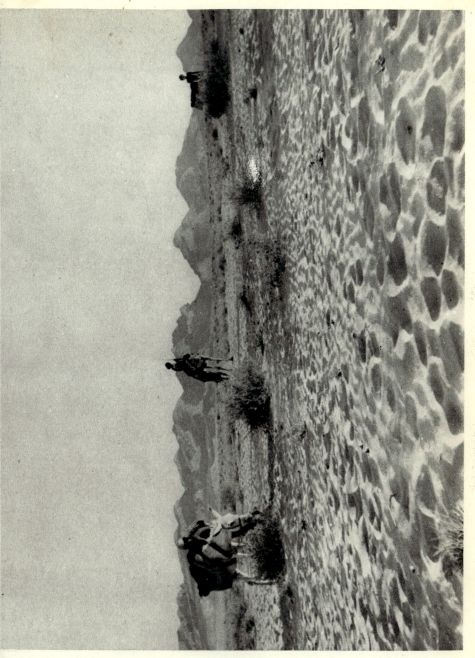

THE KAUT

GATHERING FIREWOOD ON THE JŌL

go anyway if I had known that no one would appear to assist at the other end. So we have sent a runner to Seiyun and he should bring a car in three days to Zahir, a day's ride away—and that alas is the end of my journey on the Incense Road.

I am glad even so to have seen Wadi 'Amd, for it is still quite untouched and has the feeling of remoteness about it that even Huraidha has lost: it is like a country in a William Morris story, a little feudal country living its own life, tilling its own fields and only murmurs from stray travellers to bring the news of the outer world.

Yesterday at lunch a woman called me aside and asked if I had a medicine which would kill her husband. A fierce spoilt little girl was then brought by her father, who evidently adored her; the people here are just as fond of their girls as their boys, unlike North Arabia. This one was called Barka, and was teased by being told that I would take her away, and when I put out my hand she first tried to bite it and then hit it with a stone—a venomous little spitfire with ears made enormous by half a dozen earrings and completely black with grime. I would love to see one Hadhrami child *clean*.

7 March, 1938.

The fever dropped and the heart steadied a bit, and I found by the map that if I go one day's journey on my way south I can still choose and break off eastward and a day would take me to Du'an: there I have friends and a litter would carry me to the new motor road which is approaching fast—so I am going to chance it, and have sent another courier to stop and countermand the car.

My room is beautifully quiet and Sayyid Ali has kept most people away, but a horde are waiting below and I must go down.

I went only a little way and came back all clammy with cold perspiration from weakness. 'Amd is only an hour off, in sight, I hope to get there after an afternoon's rest—I do hope I shall do this little trek without disaster.

SHI'BE, 12 *a.m.,* 8 *March,* 1938.

This adventure has begun and it is really an adventure with myself—because I decided I really would not be beaten by my silly old body. I may not get down to Bir Ali, but I am doing a *little* bit of new ground and getting up to the ruins of Redet ad Deyyin and then, if still ill, to Du'an—a two days' trek from there. It is four days from

[217]

'Amd instead of two, as they told me, and if I had known that I would not have risked it: but now I am at lunch under an 'ilb tree, and everything seems more hopeful. I had a miserable night, going into semi faints of weakness. It is one's *morale* that counts in Arabia: it is that which gives way under the constant strain of people: I realized it strongly by the immensely restful feeling it was to get on my donkey and be off, with nothing but the exertion of riding!

This little bit of my ride has not been done by a European, it is all very feudal and pastoral. We left the old headman at Redet very friendly but I was too ill to rouse any feeling but pity: he was a nice kind old boy. His four bullet wounds were got only $1\frac{1}{2}$ years ago from the houses opposite in the wadi, and he told me how he put a concoction of three plants on them and they recovered in 35 days. I lay on my bed and talked, and Qasim made a nice dinner of liver boiled in milk: but then the proper meal was brought in and I saw that I would offend if I did not get up and share or pretend to: there *is* no way of getting on here except by sharing the life, and that is what makes this country so hard. Now I am eating my own tinned food, and it makes all the difference with my new bedu: the others had become friends when we shared the lizard. I know now that I am right for I have tried both ways.

When we had dined last night various tribal notables came in and sat round and came to the never failing topic of the slave governor in 'Amd: why do the English allow him? Every tribesman hates him, he knows nothing of the local customs, and takes two dollars from every plaintiff or defendant who comes before him. The old men wagged their long beards and the younger ones their black curls tied with head bands. The old headman had a lovely red and brown turban nicely put on: otherwise only his futah and a black cotton shawl. Some here wear leather necklaces, with silver beads and tassels, wrapped two or three times round the neck: that, with a little tasselled bag for coffee beans, which the guest offers to the coffee hearth where he is staying, make the top of a naked body look quite clothed. Here too they wear the little red talisman which stops bleeding, with a silver ornament each side, much more elaborate. The women are much freer: they came and sat among the men and did not bother to veil unless a stranger came in: they were very friendly, but presently crowds and crowds began to pour up my narrow little stair, and children, and it felt like a railway station on a bank holiday, and altogether I was never alone from when we arrived till 9 p.m. Luckily I have a little brandy and that supported me through the night.

The Wadi 'Amd is so pleasant. Its little towns are on small hills that stand out into the wadi, the houses built like towers and all brown. Windows are only just beginning: each house has one good room and perhaps a little one for the harim with lattice windows, the rest are small openings for shooting from.

There is no comparison between the industry of Huraidha and 'Amd: here every flat bit that can get water is tilled and every field is terraced: long lines of regular stones like embankments hem the seil bed in, and one can see them rising, sometimes four, one behind another. We came into Shi'be wadi by a most picturesque village of tower-like houses, their battlements all separate and individual against the blue sky. As one looked up the main wadi, other jagged village outlines were in sight, with their topmost towers made purely for shooting, so that one felt Huraidha a civilized centre of modern life and this the true medieval. One hardly ever sees anyone here dressed in anything but futah, bracelet, and cartridge belt, and they all carry guns.

Camp below RADHHAIN *and* AQABA KHURJE, 5 *p.m.,* 8 *March,* 1938

I have got to the end of this day, and have been enjoying the afternoon and hope for a better night out of doors. Ali very agitated about it, but I cannot *bear* the idea of another late evening with unknown crowds. It is lovely to have the feeling of enjoyment creeping back: I can get it so easily, it seems very hard not to have it at all, but these last days have been too much for me.

ZARUB, 9 *March,* 1938.

It was lovely to get on to the stony sunny jōl once more and delicious to taste the good thin air. We have been riding nearly five hours and I feel so much better that I think of attempting Bir Ali after all. The difficulty seems to be my suite, all except Qasim very nervous because Wadi Hajr has a bad reputation for fevers at the time of fertilizing the dates. It seems peculiar that I should be urging on these perfectly strong and healthy men.

It is curious how one finds what one is looking for. The jōl above Khurje was strewn with palæolithic flints which I would never have recognized before. I expect there are some to be found all over, but there they were thick, just at the top of the pass, and then seemed to peter out.

CAMP, 2 p.m., 11 March, 1938.

The jōl now with the flat samr trees and far shallow cliffs looks just like a water-colour by Lear. There are lovely effects sometimes made with stones, the wadi bed and gravels of 'Amd all silver in the sunset like waves of a river: and yesterday the sun caught all the polished flints like little mirrors.

The camels have just gone on and I am being packed: a sort of third degree torture of constant attention till one gives in and goes.

NUQBAT AL 'ILB, 6 p.m., 11 March, 1938.

Ahmed has just started the chant of his evening prayer, his gaunt peasant neck and shoulder dark against the yellow sky which has one yellow star. The moon is high up, but only just above us, entangled in the branches of a samr tree. If I get through to you and Europe, I shall often remember this loveliness—and all the human beauty too with it all, the kindness and the courage and the gaiety. A good world.

Ahmed has a face with Mongol cheek-bones and kind eyes screwed up in a smile nearly always—quite stupid but so nice. He is busy asking the price of commodities in Yeb'eth and I think means to be a merchant on his way back—when one meets someone from another town, one gets over the greetings and then comes to the prices of things—oil, sugar, cloth, rice, paraffin. A load of rice costs 3½ dollars less at Yeb'eth than 'Amd. Ahmed, walking with his perpetual absent-mindedness behind Robin, (the donkey), his mind wrapped in finance and bakshish, told me he has a wife, two sisters of his own, and three orphan children of a dead brother to feed, and would buy a little rice to take back. When one thinks of these people as grasping, one might remember what they are so often grasping *for*.

CAMP near J. HIMAR, lunch time, 14 March, 1938.

The journey from Yeb'eth to Azzan was said to be two small days: this is our third and it is doubtful if we get there to-morrow:

[220]

it seems safe to double the estimates. Luckily I am getting stronger day by day so it does not matter. It is lovely to sleep out on the jōl. Yesterday there was no dew and it was far less cold: we sat on a little circular shelf of limestone over the deep ravines.

I hope to make a good map. No one has been this road but Colonel Lake who has been everywhere and went to Azzan twelve years ago and is well remembered. I think that many intellectual progressives do less good than these officials who just *walk about being nice* and get known: it is nearly always ignorance which causes the troubles here—one can see them melting away as one talks to people.

HAZINE CAMP, 8 p.m., 15 March, 1938.

We have just had three hours of sand, crossing the Kaut (sand drift)—not hot because our bedu are so late in starting and it was 4 o'clock, and we entered the long winding defile of our camp with a round moon in a violet sky and the hills we have come from turned to violet shadows washed up to by the sand. The two little oases we passed showed green patches, and the whole land slid down S.E. to the sea (invisible) with ridges on three sides, the one before us being luckily the lowest. It was lovely, the sand soft and ribbed by S.E. winds; our caravan moving with long shadows; and as we got to the middle of the Kaut a messenger on a donkey came along with a letter of welcome from Azzan.

AZZAN, 18 March, 1938.

I am having two quiet mornings' rest and found I needed it quite badly. It is comfortable having a room not to oneself (there are usually ten tribesmen or so in it) but to spread about in: it is in the palace of the Sultan's uncle, a square proper fortress, and it is a lovely room all matted with a magenta mat made locally, six windows on floor level and five little ones above, besides three shot-holes and eight niches: two carved columns and a table and four chairs: besides a bathroom of its own.

later.

I got good proof of the difficulty with the bedu in the afternoon when I went to see the famous ruins of Naqb al Hajr. Sayyid Ali as usual was absent when wanted and nothing prepared. So I got on his camel and went off with a guard of a vague number of bedu with rifles and an old white-haired man leading the camel whose saddle began by nearly coming off with me because the ropes broke. We were very late and the sun low, so I hurried them on, and we began to trot, the Bedu giving unexpected whacks from behind and the camel's baby trotting on ahead in the outraged way they have when hurried. There is a row of little villages on the left as one goes down, across the broad sandy wadi plain, and from each of these the blue bedu came pouring out, cheerful but determined to get money if they could. By the time we reached the ruins I was in a crowd of about 300 people. The 300 moved about with me in a solid mass, touching everything and talking of bakshish. I copied the inscription, but having to keep up a running conversation all the time. They would have been charming if you had gone with nothing as a guest to their homes, but the idea of money works like blood in a tiger.

WADI MAIFA'A, 22 March, 1938.

I was so tired that I went to bed and stayed and did nothing till we started at 2 p.m. on our trail to the sea. The old 'Wolf' got up on to his camel and held a black umbrella for the sun. Sultan Husain saw me on to mine and then went arm in arm with Qasim to the gathering place. We defiled down, seven camels and a handful of soldiers, and began to discuss whether Nasir [the Sultan's nephew] was or was not coming—even at this time it was not known for certain. Nasir appeared however with the Sultan's brother Ahmed dressed in the gayest harmony of green and yellow, with a bunch of scented herbs in his black hair. As we passed the north gate of Naqb al Hajr in the afternoon it looked far finer than when I saw it in that hustling crowd, its buttresses square in the sun, and the gate overlooking us and the caravan road as it must have done to innumerable caravans before. Our numbers increased as camels joined us for safety, carrying tobacco to the sea. We were taking the unsafe route which ordinary caravans are now afraid to use.

On our left, below N. al Hajar, were the towers of the wicked Ba Rashaid who have killed the Naqib during the truce and are due for the R.A.F.'s next visit. The friends of government have little shooting heaps built up of boulders to snipe from in the area of the law-abiding villages. We went right down the Wadi Maifa'a and it should be a wide and lovely region of groves and gardens, where the water lies at 16 to 25 feet: but of the 350 wells nearly every one is in ruins and the villages, when you come near, are just shells of houses mostly empty and empty enclosures of untended fields. All this because of wars. There is something terribly tragic in going through a war-devastated land; its feeling of unnatural and *dead* peace, its solitude filled with ghosts, and fears. No dogs barking near the villages: hardly any crowd of children; and poverty everywhere.

By 6 o'clock next day, just as it got light, we stopped to water the camels at Juwairi, the next oasis, where the water, pleasantly hot, runs in little channels nearly covered over with turf into small palm groves. It was very decorative to see the camels stooping their long necks one behind the other, their colour and that of the rocks and turf all dim and gentle in the early light and cloudy sky. From Ain ba Ma'bad we had been in sight of the sea, and now we rested till 8.45 and then kept inland again, with the mountains of Bal Haf opening out before us, and at last came through dunes of grey and yellow parti-coloured sand to the open beach and Bal Haf a violet headland very far away.

It is five hours from Juwairi, but it was such a delight to get to the edge of the waves into a fresh sea wind that everyone felt cheerful and our long line went jogging along the sand disturbing armies of crabs. There is only one tower and a house or two in all this stretch, guarded by the Bal Haf soldiers, as it is from there that Bal Haf has to fetch its water. When we got near Bal Haf my camel was stopped while the old 'Wolf' said his prayers by the sea edge, so that I should not enter before him: they all then got off, and so did I out of politeness, and walked into Bal Haf while all its inhabitants were gathered in one long row to shake hands. Here too there was some little sign of reluctance at sight of a woman, but it was swallowed up in the reception and I was given a little room filled with bugs and indigo stains but cheerful because it had windows on the sea. Nasir is very expert and recognized the bugs by stains on the walls: then seeing my dislike assured me there were none, till I told him I had just killed two, when he gave it up with a smile. We arranged for the sambuk of the garrison to take Nasir and me to H. el Ghurab next day while the dhow that was coming in would wait for us to board her. It was only an hour or two's run, he said. Sayyid Ali would go with us and on to Bir Ali and Mukalla.

[223]

5 p.m.

I am now lying in comfort on the deck of the dhow swinging easily in the sunset and feeling very near the water. The Arab coast, whose mysteries I now feel I know better, is just in sight, and the chief mate, a fat old stubble-bearded man from Dis, is standing near calling the sunset prayer. The old Nakuda skipper, also with a grey stubble beard but a red henna moustache, a blue serge coat, a white and red futah rather like a dish-cloth below, has been sitting by me giving me tea and telling me of the remains of a city on a hill called Gatli near H. el Ghurab—another strengthening of its position as the site of Cana.

It has been fun to do this all in the proper Arab way—to join a caravan to the coast, to be in for a threat of battle between the neighbouring ports, and to start off in a sailing boat which traffics from Basra or Calicut to Zanzibar or Jedda, wherever its merchandise carries it. It looks like a fragile little cockleshell for the Indian Ocean, with a prettily decorated coloured stern. We have little merchandise but 32 passengers, most of whom were sitting on a rock in Bal Haf harbour waiting to be taken off. They had been camping for the last few days and it was amusing to hear them under my window—an Indian unable to talk Arabic, a snatch of Italian or English on this little desolate patch of Arabian shore! Two came to us for water which only exists in Bal Haf through the Sultan's efforts; he gives a skinful or two to every household every two days when the soldiers go for it in the sambuk.

3 p.m., 26 March, 1938.

We are in sight of Shuqra and if we get there in time will get a car to Aden to-night: if too late will stay on board and hope the wind may blow us in by morning. It fell and we lost five hours. It has been quite pleasant, running along in sight of the misty coast volcanoes with a running commentary from the people who lie in a thick dark carpet of bodies swathed in futahs on the deck: they have mostly done the journey by land which takes ten days.

They say there are no Himyar inscriptions here, so it looks more and more as if Cana and its three roads, Maifa'a Hajr and Du'an—all leading to Shabwa, is the key to the south. I wish I could have done the west road from beginning to end!

[224]

'AZZAN

'AZZAN: DOOR OF THE PALACE

one that I know of believes it except we ourselves—and we have let things get to such a pass that hardly anything short of actual war will make them believe it. I still think that a decided slap to Italy, on some point that Germany does not care about, would save a European war. But evidently no one else thinks so. And I suppose we will give them a loan which will just save them from collapse in Abyssinia. It is better to forget politics if one can.

c/o MRS. DEVONSHIRE, MAADI, CAIRO, 12 *April,* 1938.

Darling B,

I had a very agitated time in Port Said owing to an idiot who took my suitcase with *all* my cameras at the Customs and never noticed it till she got to Cairo next day! I spent till 1 a.m. hunting round and all next morning before my train left. A little New Zealand elderly spinster whom I had helped off the boat came with me: she was a most entertaining person, so full of common sense, a sort of Mrs. Allshine equal to any emergency: she noticed everything. She was a person of some consequence in her own community and interested in a hospital in Jerusalem and various good works. When she had got through the Customs and I had to go all the way back there for my bag, I naturally thought she would stay and have her supper and go to bed: but not at all, she wouldn't let me go alone, and back we went, and back to the *Orontes* in a motor launch and only subsided to think of supper about midnight. Then she drew me away from the hotel because she had seen a man embracing the Hungarian dancer at the cabaret show there and she thought it not a very nice place: so we stopped at a café on the pavement and asked the Greek fat proprietor the price of omelette, and found it too dear, and so bargained for beer and cheese for 2/-: the proprietor winked at me and I am not at all sure that he was any more respectable than the cabaret hotel.

4

Greece and Syria: The year of Munich, 1938–1939

THE English are so used to unpopularity that it is a pleasant
surprise to realize how much they are liked by the
Greeks. Lord Byron no doubt began it, but it has been
helped, I think, by the fact that Greece is the only country in the
world which the British traveller of the industrial age approached
with humility: he came to learn and not to teach, and the bad-
ness of hotels possibly kept the non-learners away. When my
mother and I reached the country in the spring of 1938, hotels
and roads had improved under the dictatorship of Metaxas,
but the British one met were still mild and open-hearted, delighted with beauty and reverent to the past. All but the most
insensitive blossom out in a land which is so obviously our
origin and which still holds nearly everything that, in our
noblest moments, we wish to return to or to find. Nobility
is the word. The landscape is held in an austerity of light and
there is none of the Latin waste of beauty: the ingredients used
are basic—light, rocks, dark sea, an incandescent sky—with a
bare minimum of accessories, trees, fields or streams or towns,
that make it possible for human habitation; and of these, the
buildings of men are either subordinate or unimportant, and the
things of nature are spaced with an aristocratic elegance, as if their
rarity were not necessity but choice. The people too have
that natural aristocracy which will dispense with luxuries, comforts, and even necessities for an abstract cause. They are the
only nation I know where a beautiful mouth is frequent; where
the peasants answer a question with a look of intelligence (this

is so in Tuscany also); and where the dullness of clothes and poverty of houses is unimportant because of a living exuberance, the spiritual fountain. This no doubt is the secret of courage, which no one would deny to that small people at this time; and perhaps that too, together with humility and Lord Byron, is a bond between us.

It was pleasant to feel the friendly atmosphere in the rising temperature of Europe. Over the sea-laced land the spring had thrown her flowers, the only lavish ornament, too fragile for custom to make common; and there was that feeling of youth which only the most ancient lands can give, founded in renewal and resurrection through thousands of years, and as much richer than a barbarian spring as morning in Paradise must be richer than the débutante's ball.

We were all happy. It was my mother's first sight of the young and ancient world, and I too had never been so near the fountain of the Levant, nor stood on the ramparts of Tyrins, nor seen Taygetus in his spring splendour, crowned and blanketed with snow, as you top the zigzag road and reach the dip for Sparta.

The life of Athens, with its long talks, and picnics under Hymettus, and late evenings in *tavernas* where, as you walk in, you choose your food from the saucepan where it simmers and the canaries are kept awake to sing till midnight, by electricity—was gay, with moments, too, held and made beautiful in the marvellous light. My lizard Himyar was bound up with it, for I walked him about in a small silk harness to browse on the Acropolis every morning, and he grew tame and contented, pushing briskly with his nose down and his tail up in the sun and distracting the tourists. When Jock Murray flew out from London for a long week-end, we lost the lizard in Delphi; he crept into the cranny from which the Sybil used to speak, and the string of his harness snapped. He thought himself safe there, wedged between two mighty blocks of stone, and no pushing or pulling from Jock on one side and me on the other could make him do anything but swell himself out so as to fill the

[229]

narrow crack like a small dragon. It was Jock's only day in Delphi, and hours went by. At intervals he suggested that nothing more could be done, and Himyar must be left: but I thought of the winter, and the huge eagles of Apollo circling all day with their far-seeing eyes above the Castalian cliff—and refused to give up; till at last, with agonizing delicacy, we inserted an iron hook into the part of the harness that had luckily remained intact, and the little voiceless pythoness was pulled out, flustered and scraped by the granite walls, perhaps the farthest-travelled of all the Delphic pilgrims.

I have been twice again to Greece, always with the same rapture: but now we sailed for home, on 13 May, by Corfu and the Empress of Austria's villa, which left one depressed as the Greeks under Rome must have been depressed for centuries by one thing and another, when they travelled towards the barbarous West. On the Dalmatian coast, we strolled in the early morning while our boat lay anchored at Vallona, and saw preparations for war, in the obviously military harbour built while Britain cherished Mussolini as a pillar of peace.

In the summer I was in Bavaria for a cure at Partenkirchen, and found much more prosperity there than in 1934, and a busy, pleased, hopeful feeling. The young, one could see, were at home in their separated world, where I was welcomed as if I had dropped from Mars, but with friendliness. No one I met expected or believed in war: but the concessions to avoid it were to be entirely on the other side. The Czechs must be put in order; the rest of the world must understand; and how wonderful for them all to see how well Germany was doing! It was like those family quarrels where direct communication has ceased and no inkling of an opposite point of view finds entrance any longer; they went on, painstaking and kind, in a world of their making: and in the whole of the little district I visited, crowded with happy people in the *sommer-frische*, I cannot have seen more than three other foreigners and two Englishmen sent there by the Oxford group, apparently to play tennis with each other. Beneath the contentment and general well-being, an unpleasant undertow would show now and then: people speaking freely turned their neck, to see that no one listened from behind; and the secretary asked me for my old copies of *The Times*. I gave them gladly, but remarked that there was a whole stand of foreign papers on the pavement just outside.

"We daren't buy them," she said. "They have a camera bracketed, and everyone who buys is photographed."

My German, though poor in words, has a good accent, so that I was never taken to be English at first and many people spoke to me very freely—the middle-aged sadly and the young mostly eager to convert. They worked hard, they asked little; they were content to live without all the visions that make the Greek poverty splendid. And not far below the daily level was the poison of fear. The Jews were being baited; as I walked up a little hill under the trees one day, I came upon a wayside shrine; two German paterfamiliases with a cluster of women and children stood there regaining their breath and looking at the crucifixion: I did the same, and could not resist the temptation of remarking to the atmosphere in general: "Es ist ja merkwürdig dass Er doch ein Jude war" (It is a remarkable fact that He was a Jew). A silence surrounded me, and when I turned round the whole group had evaporated—they must have moved with astonishing swiftness, and were nowhere to be seen.

I made two charming friends, an Austrian and a young woman from the Rhineland with a French mother—all of them strongly anti-Nazi and living outside that manufactured security of content. They fell back—as the world must have done through many dark centuries—on the small pleasures of every day as it appeared. "I loathe this treatment of the Jews," one of them told me. "If I see one being beaten, I never go up that street; I take another way."

"But surely," said I: "that is why they go on being beaten—because everybody takes the other way?"

She smiled, for it was hardly worth arguing. And now that the pattern has appeared more clearly, I think I would not

[231]

challenge her. We are happy in a country where we can still choose on which side to stand.

I worked during my cure, in spite of trouble over headaches, and sent the MS. of *Seen in the Hadhramaut* to Jock Murray, while the chapters of *A Winter in Arabia* slowly increased.

There were strenuous arguments over this book and it finally emerged far less outspoken than I had written it. The dislikes of the Arabian winter dissolved, as far as I was concerned; but I was reluctant not to describe things as they were. This compulsion has nothing to do with people; it comes, I think, from a respect for words, an ineffectual desire to avoid, as far as possible, the inevitable discrepancy between the word and its fact. It goads me, and always will, into difficult sincerities. It makes inaccuracy—not so much superficial inaccuracies of statistics but the deeper ones of meaning—painful as a discord; and when I write I will take hours, days, weeks even to find the word I wish for, seeking it not for its beauty, originality or strangeness, but merely because I want it to say what I mean.

For this reason I am puzzled when asked what makes my style, for there is nothing to it except a natural ear for cadence and the wish to get the meaning right. The picture is there, and I hunt for its words as a painter ransacks his palette for colours; apart from any incidental harmony, my writing is like a telegram—an effort to say all that I mean and nothing over, in the shortest way. This is not modesty, for how few people do we know who can write a telegram. The target is unattainable and facts are not transmutable in words; but the approach gives happiness in its relative way; and any voluntary, or even avoidable distortion seems like a mutilation of articulate speech, a negation of the prerogative of man. Most people would agree with this, but not so many believe that omission is equivalent to distortion, and that the whole object of speech—the clean fit of the garment on to the body of fact—is as much frustrated by the one as by the other. What a lot of trouble Cordelia could have saved by talking! For neither silence nor inaction are neutral,

[232]

and the builder of ideas uses words and their opposite silences as the builder of palaces and churches uses the voids and the solids of his design.

The pleas of Jock Murray and dear Sydney Cockerell fell therefore on rebellious ears as far as my book was concerned, until they shifted their ground and asked me to distinguish between my permanent and temporary feelings; yielding to persuasion, I took out all that seemed to have no bearing on my chief theme, the problem of East and West. But here again comes the main difficulty of writing, the disentangling in its transient cocoon of what is enduring. For how is one to know, among details of which none is too small to have its eternity somewhere, where the apparent greatness may dissolve on feet of clay. On the sure discrimination, the writer's immortality depends.

All these things I pondered during the months of the year before the war, as I had done ever since I had first begun to play with words. I returned from Germany in August, and the few remaining weeks in Asolo passed as if in a spotlight surrounded by storm. All the various threads of my life seemed to wander through these summer days at home: even my brother-in-law came with Costanza his daughter, now grown into a slender, lovable creature, seventeen years old, with my sister's laugh and long dark hair and eyes. The Leonard Woolleys and John Kirkwood and Moore Crosthwaite came, friends from Baghdad; old childhood friends from Devonshire; and Sydney Cockerell who made a bridge from my London youth unbroken to this day.

With him one night we went to see a pageant of war on the banks of the Piave. It was one of Mussolini's efforts to inject military ardour into his Italians, so much more inclined to civilization than to arms. They responded, as one could not help doing, to the beauty of the spectacle, and several miles of motor cars lined dusty lanes and shallow grassy banks beyond which the stream meandered in its easy summer bed of smooth white stones. Camp-fires smoked with silhouettes of tents

[233]

before them, and figures crept bending in the gentle night of June. Verey lights hovered as I had seen them so often over the death-strewn ridge of Carso twenty-one years before; and the guns flashed through their own smoke and rolled their echoes round the hills. The horrid crackling spit of the machine gun kept the white river-bed clear, and searchlights moved like the slow gaze of history, partial but investigating, over conflicts of men. An immense sadness filled me together with the beauty: there was such terrible levity in the Italy of those days, rushing to a chaos which none wanted, which was so easy to avoid—hoping against hope that the two and two they were so busily putting together might for once make something different from four. The whole of the Piave basin, its dipping combes and broader step-like rises, and farther foothills hiding deeper gorges and unseen Dolomites, and fruitful slopes that settled like birds in their nests to the plain—all were now glaring in the pink fumes of explosions, lit by tracers that rose and burst like sudden tulips on long invisible stalks, and deafened by the noises that hit each other and rebounded. So might some emperor have given his gladiatorial show in Rome debased—with this difference, that the audience itself was the victim designed.

As the gathered harvest let war draw near, English friends left one by one; the peaceful autumn, collector of riches, had changed into something very austere, stripping for nakedness. My mother and Herbert Young had long decided to expect what might come in Asolo, and I waited for a warning from Lady Iveagh before moving. On September 26th the telegram came: "Olga dying": poor Olga was Peace. I had a few hours to telephone for the last available sleeper, to pack, and catch the Orient Express in Padua: everything had long been foreseen and was ready; and I awoke at Vallorbe next morning with a well-organized feeling, and leaned at my window to watch more agitated people of less certain nationality being bundled out of the train and rejected by the French. "What a good thing it still is to have a British passport," I thought in my rashness. I met with no trouble of any sort before I reached Paris, where Jock had sent money to the American Express (for one could not take more than £10 out of Italy at that time). Hitler's ultimatum was being broadcast about the streets on large sheets in thick black letters like funeral announcements: half the porters had left the stations, called back to the army: I noticed with surprise, even then, an absence of air-raid shelters, and wondered at what I thought of as the supreme confidence of the French. The American Express was filled with women trying to get boats back to America, and very like what an ant-hill stirred with a stick would be if every insect had a voice. In the middle of this confusion, the man who had gone for my money made his way back and remarked politely that there seemed to be something wrong with my passport. There was; our maid had put my mother's passport into my bag by mistake. Even at that moment, I noted regretfully that no official had noticed how thirty years had been added to my age. I persuaded the American Express to give me my money just the same—they were ready for almost anything if they could have one woman the less on their hands—and I spent two nights in Paris before getting away, in a dark empty hotel in the Rue Rouget de Lisle, filled with dim gilt consoles and mirrors that reflected nothing. The everyday life went on, not yet thrown out of gear, but stiff, like those bodies of the dead inhabited by ghouls, of the Arabian tales. I found an atmosphere of security and comfort only at Mme Suzy's in the Rue de la Paix, where Mlle Suzanne, sadly, but with no swerving from her Art, designed me a hat of feathers light as a dream. People have different ways of being courageous and a lot of bravery has gone into the Paris hat—the little nothing that in the worst days of the Occupation blossomed into tulle to show the Germans that France was still there.

Strangely fortified, partly by the hat and partly by the sad, firm, resigned philosophy of Mlle Suzanne, I went back and fed my lizard Himyar on the last dandelions from Asolo and tried to console him for the marble gloom which had taken the place of his sunny garden. In the crowded restaurant car of the Calais train next day, he added to the already tightened nerves of American ladies returning, by crawling half out of his nest in the breast of my jacket on to the dining table: and a frozen atmosphere, a dumb but noticeable rejection of *all* British and European eccentricities altogether, surrounded the rest of our meal. I had a paper obtained in Paris to allow me to enter Britain, but I knew it would cause trouble and delay; my mother's passport had served me so far—I thought it might continue: it was examined and passed by four officials at Dover and let me enter war-time England unopposed.

I think that, by the time I reached England, the tension over Munich had been relieved. Even if it had not been so, the English feeling of a rooted security would no doubt have welcomed me, for it persisted—however unjustified—right through the blitzes, and was there, inexpressibly dear and familiar, when I landed again after four years of war. It became firmer, in fact—for after Munich there was a wave very like hysteria, which made me wonder what had happened to the England I knew. Those two unhappy little sentences, "peace in our time" and "peace with honour," seemed to me incredible for a statesman to have uttered and for a nation to believe: and though I knew too little to be sure that Munich was a mistake, I felt that only the most appalling condition of our defences could explain it. I realized then how much I cared for the honour of our island, since my grief and shame were greater than I had felt for years, if ever, over any private matter; and there is a walk by the park which I can never take now without an obscure feeling of discomfort, which I trace back until I find its first occasion—the reading of Mr. Chamberlain's speech on his return from Germany, and the sudden facing of the fact that war was now inevitable, though postponed. Before the end of the year, Sydney Cockerell took me to call on Earl Baldwin, who asked about life in Italy and looked up, surprised even at that eleventh hour, when I answered that I thought she was preparing for war.

[236]

"War?" said Lord Baldwin, at his desk, with a row of pipes ranged rather ostentatiously along one side. "War with whom? No one wants war."

"I don't think they mind," I said. "Mussolini thinks war will be good for them. He wants to make them strong."

Lord Baldwin tried to make me unsay myself and obviously disliked this statement. But I felt passionately; I refused to talk on less controversial subjects; and left in a disappointed atmosphere—Lord Baldwin bored with politics from someone he had thought of as pleasantly remote and Arabian—and I depressed by the meeting with such pure British provincialism in one who at any moment might have to be a leader in Europe.

In my Cassandra-like depression during the months after Munich, I met Harold Nicolson. Quiet and unemphatic, with the look of a dignified and serious small boy, so much more grown-up than the adults about him, he sat next to me at a dinner in the Junior Conservative Club, where he was to debate against Mr. Chamberlain's policy. He was silent and absorbed in his thoughts till I made some comparison of Greece with Persia. "Oh let us talk about them," he said, turning his chair a little round, as if the whole Conservative Party and all it was interested in were to be forgotten: "Those are such nice countries to talk about." It was only near the end of the meal that I discovered how much we felt the same about this moment in England. There was an extraordinary fervour in the Conservative devotion to Neville Chamberlain at that time, and, in the debate that followed, Harold was—except for my silent alliance—in a minority of one, though that pleasantest of English qualities, the decency towards opponents, gave the room a feeling of cordiality towards him: and there was also, I felt and hoped, a beginning of revolt against the desperate slogan of 'appeasement' which had led us to the edge of our precipice. If Harold had bowed only slightly to the Barbarian, to what we have brought almost intact out of forests that fringed the Roman centuries in their decline, the strain in us that likes sentiment and humour and the fight against odds—he would have captivated

[237]

his whole audience completely: but he never wavered—then or
ever—from that clear and sharp Mediterranean standard, the
cool merciless flicker of wit, the clean disinterested verity, which
is still the norm of civilization, even to us who fear it and carry
half the barbarian in our hearts. Whenever I can, I meet him,
and every meeting is made memorable by this impression of
'civilitas'—as if it were a talk with Boethius or Cassiodorus in
the days of Theodoric the Goth.

In spite of the shadow of Munich, and that I began my stay in
London with some weeks in and out of a nursing home, the
autumn and winter of this year were among the happiest I have
known. Leonard and Katharine Woolley were going to India,
and lent me their little house in Royal Avenue, Chelsea, and for
the first time in London I was under a roof of my own. It was
a separate pleasure every time I turned the latchkey, a delight to
from open out narrow stair and entrance into the civilized rooms,
filled with Katharine's taste, quiet and urbane, with bay windows,
and the branches of trees outside: the first requisite in a London
house is to look at trees.

Here I was able to give small luncheons and dinners and to
see my friends; I was planning a journey across Arabia with
Stewart Perowne, from the Mediterranean to the Indian Ocean,
and he visited me, with Michael Huxley and Larry Kirwan and
others interested in exploration. I came to know and like
Ella Maillart, and we lost ourselves one morning, crossing Hyde
Park, pretending it was the middle of Asia. I had begun to
think, after the last year, that I might be one of those women who
hate other women and are only easy with men: but I now realized
that what I dislike is the arrogance of the unfeminine woman,
neither one thing nor the other. The lovely and the brilliant or
good of my own sex, Celia Johnson, Biddy Carlisle, Phyllis
Balfour, Vita Nicolson, Virginia Woolf, Dora Gordine, and
many others, I met and admired and easily love—great people,
all moving like queens in their own atmosphere, and none of
them, it suddenly strikes me, fond of working in committees.

I now know that it is this individual quality in the human

being that I care for, apart from sex or age, and my pleasure in the world is made out of the variety of the ties that bind us. I like to remember these people, and regret that my visits in their lives are so short: the thought of so many incomplete friend-ships, to which Time alone is wanting, makes one long for an eternity whose intimacies can presumably be simultaneous and unimpeded, timeless and therefore secure.

The variety of London was enchanting, for I would spend my week-ends sometimes very grandly, at Petworth or Elveden, where I met royalty for the first time and noticed the finished art of my hostess's curtsey and felt the carriage of life running so smoothly on its wheels that one would have to give oneself a jolt out of it now and then if one stayed in it for long: or some-times I would go with Jock to his new house, planning Regency wall-papers and chairs, and warning him that his rashness in buying this little gem on Richmond Green would be followed soon and inevitably by a wife. Or I would stay quietly in my house with the pleasantness of a London Sunday at home and so many new people to know. Not only the characters of people, but their lives were absorbing: Humbert Wolfe with sad eyes and the poetry of London in his bones; Sir Charles Bell, fragile as a mist, talking of old friendships with Tibetans; Tom Boase and Leigh Ashton, wanderers in history and art; and Victor Stoloff, an eager young man with new ideas in films. A few plays are noted in my diary—*French without Tears*, and *Hamlet* in modern dress—but most of the pleasure was people, and they left little time over. Many of the friendships endure, and many were confirmed and strengthened through the war—like that with Fitzroy MacLean whom I first met in the house of the Peter Flemings, a languid young man with a drawl, just back from his travels round Bokhara where—so he said—one could go about anywhere so long as one slept in ditches and never registered at hotels—and whom I next met on his return to Cairo from a raid on Benghazi.

I was busy with Arabic talks at the BBC with Stewart, who was there on loan for a year; and I was being televised at

Alexandra Palace, a draughty unfinished place, where one stood shivering with enormous searchlights bracketed upon one, and an audience of oddities—a Zulu chief in feathers who was to dance, a Korean schoolmaster, a Viennese caricaturist,—among whom one presently took one's place to watch the next number come on. Before going through this ordeal, my face was made up on a dull green foundation, on which a pink mouth was painted very large.

"Must you go on widening it?" I complained. "Surely my mouth is quite big enough as it is?"

"We like them big for television," was the reply, typical of an age when everything is being adjusted for the Public.

But this was not the atmosphere I lived in, and when I lectured again, to the Royal Central Asian and to the Royal Geographical Societies, the friendly audiences were interested in what were to me realities, and my dress from Paris, white tulle with silver medallions, seemed to me not only unique, but very near the Absolute.

The winter had gone and 1939 had started with a war in its heart. I was taken to call at the USSR Embassy on the Maiskys, and noticed the friendly look of Asia grown rigid as it were, with a conviction that no intercourse was possible: it was like talking to somebody's back. Early in the year I wrote to Cairo, offering myself and asking for instructions, and was told to present myself at the F.O. or in Egypt as soon as the crisis came. I was anxious to become as fit as I could in preparation for this moment, and decided to spend the spring in the strong air of the Levant that cures or kills.

My mother had been taken off by a friend to California; after a few weeks in Asolo I started in the opposite direction, eastward. The best train journey I know is that of the Orient and Taurus Express round the corner of Europe and Asia: there is the feeling of an opening world about it, the old and the wild alternate, and the countries change as you sit, swiftly enough never to become monotonous: the food alters in the dining car, the shape of peoples' heads changes, there is a growing emptiness

[240]

in landscape as you pass through wastes trampled by the wander-
ings of nations and climb along valleys beyond the Bosphorus
where spring makes her difficult way on to the wind-bitten
plateaux of Anatolia. And the Cilician Gates in the early
morning hang over the Aegean like a balcony for the gods; the
old mule-track still zigzags under cobbles here and there, and
the whole spirit of travel cries out from its sharp corners.

I spent a few days with the George Rendels in Sofia, and saw
my first and only glimpse of the Balkans—the small and muddy
capital surrounded by melting snow, with unfinished patches
round its public buildings, and a feeling about it of Barbarian
Invasions turned to Peasantry. Bulgaria was being pushed into
the arms of the Axis by the fact that the English were not fond of
attar of roses, and our Treasury's notions of economy did not run
to preserving an ally by buying useless stores: we were still
busy offering guarantees to countries unapproachable by sea.
George Rendel, who had been in London and helped me with
the greatest kindness over my south Arabian journeys, was now
fighting here in the last redoubt of a position already lost at home,
depressed by the feeling of the Bulgarians themselves, friendly
but hopeless. The country had been scraped clean into poverty
by its successive wars: nothing of luxury—no fine silver, linen,
furniture—existed any longer: and the receptions, to one or two
of which I was taken, were very like what we became accustomed
to in later years of war.

I was making for Crusader and Assassin castles, and—not
stopping in Stamboul—very nearly stepped off at a wayside
station between Adana and the Syrian border, where romance
opens northward in wide shallow valleys with ruins on surrounding hills. Luckily I reflected on my want of Turkish
combined with the international situation, and continued till the
train reached Aleppo. Here an anti-French strike had been
going on for a month, and there seemed to be no way to buy all
I needed from the shuttered bazaars. Soldiers in battle dress
stood at street corners, and a sullen and ineffectual bomb of
protest went off regularly every evening in the town: I realized

R

what a hopeless place a hotel is for dealing with such an intimate oriental situation, and asked how people managed to keep themselves fed: no one in Aleppo, they explained, would be without at least a month's provision—oil, corn, sugar, etc.—stored in their own house. This is a fundamental precaution which a century or two of security has made us forget; I found it working again in Italy when I returned with the normal bloodshed of the world about us at the end of the war: in Aleppo it seemed to promise endless delays, and I decided to use a letter of introduction to some merchants in Hama.

Hama, supposed to be a hot-bed of anti-Christian feeling, had recently murdered a Frenchman. As far as I could see, I was the only European there, and it was an enchanting little town, built on the Orontes with black and white stone. The noise of the water-wheels, high as houses, wooden, without even a nail of metal that might rust, sang like a harmony of organs, near and distant, through the night. The merchants were kindness itself, provided everything out of sacks and jars in their stores, and sat with me at intervals of the day at crowded café tables, where among hookahs and swinging tarbush tassels the news-sheets with their well-worn platitudes were handed up and down. I found, as I had often done before, that the way to carry out an adventure is to organize the jumping-off place as near to its borders as possible. Masyaf was the beginning of the Assassin country: the merchants found me a citizen who would procure me two horses and a guide; we drove there all together and faced the French officer in command, who was polite, doubtful, pleased to see an interest taken in his district, reluctant to let anyone loose in it unaccompanied, obviously unable to dispense an escort himself at that time, and finally—faced with everything already settled and established—resigned to letting me do the best I could. In the afternoon I was alone with my small and not very reassuring caravan, climbing up stony tracks towards Husn Sulaiman, the temple of the Phoenicians in the hills, and along the crocodile back of the watershed to Krak of the Crusaders.

I had a bad supper that night among mountain hovels, with a crowd of children round me. My poor depressed Ismaili guide knew his life was in danger in a Nosairi village, and showed no promise of guide-like virtues at all. The old lady, in whose room I slept among household stores, settled into a sheepskin bunk after taking off one head-kerchief and one skirt and lighting a little oil-lamp to discourage bugs: and the gloomy ideas awakened by this process were justified. I wondered, in the wakeful hours, why I was there—a doubt that rarely troubled me except sometimes in the Alps before a climb. I wished that there might be no war, and that I could sit in Asolo and read old histories in peace. But when the morning came and we rode on, and the beautiful land spread its high places, its secret pastoral solitudes about us, and I sat by a spring and ate my eggs and bread and cheese, and read William of Tyre and watched the poor old thin horse grazing—the silent hours so quietly lifted out of the world seemed worth all the trouble of their attainment.

We walked and rode for three days along this high land, dipping one night into a village and sleeping the next in a little rest house under the high walls of Krak; there too was a peaceful hour in the great fortress, watching from the battlements the swallows circling and the triangle of the northern sea. Through centuries that triangle must have been watched by those to whom it spoke of home. In the rest house a young Syrian and his sister were hoping to make a living after years in America: they had come back to Syria because: "It is good to be poor with one's own people." When I left them, I rode by the Crusaders' way and the monastery of St. George to Safita, in sight far away, and, in the immensely thick fortress church of the great Templar tower there, attended a Greek service for Easter by candle light. On this day a young man was killed in cold blood by the Germans in Stuttgart. We had met in the winter, and before he went to Germany, in a letter full of hope and foreboding, he asked me to marry him: I found this letter on my return to Aleppo, and another from a friend, written later, to tell me of his death.

[243]

Knowing nothing, I continued my ride from castle to castle, with two guides—one for each religion, Ismaili and Nosairi—making for the country of the Assassins, Khawabi, Qahf, Qadmus, 'Alleiqa—fortresses roughly built, lonely and ruined, with the flavour of their rebellious origin, the defiance of a minority that has taken to the hills, still strongly about them. The Ismaili, devotees of the Aga Khan, were now being slowly pinched into extinction, while the Nosairi, tree-worshippers of some forgotten day, pushed into their conquered villages: the fierce little struggle went on beyond the range of law, in a wild country, steep and lonely, where patches of cultivation scarcely showed, and paths, tilted at strange angles, made even our agile horses slither on the mica slabs. The hot Mediterranean scents were all about us, pungent and aromatic in the sun; the people were fearless and friendly, tall and loose-limbed with light eyes, descendants very likely of Crusaders, and busy with shallow ploughing in stony fields. From their high world we scrambled down, and crossed from the Crusader ruin of Abu Qubeis, through the rich Hama loam where the plough cuts a mile-long uninterrupted furrow, to the swift elbow of the Orontes and the castle of Sheizar, the home of Usama, most charming of Arab historians and Saladin's friend; to the mound of Apamea whose ruins lie deep in asphodel; and back to Hama, to find the spring in full blossom and the city folk enjoying it in tents along the cliffs that line the river and catch the desert breeze. We left them again for the coast and the settled fiefs of the Crusaders—Tartous where I found an Arab house to sleep in and wandered for some days among the Templar ruins into which the town is built; and among lesser castles, Areimat and Yahmur, pleasant surely to live in in their time, lost among wheat fields and out of the sound of the sea. The people were hunting small birds with falcons on their wrists in the corn.

It is curious how little there is of Muslim feeling in Syria as soon as the line of the great trading cities, from Damascus to Aleppo, is left behind. The Christians have impressed a stronger footprint, but the real lords were pagans long before. Their ruined walls and temples, few and in lonely places, seem still to be the true holders of the land, and the groves of their trees are worshipped, crowning heights where some Muslim is buried, a parvenu in Time. Near Tartous, their once-rich city of Arvad shows a few tombs: and the only *living* tradition of their world, apart from the high mountain sanctuaries, is the little island of Ruad where the seafaring Phoenicians build boats and dive for sponges to this day. For many years I kept a sponge I bought there, and its clear salty smell, different from shop-bought sponges, brought back the sunny day, the light colour of the spring waves moving gently round the high blocks of Phoenician walls, the clean drowsy streets, salt-encrusted and washed with air; and the looks of the inhabitants, careless and free, and nonchalant in their island privacy with strangers.

I made for Beirut by car, and stayed there with the Seiriqs and Schlumbergers, and came back with them, visiting Merkab, Ras Shamra, Latakiah and Sahiun: and then took horse again with Mme Seiriq and rode over the ridge of Slenfe into the Orontes valley to Jisr Shogr, Eriha, Idlib, and to Aleppo by car. This three days' ride took us up again into the loneliness, wilder than most because smugglers, who cross it with sacks of Latakiah tobacco on their backs, are prepared for violence and quick to shake off the police if they follow them into the lacework of the Orontes marshlands far below. The owner of my horse was a smuggler himself, and the horse had a neck pitted with bullet marks where the hair had grown again a different colour. This dangerous sign I noticed only when we got down into the silence of the Orontes valley, fertile under heavy-headed crops, but so deathly from malaria that no one will sleep there in summer: in the loneliest stretch the man forced me off my horse and started to make away with the luggage. My new and devoted guide Isa was with me. Together we turned on this man and told him that he was going to prison as soon as we reached the journey's end: the other two owners of horses looked frightened, hesitated, and took our side: and I walked on, refusing to mount, with both hands in my pockets, to avoid having to pardon the man if he succeeded in kissing my hand. He tried to do this at intervals, with sudden grabs, but I walked on, stolid and angry, with an occasional remark, on the wickedness of robbing travellers, thrown behind me.

In Aleppo I rested for a fortnight in the Altounian house. Their kindness I shall never forget, for I needed my friends in those days. The world seemed to be cracking, every crack widening, and no escape from its ruin: yet its beauty and strangeness were never closer to the heart—and this I have found often in times of sorrow. Perhaps, when the account is made, those times of happiness, sorrow, or love will alone show themselves alive?

With the Altounians I rode about the red Aleppo cornland rich with flowers, by beehive villages of mud; drove to St. Simeon in its dove-grey frame of stones; visited the Woolleys digging at Atchana, by the ancient fords of Orontes; and went alone to Antioch, just taken over by the Turks, who sat drinking arak that looked like milk. Alcohol, and the green lanes shadowed with trees, and abundance of water, gave a feeling suddenly of Europe. The whole of the prosperous country of Alexandretta had been ceded, with such brutal swiftness that there was no chance for an Armenian landowner who wished to remove himself to get a fair price for his lands. Tension and fear were there, even in Aleppo, behind the curtain of everyday living. For three last days, with the Altounian girls and a charming Armenian, hero of the Musa Dagh and one of the dispossessed—we made for the Euphrates and the round Saracen fortress of al-Nejm that overlooks it, and crossed to Sirrin on the Eastern side. With that last vision of space, the bare river and open cornlands that clothe its treeless landscapes, the slow Assyrian ferry that never changes, and the flocks of sheep that walk under their dust—with this in my eyes, between one European crisis and another, I left Aleppo to look again at Greece before the curtain fell.

*　　　*　　　*

ATHENS, 4 *May*, 1938.

My dear Jock,

I am glad I didn't see you fly off into the air: as it is, I should not be at all surprised to see you sitting on the terrace of the Grande Bretagne in the sun, transported by your thoughts which cannot be glued to an office chair after wandering over Delphi. I spent two hours among the funeral stelæ of the Museum: you can't surpass the beauty and dignity of those monuments: so profound and serene an acceptance of death, such tenderness and such restraint: I can imagine no sorrow that would not be lessened by a walk among those immortal things. I got you a catalogue, but it is very poor, and so I have bought some of the things I liked best in picture cards and will send them together; I had no idea also to what beauty the Greek vase could attain. The Mycenœan things (except the two cups of the bulls) suffer from being seen after the full loveliness of the classic. There is no doubt that something must be done about coming next year, for such things you must see. And I hear that in all the country where no one goes, between Helicon and the sea, there are little bays with 5th century fortresses, one more perfect than the last.

Himyar [my lizard] has been taken to the Parthenon and the temple of Zeus, but what he prefers is Hymettus. We took him to picnic above your most beautiful monastery (no priest or brandy for us alas!) and it climbed so to the poor little lizard's head that he went quite gay and walked about with a purple flower sticking out of his mouth on one side, like Carmen!

12 *May*, 1938.

My dearest Jock,

Is it proper to address in these affectionate terms? but it was *nice* of you to write so quickly from your Roman splendours, and we have been missing you so much on the way to and from Sparta. We found a delicious hotel, a little island fortress off Nauplia where the Executioner used to live, but now not reminiscent of that and beautifully arranged for anyone who wants to be comfortable and lazy and to look out from morning to evening on the great bay of "horse-breeding Argos". I can't tell you about it all: Mycenae and Tyrins more impressive than anything except Delphi, and the incredible beauty of that open landscape of hills. We were on the Mound of Tyrins at sunset and a golden halo was against everything that

touched the sky. I have come to the conclusion that the Byzantine does not belong here: the country needs the straight and severe
line of its square temples—so that Mistra did not thrill me as much
as the rest; but the hills of Arcadia did, and Taygetus covered in
snow with Sparta at its feet: and the people here and there just like
their old statues.

Himyar sends you his greetings. He *very nearly* got under the
Parthenon but I had him by the tail just in time. He is getting
tame now and eats while I talk to him.

VILLA FREIA, ASOLO, 23 *May*, 1938.

Is it you or I who owe a letter? I know that it is *really* you,
because of a long letter I had it in my mind to write, but I am not
quite sure that it ever got written.

A woman here typed out my articles *so* badly: when I protested
she explained that "she was not interested in words".

6 June, 1938.

A dreadful thing has happened. My poor Himyar is lost. He
slipped out of the little white belt I made him, *so* tight I thought, and
he was seen yesterday across the road and the tennis court next door.
I don't suppose I shall ever get him again; we have been looking and
looking and offered a reward. I didn't think I should ever miss a
little creature so much: he had become so tame and was so engaging
and when I think of him dying of cold in some damp cleft—I just
weep. It shows one should never love any belongings: one can't
help winding one's heart round even the littlest if it depends on one
and then one is sure to be lacerated sooner or later.

SANATORIUM, "DR. WIGGER'S KURHEIM," PARTENKIRCHEN,
25 July, 1938.

This heading makes one feel rather unwell just to look at it, but
all the rest of this place is lovely—only who would work here? There
are hills and hills and rolling meadows and woods below. Anyway,
my dear Jock, it is no use wailing about this hurry hurry in every
letter of yours when you give me nothing to hurry with. Even the
people one can no longer mention were incapable of making bricks

without straw, and as you told me only to bring the catalogue if the negatives were *not* sent, and as the negatives *were* sent, I didn't bring the vast tome and your little figures by themselves are useless.

I am sorry to have to leave my book which I am just interested in. Whether you will ever publish it, is a question, but it makes a fine drama of East and West and Mama says you will refuse to take any of the venom out when you read it. As a matter of fact it is a curious thing how any personal feeling vanishes and only the pleasure of creating a harmonious whole remains.

I don't yet know what sort of a cure they are going to impose on me. I know that all I need for health is total absence of work.

VILLA FREIA, ASOLO, 25 August, 1938.

I am *awfully* sorry but I *do* dislike 'window'.[1] Two very real objections—one that it isn't a true title. You can't call a thing that moves 300 miles all over the country a window. And secondly it is the sort of title that R. would have. Perhaps you got me mixed up with her in your mind under the intoxicating stimulus of your bath? I don't think I can bear to leave it, and I am told that books are always appearing with different names from those announced. And it would remind everyone of *A Window in Thrums*. I have always wondered what Thrums is and whether it has a singular. I hope you won't mind—but it was rather rash of you not to consult the Mother for the christening.

I am very glad to be home again and think cures a dreary business, but it was interesting to be in that country and I met such nice people, Austrian and German girls all feeling very caged.

Himyar showed no very exuberant feelings, but he rubbed his nose against my finger this morning. He has worn off all his finger nails: either by running round his cage or else he must *bite* them!

17 September, 1938.

Thank you for your nice long letter: I agree about the delight of detail for its own sake—a pure form of happiness? I think too that it is a mistake to think one sort of work intrinsically superior to

[1] The title *A Window in the Hadhramaut,* later altered to *Seen in the Hadh-ramaut.*

[249]

another. But I do think one can protest against the collector of detail saying that he and he *alone* is scientific, and there is a tendency among them to do that. I am quite sure that one can be accurate and imaginative—but not at all sure that one can be accurate in any real sense and unimaginative. The fact is that the fable of the hare and tortoise is only true as an exception and not as a rule!

I have got to page 180 of the great work. Hope the state of Europe will let it be finished.

PARIS, 28 *September*, 1938.

Dearest B,

Such an awful discovery. I have your passport—and you must have mine! How it got into my drawer I cannot think. Anyway no one noticed luckily till I went for my money to the American Express—you can imagine my feelings, as everyone was rushing off with news of the German ultimatum. They were very nice, gave me my money, gave me a temporary pass (but I spent all day over these operations, in fearful crowds). Now I have a ticket for Friday and give up Belgium, as we are advised to go as soon as possible. And I will send your passport by the Bag and Tony Torr when I get to London, and H.A.O. can bring me mine. Meanwhile I did not dare buy a ticket till this afternoon and can only get a faint hope of a seat on Friday—hope for the best.

Poor little Himyar is so unhappy. I wanted to go to a theatre to-night but haven't the heart to leave him. He sits in the dark on his hot bottle with his eyes wide open and only shuts them when I stroke him and has refused to eat: and when I came home this afternoon he was hanging by his neck. That was my second shock to-day!

At the Consulate the Consul—such a nice-looking man—came along and chatted politics, which helped to get my passport through.

30 *September*, 1938.

News seems better—the crisis at any rate put off till next time and perhaps it has dawned all round that one means business. It was rather pathetic coming along to see French reservists guarding the railway bridges, etc., in a blue uniform coat snatched up and worn over their ordinary clothes.

My hat has come and I wonder if I shall ever dare to wear it: it

[250]

has a pink and a yellow ostrich feather over one eye and a red one down the back!

LONDON, 23 October, 1938.

Am dining with the John Murrays and lunching with the Halifaxes Tuesday—to-morrow a Sherry Party of farewell to Katherine Woolley. All this in between mud packs and bed. Poor little Himyar enjoys this invalid life—he snuggles in beside me and is so tame now, he looks up when I talk and makes his eye quite small and friendly. He has just crept under the gas stove and I have had to unscrew it to get him out.

12 ROYAL AVENUE, 12 November, 1938.

On Wednesday I dined with that nice young Peter Carter who came out to Asolo. He and a friend, John Davie, live together in Westminster and it was a party of six with Elinor Glyn, and a Mrs. Ghika from the Rumanian Legation. Elinor Glyn is 74, without a wrinkle, with red hair, green velvet and pearls, lovely eyes heavily kohled, and an emotional very delicate manner. And she told us all what we were in our former lives. It was rather trying, as she says she is inspired direct by God to say these things across the dinner table and the young men were all treated rather unkindly: but *me* she fixed and said: "This is not a woman that I see—it is a 'man, a young man pure and enthusiastic: there is no falsehood here, no pretence: he speaks simply: he is caged in a woman's body and he hates it, but he is too great to rebel: he uses it gracefully, but remains aloof inside it: nothing but goodness and truth can come from him'." So now you know.

21 December, 1938.

Darling B—and Herbert,

Last night Jock gave a dinner and I sat between Max Beerbohm and Vernon Bartlett—a contrast. Max Beerbohm *just* like his books, the most charming adjectives popping out of his mouth, and his remarks all made with a sort of charming innocence not innocent at all. He talked of somebody's 'arid' profile and the 'immense cosiness' of Trollope's books. They were both like something so remote, belonging to a world quite gone now, and so charming.

[251]

6 January, 1939.

Darling B,

I have a sad little piece of news. My poor little Himyar is dead. It was too much for him here and though I kept him warm, he just could not bear the absence of sun. I don't think he suffered, because he slept peacefully but just got thinner and thinner and the day before yesterday I found him dead, and even now I can't think or speak of him without crying. It is absurd for so tiny a creature—but I think he and I were alike in lots of ways, both rather small and lonely in our hearts and he was a gallant little fellow. The nice maid here came to ask me for his little body to send to her brother in Austria who has a passion for these things, and has a school—and so I let her send him so that his small existence may be as useful as it can. It may be ridiculous to care so much, but after all there is less difference between us and a lizard than between us and God and we expect *Him* to feel an interest. I will wipe my eyes and go to less sorrowful things.

SIMPLON EXPRESS, 20 March, 1939.

I am just off—a fine sunny day. Herbert came to Venice and Bertie too and we lunched at Dorothea's with the Napiers there also —I would have postponed altogether, but I would have to get out of the country *anyhow*, so may as well go on—but I don't think I have ever felt so sad at leaving. All the things in the house that mattered most are arranged for. I sent the silver to Cantoni, and Dorothea will provide Herbert with money if the worst happens. I still think it may be delayed, though not for *very* long. I am writing to London to ask if I should be wanted there or in Palestine or Egypt. I may find that I am suitably placed where I am and will let you know as soon as I know myself.

I think of you sailing in comfort in this lovely sunshine and just about to arrive now I suppose. It is a great comfort in a way to think that you are so well and comfortably *out of the way*!

There is something very exciting in being in the Simplon-Orient Express. I suppose I am destined for ever to be a wanderer on the earth—and yet I felt so sad to leave the quiet things of home.

TURKEY IN ASIA, 24 *March,* 1939.

I have lost my heart to Constantinople, only through the sight of it crossing the ferry this morning—a quite incredible splendour spread out in gentle bays and the houses all built of wood, but three or four stories high and decorated, and blossoming trees and cypresses about among them. It feels hot now, as Bulgaria was all under snow and the Rendels were off skiing. I had two very amusing days. They gave me a dinner party and I had the American Minister next me, called Atherton—such nice people from Boston who asked me to tea next day. Some old friends from Teheran were at the Legation too; and then I was taken to a proper Bulgarian party the evening after. It is a pathetic country: their two wars have left them with *nothing*, no houses, no linen, no silver; everything even in the best houses is rough and poor, and the bit of country that grows wheat was taken away from them. They are now just waiting for the next chance to snatch it from Rumania. They are a fine people with a *passion* for freedom: so great that it made them able to remain 500 years under the Turk and come out pure Bulgar at the end. Because of this bad peace settlement it is quite likely they may throw in their lot with Germany.

We are hovering now on the very brink of war and the Legation atmosphere was not reassuring. The American thought there was not a chance, but the Rendels still hope for peace. If war comes I shall probably begin by going to Egypt. The Italians have mobilized on the Jugo-Slav frontier and the rumour goes they mean to attack France through Spain, but this seems to me rather wild.

Meanwhile here one is back in the spaciousness of Asia, rattling through glorious country of wheat-growing plains with mountains around them still sprinkled with snow. But the villages are rich with blossom and a thick carpet of anemones runs by the railway track. I seem to be the only woman on the Taurus express! Very few people travelling.

ALEPPO, 27 *March,* 1939.

I spoke yesterday to the hero of the Armenian defence of Aintab— the only bit of the world where the Armenians fought and won, holding their rock-bound village right through the massacres. He was telling me that the Turk Army is all pro-German and Ismet too, but I am not very ready to believe it. If we cannot keep them with us, we may as well give up any diplomacy *ever*.

I can't tell you how wonderful it was to come pouring down with the rivers from the upland of Anatolia through the Cilician gates—huge rocks and pinnacles, towering from the plain. I don't think it is true that one gets no idea of a country by just going through it: it depends on how skilful one is at gathering evidence quickly; but one can see a great deal from the kind of agriculture, the climate, the roads, and the structure of the land, and the people as you pass. Not one of the men on those high windswept plains had the slack mouth of a townsman. There was something quite indescribably touching in those small villages with a mist of blossom—apricot and peach and cherry—so fragile against that landscape of immense rocks and snows. And then it was lovely too to reach the high tributaries of Euphrates, shining through great green plains, with castles and ruins on heights about them: and to come over more but lower ranges, wooded with pine and myrtle and juniper, to these plains of North Syria shining in the sunset, laced with ribbons of water, and in their solitudes here and there broken columns of forgotten temples, and flocks of sheep. There are ruins everywhere here, half of them never visited or known.

28 March, 1939.

I must say that there is something rather sinister in going to bed with the sound of a bomb every other night. This one has just gone off in the suq: it sounds quite ordinary, but there is a horrid sort of stillness after, as if every conversation in Aleppo had stopped. The last one they say did not matter as it was filled with only gunpowder: in my ignorance I thought that was all that one ever did fill up one's bombs with. It would be too long to tell you all the ins and outs of this unhappy little corner, but what with Arabs, Turks, and French there is a tangle on every hand. I have come into an anti-French strike and to-day the troops have marched silently in and are standing scattered about with bayonets here and there: one amiable Senegalese seized me with one hand and his bayonet in the other and made me go across the street, I don't yet know why. The effect has been like a holiday: no traffic, so everyone had time to walk about and look—only it is a rather nervy sort of crowd, and no women (except me and one other) walking about.

This morning I was given a glorious ride by Captain Altounian, such a nice Irish-Armenian, friend of Lawrence, and as we came back saw the troops marching in, *so* tired as they have just been fighting on the northern hills we see in the distance, and we have three armoured cars at the entrance to the town. It does not make me feel uncomfortable at all (except that I wanted to get my provisions and all the shops were shut). I suppose it comes of growing up in a war: but it just struck me that nearly everyone I know in Asolo or London would feel it to be quite abnormal to walk about among bayonets like this. Here however no one bothers very much about it, and my Armenian friends are only very unhappy because they will lose all their lands and become exiles as soon as the Turk is nominally as well as actually in power at Alexandretta. The wife is English and the old father is a wonderful character, who built and ran a hospital and still operates at the age of 85; and stayed right through the war in Aleppo, never stooping to compromise with a Turk or anyone else. He had to wait for years for permission to open his hospital because he would not give bakshish—but he got his way without it in the end (as everyone could do if they stuck to their principles). And now he is respected by all and has known everyone of note in the Near East, and has the most charming head and expression you ever saw. They have been so good to me. Yesterday they took me to one of the old Venetian houses that all communicate with each other by the roofs: a whole green city lies above the suqs with holes let in that light the suq below. Trees grow there, and there is even a well to keep these hanging gardens—and the citadel and the minarets float above them. All the suqs were deserted and closed and many people kept indoors, but everyone was as pleasant to us as can be, and we looked at shrines outside the city and bits of the old walls, and to-day rode in the morning and this afternoon went to see the salt pans, all surrounded by anemones and iris in the grass.

To-morrow I go to Hama and then vanish for a fortnight into those peaceful hills. There will be no trouble once outside the towns. It is all very touristy, but I shall get into side tracks and wander through those lovely hills and may not be able to post for some 15 or 16 days—but will see.

My provisions have been bought by way of some back door. Lots of the shops sit with their shutters *half* down so that they can close quick if some official comes.

This is the sixth day of riding in the hills and I am about half-way, having just touched the civilized high road at Qal'at al Husn (Krak)— the show-castle of the Crusaders. It is not *what* one sees, but *how* one sees it that counts: by coming riding across country in the sunset when the tourists had gone, and spending the evening wandering over that enormous pile, and going again next morning, having it all to myself, I really walked back into the crusading age. It is quite unbelievable: seated on a pass in the hills, a snowy ridge behind it, the plain of Homs below, its great outer circuit was able to hold 2,000 men. From it we rode by the old road—a romantic way, with a river and corn and flowering trees, to the other great castle in sight— Safita, which held the coastlands, a country of small stony hills and corn-growing hollows. My Ismaili guide brought with him an assistant who was (not metaphorically but actually) dotty: amiable but just loony. I felt like someone in Shakespeare, riding along with an Assassin and a Fool. My Ismaili was, it seems, in danger of his life among the Nosairi but for a letter which the kind wife of the Qaimakam of Masyaf (who is a Nosairi herself) gave him. Anyway we had rather a difficult time with a certain want of cordiality and at two places they gave us no food. The second time I got angry and said that they would be known as the only people in Syria who refused food to strangers!—whereupon a widow led me into her house and fed me, and refused payment and all was well and friendly.

But at Safita, before going back through the Nosairi country, I have got one of their own people, and he is the handsomest young man I have ever seen. He says that they are descended from the Crusaders, and I believe it, for they are quite different—with big bones, tall, and fair as often as not; and even their gruffness and anxiety to keep themselves to themselves is more Nordic than Arabian. Anyway my charming Isa (Jesus) might be one of the best looking Crusaders—so well-made, with clean-cut features and green eyes and the most beautiful smile you ever saw: and he wears a black kefiah like a helmet, so that I think of him as one of the young Franks who settled here, and who knows to what small French or Norman town his ancestry might lead?

This castle is Arab and belonged to the Assassins, but the Muslims are in it now, and have built a village inside its walls, so that little of the old is left except the pleasant feeling of being perched high

[256]

among walls. I was given a lovely clean bed here, a great luxury, and they have been all so friendly.

I hope to be in Hama in a week's time. This country is all on edge of revolt and the strike continues, but it is quiet enough in the hills. What will happen in Europe no one knows. Be careful about coming back in a freighter: it would be horrid to be caught in a slow boat by a war.

ALEPPO, 19 April, 1939.

My dear Jock,

I am not going to write an answer to your long good letter, merely because I have had a great shock and sorrow and can hardly think what I write. You have probably seen it and may know what really happened—D. died on the 5th in Berlin. I don't think in this whole world there was a truer, more chivalrous, more pure and gallant soul; and he and I were very true friends; and I have his last letter, waiting at Hama for me, by me now—so full of all the future he will never see. Among my friends, he is the first victim of this war.

Perhaps, dear Jock, it is because you have never been through the abyss of insecurity that you have not yet made a Unity of your universe? I was very young when the war came, and no one could emerge sane unless they blunted one part of their mind or else penetrated to where—differently perhaps for every living creature—the secret runs one and indivisible, the same in the stones and flowers and in the hearts of men. You are not yet your Master if you feel it all divided. But whether you can reach that ultimate security without great unhappiness I do not know and perhaps it is better not: I would not have the courage to desire that depth of adventure for any of those I love.

I wonder why you thought of the sailing ships? Is it because you are safe in harbour, and wave them a farewell? It is not easy to sail on the high seas, and often lonely—and yet at the end of life one would not wish it otherwise.

9 May, 1939.

My dear Venetia,

I got down to Beirut to see some friends and got stuck there by a chauffeurs' strike, so rode back with a nice Frenchwoman across the

S   [257]

hills from Latakiah and down into the valley of the Orontes, one of the loveliest things in this world to do. It is so unhealthy that very few people live there, but the corn and meadows are rich and green and the flocks pasture in that solitude of cities long dead, and it has just been for many centuries a passage-way for armies. Castles in ruins stand on ridges at the edge and the Nosairi mountains pour down into it range behind range.

I have given up thinking over Europe; have made all arrangements for the worst if it comes, and now carry on as if no war were anywhere about. I have an idea we may yet evade it, if only we keep firm. We are so incredibly stupid. It is only by an undeserved mercy of Providence that the other people are more so. Anyway I have no doubt of the final result, and that after all is what chiefly matters. And the fact that people in England begin to realize that there are things worth dying for is surely to the good. I find this atmosphere pleasanter than the smugness of five years ago—and I believe one will get tempered to live in an atmosphere of danger and not mind it any more than other healthy animals mind it.

10 *May*, 1939.

My dear Lionel,

I must write and talk to you about Crusader Castles—I have been thinking of you so often these last weeks. You would have enjoyed yourself with me, and Mary would have loved the flowers—pink primroses, and cyclamen, asphodel, red tulips, scented hyacinths and red and purple anemones—and ever so many more. I started at Hama, which is an enchanted place at blossom time, and drove to Masyaf and from there got a mule and horse and an Ismaili guide who had huge yellow boots like Charlie Chaplin. We rode along through the Alawite mountains by the Phoenician temple of Husn Sulaiman to Krak: it was so pleasant coming to it in that proper leisurely way and spending the evening there, and then riding by small paths to Safita. Here I asked for an Alawite guide, as the Ismaili could procure no food in the pagan villages (there being a feud), and I got the handsomest blue-eyed Crusader you ever saw and so nice that I am going to try to keep him, though he will break all the Asolo hearts. I don't know what Monsignore will say if our maids want to marry a Tree-Worshipper? With him we rode north to the Assassin fortresses—Khawabi, Qahf, Qadmous and 'Alleiqa—

[258]

all in the most inaccessible steep places, not so well built as the Crusaders', but fine romantic ruins—and then out to the Orontes plain by another castle (Bukbeis of the Crusaders) and by Sheizar to Apamea all buried under asphodel and grass. I then came back by Hama and made another tour largely by car from Antioch by Tartous down the coast, and saw Markab and then rode back from Sahyun over the hills. It is quite incredibly lovely to ride down into the Orontes valley, so lonely and scattered with its forgotten *tells*. We had an animated moment with a guide who went mad and forced me off my horse and was for going off with my luggage—however my tree-worshipper and I dealt with him between us. I carried William of Tyre about with me, and sometimes hardly knew whether I was in the 12th or 20th century. There was a good deal to be said for the 12th except for the peasants who must have had a thin time being raided from both sides.

TAURUS EXPRESS, 17 *May*, 1939.

Dearest B,

I have booked myself a little berth in Egypt and will go when and if necessary, and meanwhile carry on according to schedule and c/o American Express, Athens, should find me for some time to come.

We are sweltering along up the Amanus range out of Syria, the rolling plains yellow with corn below. I had three very good days to finish up with—the two Altounian girls took me with an Armenian friend to see the 'Castle of the Star,' a fine old circular Arab 13th century fortress on the Euphrates—a stern dramatic place with yellow stone-built sloping walls on the wide loops and bays and arid cliffs of the river. What a great river is Euphrates—winding its immense lengths from the hills of Armenia to the Persian sea; one comes to it over a rolling *world* of corn: not fields, but just a sheath to the landscape, green here, yellow there, deep or shallow according to the soil; the winds and clouds make patterns on it: the horizon is softened like velvet: you feel that half the world could be fed here for your car goes through it for hours and days. The little villages, flat or beehive-roofed with their dogs lying in the sun around them, are out with clumsy sickles or bare hands pulling the harvest: all this immense country is reaped by hand. And it is lonely: we never met a car for two days. The crossing of Euphrates is an undertaking one should never attempt in a hurry: it may take six hours. It took us three to go and five to come back. The old ferry-punt is pushed into mid-stream with poles and then drifts to the other side miles down, and is towed up again with ropes. One would think that in 6,000 years or so they might have invented oars! Where we crossed on our return, just below the Mound of Carchemish, the river was little under a mile broad and perhaps more: its mud made it pink in the sun like a pink pearl. We bathed in it, held by a rope, for it was sweeping down.

The Altounians have a farm the other side and we spent two nights there sleeping on the roof with the whole circle of the horizon about us. Such stars made a science of astronomy. When one first woke it was almost startling, one seemed to be immersed in depths of space, the Milky Way flung across it like a scarf of tulle. The moon appeared low near morning and then the red sunrise began to flare up from the low rim of hills. All this was once civilized prosperous land: mounds of buried cities are scattered by every stream and in the plains, and little dwindling communities still cling to their low slopes. A broken pink marble column lay in a ditch of the farm and there are still two funeral monuments—the 'minarets of Serrin'—on the tops of the hills: Gertrude Bell rode up to them, and so did we; but half of the best one has fallen down since her day and within the last five years. It was a good ride except that one of the mares got out of hand, and mine raced her and both bolted. An Arab padded saddle gives no grip and they had only a halter and no bit: I could do nothing, not even turn her head: the way home was all downhill: I decided grimly to hold on as long as I could and hoped my feet were not caught in the stirrups; shot full tilt down a steep bit, and was finally thrown on the stepping stones of a stream with no hurt except a bruised arm and bleeding head not even concussed. By the time I got up the other mare had galloped up without a saddle and her rider came along with a sprained muscle; but we were able to continue our ride and end a long circle at beduin tents where the Sheikh had got a roasted sheep all ready stuffed with pine kernels and rice. We rested there, sleeping under abbas in the guest tent. It was the girls' first experience of the sort. They are nice young things, 20 and 22, and it is so pleasant to go with them, and let oneself be looked after, and see their open eager young minds swallowing all that comes.

c/o AMERICAN EXPRESS, ATHENS, 21 *May,* 1939.

Dearest Herbert,

I had a very easy smooth sea here yesterday, and a violent Nazi on board. I got tired of being bullied, so eventually gave back as good as I got—especially when he said their papers are all truthful. He said what a pity it was that we have doomed ourselves to extinction; I remarked that one had heard that statement 20 years ago! The result of this repartee was that he asked if he might make love to me in the starlight: but I did draw the line at that.

You never saw anything like the Greek Customs officers—they sent David Wallace back with my sheepskin coat to get it marked before leaving the gates. David asked whether *I* ought not to have a chalk mark too, but this was wasted on them.

ATHENS, 25 *May,* 1939.

Darling B,

Poor M. I knew it was happening, but I think it is because there is someone else waiting for her. C. is German, and however nice and good they are, they seem unable to realize that everyone must have a little privacy to live in: at least that is what she told me. There was such a good play in London where the devoted wife says to her husband as he picks up his little box of pills from the breakfast table:

"Those pills are rattling, my dear."

"*Let* them rattle," says he, exasperated after 30 years. "Why shouldn't they rattle if they *like* it?" No German will understand that remark, but every Anglo-Saxon will feel irresistible sympathy at once!

2 *June,* 1939.

It was altogether a very varied time beginning with a pastoral landscape at Nemea—a temple with three columns standing and a little owl looking out at us from the cornice and vines and cornfields round it and hills with cypress trees: then up by lovely country, high encircled little plains remote and quiet, to the last of the road: and then with two mules over a pass to the Stymphalian lake where our guide, who had been to America said: "Hercules fixed them chickens," meaning the brass-clawed birds he shot with his bow and arrows. It looked a grim place in the evening, with an icy wind blowing into it from the hills all around and a marshy plain beside it:

[261]

and we got so cold that when we saw lighted windows in the school, we asked for hospitality and spread our beds beside the benches. The next day the sun shone, the lake looked lovely with dim islands of rushes about it and a fringe of trees, the ruins of a Crusader church, very fine and large, and an ancient castle on the hill. As the road climbed, a *terrific* noise rose up from millions of frogs shouting as if their throats were made of brass: they sat, green and enormous, in conclaves on the lake edge and whole choruses rose from the shallow water-plants: I have never heard anything so loud.

We rode and walked on by cornfields and villages in trees, and lunched under a walnut on a slope and bathed in a stream, and this was the one really Arcadian day we had: we camped at night in the open and next day went on to a village where the doctor gave us lunch and got us a new muleteer. Whether Greece is worse than Arabia or whether we had not the art to manage them, I don't know: but we were always struggling with our men and watching them go off long before their contracts. In pouring rain we came down towards the Styx, and when the sun came out we saw it, a small pastoral torrent, green water among boulders under plane trees. It was nice to find it so easy and friendly. We settled in a lovely meadow beside it, far from all habitations, and had just lit our fire and put out all our dinner, when it began to *pour*. In the darkness I luckily remembered one big tree and we rushed the luggage under, and then I heard a tinkling mule-bell in the night: the other two were at the far end of our camp, so I rushed out, seized a man's hand and said: "I am English"—the only words I knew! The rather surprised man turned out to be the owner of the only guest-house in the village, a good half hour away! Also the only traveller along that dark lonely way! It was a strange affair altogether. We loaded everything on his mule and went behind it, the Styx roaring to itself below, the moon appearing with dark clouds over the mountain valley.

Next day we rode up to where the Styx falls over a blackish cliff in powdery water, into a snow-drifted basin held in rocks, a solemn place. Lovely flowers grow there, pansies, crocus (mauve), bell hyacinths, pink and yellow orchids, and, next day on the meadows, masses of yellow tulips. We had crossed the Styx now, and threw no obol in. I rode there thinking of all we loved who are on the farther side, and of D. who still seems so near.

2 *June,* 1939.

The last two nights out we spent in the very centre of a small earthquake: I think it was sent after us, because we crossed the Styx. Anyway we had got to a little town called Kalavrita, dead tired because I was just not having a walking day that day and David and Prue lost me and the mules and went astray in gullies; and we all gathered in the late afternoon very tired and settled to the luxury of clean beds in bedrooms—and at 2 a.m. were roused by the gruesome noise and pattering plaster of an earthquake. There is something incredibly grim about it. The walls rustled and shook like a bower of leaves. I put on my cap, suède knickers, fur coat, shoes, watch and camera while all this was going on, with a feeling of absolute terror and a dead calm above it if you know. We went out after the two first shocks and found the Greeks appearing at intervals, all decently dressed in coats and trousers, which I think is very creditable. Nothing happened for quite a long time, and we were just going to bed again when the whole thing again began to shake: so this time we took our camp beds and slept the night out by the roadside, and luckily it was fine. The earth went on having little shivers and rumblings.

Next day we climbed up to the old castle—crusading—of La Tremouille, a shapeless ruin but with lovely view: Khalmos behind clothed with pine, Erymanthus with snow beyond a green mantle of cultivated valleys and to the north the wild steep gorges where the monastery of Megalospileion clings like a wasps' nest to the cliff. We went there in the afternoon. It is an hour's walk from the little railway below: and when we got up, it was even more fantastic than we thought, for the whole place was burnt four years ago and is now rebuilding in a luxurious modern cubist style, with sun-parlours for the monks, one to each bedroom, and bathroom, lifts, central heating—in fact every *confort moderne*! and room for 150 monks who are coming there from Mount Athos! In this fantastic place, more like a morbid dream than real life, I was just sitting at my window looking down into the valley bottom deep below and thinking what a place for an earthquake—when it began again! It was really very horrid. Prue collapsed: David splendid, so patient and quiet. It was raining gently: the house had a good arched front door. I was for sleeping in the lower bedroom close by, ready to make for this door or else go out into a little space which, being so

[263]

directly under the cliff would not be hit: otherwise there was a cave in the solid rock where we could be absolutely safe. David was of the same mind, but Prue simply could not stay: she must go to the valley bottom (which was really dangerous) with the probability of sitting the night out in the rain. So David found men to carry the bedding and all, and we started down a hillside full of loose boulders and got down and settled in a little verandah where everything could have fallen on top of us, but the darkness hid this fact: and what a night it was—torrents of rain, Prue having to be soothed, fleas galore, and little earthquake shakes at irregular intervals. Next day, yesterday, we got the train to the coast and luckily the quake subsided: it only needed to shake a few boulders down to pen us in that narrow valley with no train out! What I regretted most was that we should appear so much more frightened than the Greeks!

DELPHI, 11 June, 1939.

I am resting after a wonderful but very exhausting day yesterday —a bus at 5 a.m. to a point of the road whence I was told to make for a little village called Distomo, half an hour out of sight. An old man in a smock was going the same way and we did what we could with my fifty Greek words for conversation. They sufficed to get him to offer himself as guide with a little white horse: a man with a few American words was able to screw the enormous sum of 200 drachmas out of me, and we set off, to an old ruin of the earliest Greeks which turned out to be on the edge of the sea. You can't think how lovely it was: down zigzags scented in the sun with thyme and all aromatic herbs, to a flat of yellow corn and olives and along a path with the sea lapping up to the plants almost, clear as air or clearer, with the bay encircling it, and sunbaked hills and the snowy peaks of Peloponnese across the water encircling the bay—only two boats visible. There was a house by the shore where the people had made their beds of boughs under a huge sycamore, and gave Turkish delight to me and 'uzo' to my old man, and then we reached the jutting rock of the castle, which had only a few bits of walls left, but walls built of immense blocks laid in a manner of giants and impressive in that solitary loneliness of sea and air and uninhabited hills. From there they could see who went and came to Corinth, and could attend to all who ventured in the bay: on their eastern side a

FREYA STARK IN ATHENS, 1938

THE OLD MAN OF DISTOMO

MONK OF METEORA IN THESSALY

THE VALLEY OF THE STYX IN ARCADIA

valley runs down rich with olive trees belonging to the Monastery of St. Luke, which must have inherited the wealth of some earlier shrine.

When we had loitered and eaten, we rode towards this monastery, up a wild involved gorge, with hills folded in each other like a concertina, the skirts of Helicon, and pink oleanders by the trickle of stream below. The path was overhanging and in places practically gone, and we took three hours to pierce our way to a higher basin, with Helicon bald-headed and fringed with pines above us, and the old Byzantine monastery on a slope—a pleasant prosperous place, with Byzantine mosaics not, I thought, as good as Mistra. We rode back by 5 o'clock to the point by the roadside (nine hours walking and riding) and I slept there till the bus came along and got me back at 8.30.

I had another pleasant bus morning at Amphissa which is in the valley, and we passed it if you remember in pouring rain. It has a castle, partly very old blocks, partly later and quite abominable crusader work. It is really a pain to see the horrid slap-dash building: that people should use stones, or words either for that matter, with no attention to their permanent possibilities, seems an outrage. In fact one does like to see things done just as well as the people who did them *could* do them: so that the idea has a chance to triumph over the obstacles of matter. The old blocks, carefully cut and fitted, still look grand and *say* something, even when they are snatched and patched about with rubble to run up a later wall.

To-morrow I go up Parnassus, but mostly on a mule. It is a troublesome thing, but my lumbago really comes as a result of physical exertion. I don't know what to do about it!

ATHENS, 18 June, 1939.

Dear Jock,

I reached the top of Parnassus: for half an hour I saw the whole of Greece below me, a vision of incredible beauty, all its rusty headlands and misty seas and Olympus (which they call Olybus because mp = b) in the far north and *everything* in fact somewhere in sight: and crocus and scylla, incredibly blue ones, on the edge of the snow. When we came off the top, my guide wrapped me in a blanket and I fell asleep and woke after an hour with an icy wind and have been suffering from a miserable cough ever since: but one must be prepared to sacrifice something for trespassing on the Gods.

[265]

This has to go—Mme Schlumberger and I are off to Sparta—Monemvasia—Olympia.

ASOLO, 5 July, 1939.

I ended Greece by seeing the sun rise from Ossa over Olympus, very serene just opposite. How beautiful it was! We, Mme S. and I, got two mules and climbed by moonlight, seven hours—7 to 2 a.m.: then, just below the top we slept in little stone beds piled by the shepherds against the *icy* wind, till just before the dawn: not too clear. Athos only dim, like a volcano cone across the sea. The best was the dark starlit moment just before the daylight—and to see a shepherd's fire in a hollow of Ossa at night.

28 July, 1939.

Your letter fills me with despair. How am I to make my point of view intelligible? Not God Almighty could I let loose with scissors in my book. If ever you write a book yourself you will understand all the horror of your suggestion, though S. C. should come next after God Almighty if *anyone* were to do it.

Nor can I have her taken out. If you read my introduction, you will see that my object is not to write about Huraidha at all: it is to give a picture of *Methods of meeting* between East and West. It is not a point of literature, but something far nearer to my heart, and on which I have a thing I *wish* to say. Anything that goes counter to this primary object of my book I will not entertain for one moment. On the other hand I wish to put in no personal bitterness—(which I have really ceased to feel anyway)—so that any suggestion to *alter* passages I will do my best to follow, provided the *object* of the book is kept in view. At present you are trying to make a different book of it, and that is a thing I do not for one instant intend to comply with: you may take it as one of those points on which I would not compromise.

Sydney has not written yet; but anyway, though I would always feel him far surer than I am in points of pure *literature*, I do not feel absolutely bound to take his advice in this point where non-literary considerations, valid only to people who know and love the East, also must have their weight. These you have brushed aside, regardless

[266]

of my introduction where my whole purpose in writing is explained. Have I not made it clear? I tried to.

In a hundred years' time, when all is forgotten, the picture of the type and its rôle in our history of empire will remain: I believe that the survival or death of our empire will depend on whether her methods or mine are followed. Do you think that, feeling so, I would write just another picture of Arab life alone?

You must also allow very much for what Sydney and you *know privately* about my feelings. I have tried the book on Herbert's Victorian and amiable female cousin who can find nothing personally offensive in it. Herbert himself begs me not to alter: "You will make it wishy washy," he says.

I think therefore, my poor Jock, that a *compromise* is clearly indicated. I will do what I can to soften if Sydney will mark the offending passages: and if that doesn't do we can either suppress the book altogether or wait a year and then look at it again in more detachment.

Your affectionate recalcitrant, Freya.

7 *August,* 1939.

Sydney does not send me a criticism (literary) at all—but a warm and very understandable apologia for her. But as he suggests merely taking her out, and as I keep on saying that the whole essence of my book is the *"Contact of East and West"* it is no good at all. As far as I can see, the book upsets the people who know her and not those who do not. I have softened it a *very great deal* and will send it you next week by a friend. All that is not essential to the picture and is unkind ought to come away. As for revising, I don't mind doing it for ten years rather than sending out what is not as good as I can make it. I have told Sydney that if the worst comes to the worst you can burn the MS. in the same fireplace where you burnt that of Lord Byron—a glorious death!

It is so pleasant having a quiet summer (apart from Literature)—I wish it went on for years. Herbert seems to me to be getting a little older and frail to look at—he gives a twist to my heart as I see him walking about the garden.

12 *August,* 1939.

I send you Bertie Landsberg's letter—and will tell you to-morrow what another reader says, a neighbour who is also a good critic. I must say that everyone who gets the book remains glued to it in the most flattering way and I think myself that even if it is not published now its day will surely come. It is written with complete sincerity and if there was any annoyance it is only what comes accidentally through from the diaries on which it is based. I do not *feel* any now: and I think I have eliminated anything unduly *personal* from the MS.

I have made the preface a little clearer and the whole intention of the book is there stated. About 200 people know her: about 5,000 others will read the book; it is *their* opinion which counts and I don't think that either you or dear Sydney who is the most loyal of friends are able to get yourselves sufficiently detached. Neither of course am I. You had better get someone quite unbiased, be careful not to tell him *anything* one way or another, and see what he says. I cannot, as I told you, alter any essentials. A book is a part of oneself: you can dress it in various garments, you can't chop off its vital parts with impunity. It shocks me dreadfully that Sydney *as an artist* can suggest it. All one can do is to scrap it and go on to other things. But I do honestly think it is the best book I have written so far. The drama of that academic contrast of character with the Arabian background *is* a picture worth drawing; and I hope the softening alterations have improved it. I think they have.

I am very distressed because there is trouble about my 'Isa: it seems they do not want to give him a passport and my winter's comfort in Arabia will be dished. So I am going into the long and wearisome struggle with French bureaucracy, and it may mean a day or two extra in Paris. Normally I should reach London on September 22 and leave for Jerusalem on October 1, having got an extra week out of Stewart Perowne.

It is delightfully quiet here this summer. Never have I had such a peaceful time and I wonder what awful cataclysm is preparing to make one pay for it!

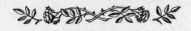

5

The War, 1939

THERE is a chapter in Gibbon's *Decline and Fall* which I
constantly thought of during the summer of 1939. In
it, Constantinople is described during the months that
preceded its capture. The Turkish ring has closed and the eye
of history watches one loophole after another shutting irrevocably
and yet the life of everyday goes on, and plans are even made for
a future already doomed; and the memoirs of this life, pre-
served by the prime minister of the young Paleologus, give the
feeling of a theatre, where the audience knows the tragedy of
which the stage seems unaware.

What happens in tragedy is the coming to life of our background. It has always been there quiescent, a vast, amorphous,
unanswered question into whose shadow we never venture
very far, but take its immobility for granted. Because we have
grown up with it, we forget it; the spotlight is on the little
foreground of ourselves. And suddenly those vast outlines are
shifting: the vagueness that we had taken for solid landscape is
moving down upon us: great rocks and obelisks are crushing
out ruin and death. Whether private or public, this seems to
me the essence of tragedy—the sudden irruption of the background of life into the small, well-ordered, tender and fragile
gardens of men.

To anyone to whom this has once happened, the voices of
the world must always have a note of foreboding; and perhaps
that is the reason of a certain toughness in the generation that
survived the 1914 war. But the pattern of the summer of 1939

was the same for most of us—a shrinking, with an extremely temporary feeling, into the shell of every day.

I was anxious to get my book finished before the catastrophe was upon us, and the threshing out of its literary problems inspired a series of letters to Jock Murray of which I have given a good many extracts, for they show what I still hold to be some essential foundations and are a proof, if any such were needed, how little I have ever thought of writing for a 'public', or even for the fashions of to-day. To consider one's duration may be arrogant, but I do not believe it to be so; and I can never remember a time when I have not tried to write for a century that follows rather than for the one in which I live. This is not because I believe my writing to be exceptionally good, but because Time is a reality to me. I feel things in movement, proceeding into their future from their past; and my immortality is no personal interest, for I feel it—for instance—when I rescue some place-name and put it safe on the map out of oblivion, to be seen by many who can never know my part in its existence there. Even on my embroidery I put date and signature, for the benefit of those whom I can never know; and the planting of trees gives me pleasure when they are small enough to move out of my life into lives still to come; it seems to me vulgarly impatient, and almost impious, to put them almost grown into the ground. Perhaps in this point of view lies the difference between literature and journalism—not in the goodness of one or the other, but in the secret of Time. The merit of the journalist, though as great, need not rely on such basic foundations—and the fact that he writes for a public is apt to corrupt if the public is bad. But literature cannot take account of a public, since even a moderate span of durability requires too many generations to be considered all at once.

These personal problems lay immediate and urgent, but small, in the foreground of the summer, while tragedy collected, now visible to all. We sat in the sun while it lasted. We spent one happy week all together—my mother, myself, Herbert (now eighty-four years old but strong and gay), and Bertie

Landsberg from his Palladian villa Malcontenta on the Brenta, which he loved: we hired a car and drove across the Swiss passes to Geneva, to see the Prado pictures, the last and the best of the lovely exhibitions of those years. There indeed were the victors of Time, Titian, Velasquez and Goya, El Greco, Rubens, Veronese, serene in their enduring present while the background of chaos darkened. We left them in their quiet rooms and tempered light—distillations of lives turbulent as ours, now inviolable—and many moments in the following years were strengthened by that mystery of beauty, which helps us to endure, and no one yet has told us why.

The days in Italy gathered themselves together into one summer splendour: morning after morning cloudless, blue, infinite, and the trees already edged here and there with gold. The lilies had faded, the snap-dragons burned in their beds; the morning letters were brought out on a silver salver; the whole gracious routine of life went on. At our feet the great plain of Lombardy spread with light summer mists, silver and blue, upon it, like a dancer of the seven veils, ravished so often, now sullen again and silent as a captive, waiting for war. The great and bountiful land lay there, ever resurgent. The foolish noise of the Fascists, who called her young, seemed to die, like the click of a typewriter in summer air: no one we knew in this quiet corner paid much attention any longer: they prayed that the danger might pass, from the minds of their own leaders and from the world, and tilled their fields. They were the descendants of Celts, Goths, Visigoths, Huns, or Franks or Lombards, who had all poured down through the blue mountain gaps in their day. The young country had even then been old, and had taken them, century after century, wave after wave, to her heart, torn with violence and blood: and the wounds had healed, and the conquerors had forgotten to conquer, and beauty had led them labouring in the everyday gentleness—of the climate and air, of the delicate far outlines, of the far traditions brought from Greece and lived in already for a thousand years—of Civilization. There they had blossomed, in saints,

in scientists, in painters, mechanics, architects, in all that makes
life noble and easy, in all that we have ever wished in this world
to live for and not to die. They are not a political people, they
are misled by the German goose-step, by Mussolini's advertise-
ments, by the flutter of a new colour in the van: what of it?
Their sanity, their deep tradition of *living*, stands steady, far below
the buffets of time; and to it they return. They will go lan-
guidly to a war in Africa where no one wants them: but when
all is over they will rebuild their roads and bridges, they will
restore—beautifully and without thinking of cost—the things
that destruction has ruined, and will be ready as ever, with the
same invincible optimism, to take the new barbarians to their
heart.

On the 26th of August I left them and my mother, and drove
with Herbert by the lake of Garda to Como, to cross to Switzer-
land. We stopped to lunch at a summer restaurant by the water,
filled with German tourists—and the head waiter came up and
asked what we were? English? He cleared a table in the
crowd, and brought us everything, with a flourish, the wine in
its straw-woven flask, the gold-crusted bread we were not to see
for years, the fruits such as those once sent—it is said—by Narses
to tempt the Franks across the northern passes: and the Germans
looked on at this obvious display with angry looks. We found
another car to carry us from the frontier; we were through in
the last hours before it closed to traffic; and I left Herbert in
Lugano in a home-sickness which lasted for some weeks before
it made him return and await whatever was to come in his own
place.

I boarded an Ostend train, and all that night we crept on
France's eastern border, where I remembered the little cities so
peaceful in the sun. We were slow because every bridge had
to be tested before we crossed it, for fear of mines, and we sat
through the night in a dim blue light in the darkened train.
The next day was spent quietly in Ostend, waiting for a boat,
which finally left crowded with the last load of refugees from
Austria: I looked at them standing about the decks, unshaven

and tired, and wondered how the secret services manage to tell the sheep from the goats in a cargo of this kind. When I reached London, gas masks were beginning to appear in shop windows, and in six days we were at war.

Here these chapters of my life should end, if one's private affairs went in step with the histories of nations. When I reached the Foreign Office, to ask for transport to Egypt, I was kept as South Arabian expert for the Ministry of Information in London: England, it seemed, was to be my home for the years of the war. Some kind friends, the E. H. Keelings, gave me a room in their house, and I bought strong serviceable clothes for walking through air raids—to the disgust of the young women in shops who seemed to think, with that extraordinary English bias for pushing ethics into inappropriate places, that it was immoral to shop after war was declared; it was only after pointing out rather sharply that I was working while they lounged by empty counters, that I was able to prepare myself for a winter of war. This had scarcely been done when Stewart telegraphed to the Ministry to ask for me as his assistant in Aden. Our plans for the Arabian journey were over: our camels were grazing at Gaza, and tents and bedding, silver cups for presents, and all the permits already gathered, were useless 'for the duration'. To go to Aden as assistant instead of being an independent expert in London meant losing some salary; but it also meant a varied life with interludes of travel. I carried among other things films for a projector and diesel motor small enough to be carried on a camel, and the film part of this equipment—which had quite an important future in war propaganda not only for ourselves but for other British stations— was added to my luggage and successfully smuggled through nine friendly or neutral frontiers on the way.

Four days were given me in Asolo, and I chose the overland journey so as to get this last sight of my home. The whole of the autumn was in it, the October sun, the falling gold of woods, the age of my two old people so much loved and left behind me. In a sullen Venice, empty of strangers, puzzled and alarmed

T

by the news published that morning, that Mr. Chamberlain had refused Hitler's overtures of peace, awakening at last to the fact that the house of cards was sliding to the ground, Herbert and my mother saw me off: on a station platform bare of all the gaiety of travel, we said good-bye. None of us mentioned it, but we knew we were not likely to see each other again, and so it was: and it was in that moment or a little afterwards that I realized how my long quest was accomplished just in time—for I thought of death with no fear, either for them or for me, but gently, as it has ever since appeared. The Orient Express carried me away, through the rich Friuli plain, the gateway of the treasure-house of Europe. Among shunting troops and a bustle of preparation, we crossed the Balkans and again climbed into Anatolia; and breaking into Syria, in spite of dimmed streets and busy secretariats, found the old Asiatic world unchanged, brilliant, enduring, hard and gay under the hammering of time: it has had too many strokes not to feel the temporary quality of each.

All the steps of this journey were now familiar, and most of its milestones were the houses of friends. Cairo, always a meeting ground of Asia and now of Europe also, had the feverish deceptive prosperity and busyness which one sees at the beginning and not at the end of a war. I left its dinners and invitations, the crowd of uniforms, the network of intrigue, behind me; the southern constellations rose nightly higher over the dark Red Sea: and already the war, with our Continent slowly darkening into silence, seemed to grow remote and unimmediate to the acts of every day.

By the middle of November I was in Aden; wrote one last letter about my book to Jock; and stepped from my own life into the life of war—less intimate, less measurable, richer perhaps and certainly more strange, with its joys and sorrows distorted, like a baroque that in moments of terror turns without a transition to the grotesque. For the next five years and more we lived it, and, when it was over, were different in ourselves. The groups and patterns we were parts of had changed. Yet,

[274]

looking back through this autobiography and its vicissitudes of nearly half a century, filled as full with sensations and passions as a glass that you ring is filled with sound—the strangest thing about it all perhaps is this—that the person who emerges is still familiar to me, the same optimistic little creature who at two and a half years old set out for Plymouth with three halfpence in her pocket to see the world, whose feelings I can still perfectly well understand and remember, whose equipment will be just as meagre, and whose general attitude of curiosity will be very little different when the gate that clicks behind her is no longer that of the home field alone.

Index

Index